love your library

Buckinghamshire Libraries

Search, renew or reserve online 24/7
www.buckscc.gov.uk/libraries

24 hour renewal line
0303 123 0035

Enquiries
01296 382415

follow us **twitter**
@Bucks_Libraries

SHIPWRECKS
OF THE P&O LINE

SHIPWRECKS
OF THE P&O LINE

SAM WARWICK AND MIKE ROUSSEL

The History Press

Dedicated to the memories of all passengers, officers
and crew who lost their lives in shipwrecks of P&O
vessels, and to those that served on the ships during
times of conflict. May their lives and stories be
forever remembered.

First published 2017

The History Press
The Mill, Brimscombe Port
Stroud, Gloucestershire, GL5 2QG
www.thehistorypress.co.uk

British Library Cataloguing in Publication Data.
A catalogue record for this book is available from the British
Library.

ISBN 978 0 7509 6292 6

Typesetting and origination by The History Press
Printed and bound in India by Replika Press Pvt. Ltd.

CONTENTS

ACKNOWLEDGEMENTS

THE PUBLICATION OF this book could not have been achieved without the valuable contributions from a great many people from around the world, to whom we would like to offer our sincere thanks.

Two of the many books that were referenced during our research were written by Peter Padfield and we would like to start by expressing our gratitude to him for providing us with a wonderful foreword. Thank you to maritime artist Stuart Williamson for his dramatic painting of the *Salsette* (2), which adorns the front cover.

Many of the shipwreck stories have benefited from the personal memories and photographic collections of relatives of the affected passengers and crew. Our special thanks to members of the extended Scotland family (Australia) for sharing the story of Paula (Erna Frieda Paula) Scotland who sailed with her baby Norah on the *Arabia*. Thank you to the relatives of Captain Cooper Kirton: Paul Allen Kirton great-grandson and Miriam Ruth Kirton Macdonald great-grandniece. We also thank the Sandell family for sharing the story and picture of William Sandell, the Gibbney family for the photograph of Captain Charles Grigg Perrins and Roger Yeatman for his recollections of the *Shillong* (2) collision.

We would like to thank the staff at Buckler's Hard Maritime Museum for allowing special access to the *Persia* collection and also to Salcombe Maritime Museum for providing photographs of their *Medina* exhibit. Special thanks are due to Joyce Banks for sharing her detailed research on the *Maloja* (1). We are indebted to the work of P&O Heritage for their continued preservation and celebration of P&O's rich maritime history. The online resources of the P&O Heritage Collection have been an invaluable reference and we are grateful to the senior curator, Susie Cox, for her support.

Many divers and personal friends within the scuba-diving community have lent their invaluable assistance in many ways, most especially by providing photographs and recollections from dives on P&O shipwrecks. In particular, we would like to thank the following: Simon Bell of Simply Diving, Callum Beveridge, Richard Blake, Richard Booth, deep-wreck photographer Leigh Bishop, Ben Burville, Nick Chipchase, Nick Ellerington, Mark Ellyatt, Dr Malik Fernando, Victoria Folgueira, Nick Franglen, Raúl González Gallero, Alejandro Gandul, Julian Hale, Ross and Annie Hanley, Ray Harrison of Totnes BSAC, Kieran Hatton, Brian Hayes, Dharshana Jayawardena, Jean-Pierre Joncheray, Steve Jones, Johno and Cathy de Lara, Ian Lawler, Alan Leatham, Don Love, Zé Beto Miranda, Luis Mota, Andris Nestors, David Ronnan and Sylvia Pryer of Dive125, Roy Roseveare, Miguel San Claudio, William Shiel, Jamie Smith and Rob King of Tunbridge Wells Sub Aqua Club, Paul Vinten, Richard Wait, Chris Webb of Mutiny Diving, David Wendes of Wight Spirit Diving Charters and Mike Wilson.

A book such as this would not be complete without a strong selection of ship illustrations and we are thankful to those who have generously contributed pictures from their collections: Robert Henderson, Richard de Jong, Mick Lindsay, Bert Moody, Peter Newall, Andy Usher and David Whiteside.

Our research has benefited from help in the translation of books and documents relating to the many P&O shipwrecks that lie in foreign waters. We would like to thank Evelyn Jones, Linda Gray and the Nash-Williams family for their invaluable assistance.

Special, personal thanks are due to Steve Metcalfe, especially for his assistance during the visit to the *Socotra* (1) wreck site in France. Thanks also to Stanley Haviland for his continued encouragement and support and Ian Gledhill for lending his expertise with digital images. We extend our thanks to Amy Rigg and The History Press for all their help in bringing this challenging publication to fruition.

We are particularly grateful to Hilary Warwick for all her time spent reviewing the shipwreck stories as they unfolded and for providing us with valuable feedback. Finally, we are most grateful to our wives and immediate families for their continued and unwavering support in indulging our mutual passion for maritime history.

FOREWORD

I HAD THE PRIVILEGE of serving as an officer in the P&O company before the days of long-range civil aircraft, when P&O ships carried passengers to and from India and the Far East and Australia. Before that I had travelled P&O many times as a youngster; I was born in British India and this was how we travelled home on leave and out again afterwards. Some of my earliest memories are from aboard P&O ships; they remain sharp and vivid: in Biscay, watching from aboard one of the great, white Strath liners – I forget which – a sister Strath heaving and pitching into great seas as she passed us on an opposite course – an indelible memory!

And what fine ships they were. Many are illustrated in this book: they have straight stems and counter sterns; a white line stretches along their ebony-black sides from bow to stern at weather-deck level, the accommodation above painted in light buff known as 'stone' colour with two or three raking, black funnels rising above and slender, raking buff masts. They are yacht-like in comparison with today's obese cruise ships. It is so nostalgic just to look at the photographs here.

During my childhood the great, white Straths were launched. I travelled in one or two as a boy and learned to swim in one. Then, as a young man, I was appointed third officer of the *Strathmore* and almost felt as if I had come home. I stood watches with the first officer, a lively character who had served in the Royal Navy during the war and who found peacetime rather tame.

Too many of these ships were sunk in the First and Second World Wars, including the newest of the Straths, the *Strathallan*. Earlier losses were victims of the natural hazards of the sea or the dangerous anomalies in the regulations for preventing collision at sea, regulations designed in the age of sail and still scandalously unsuitable for powered ships. The last wreck described here was one such, the *Shillong*. I remember hearing of her loss through the company grapevine and wondering how it could have happened. It was, of course, the collision regulations; they sank her as surely as the stem of the tanker that ploughed into her side.

Sam Warwick and Mike Roussel have given a marvellous account of these losses and many more from the earliest days of the P&O company, enlivened by reminiscences, letters and official reports, and, of course, by pictures. Sam, a diving instructor, has dived many of the wrecks himself and the underwater photographs are most poignant. I heartily commend this book to all interested in our maritime history and in particular the history of one of our most distinguished liner companies with a reputation second to none.

Peter Padfield
Woodbridge, 2017

INTRODUCTION

ON 4 SEPTEMBER 1837 the wooden paddle steamer *Don Juan*, of the fledgling Peninsular Steam Navigation Company, sailed from the Cornish port of Falmouth, bound for Portugal, Spain and Gibraltar, on the inaugural voyage of the mail service contract to the Iberian Peninsula. Three years later the company was renamed the Peninsular and Oriental Steam Navigation Company, and the same distinctive P&O flag still flies proudly on ships of the modern twenty-first-century fleet.

The voyage of the *Don Juan* was to be significant in a most dramatic way, since on the return journey the ship ran aground in thick fog, so becoming the first shipwreck of the P&O Line. One of the company founders, Arthur Anderson, happened to be on board and took immediate action to personally ensure that all the mail was saved and dispatched with minimal delay. Fortunately there were no casualties and the mail contract did not come under threat, allowing P&O to lay its foundations as an emerging shipping empire.

It was to be nearly a decade before the *Great Liverpool* became the second P&O ship to be lost by shipwreck, by which time the company had expanded rapidly, with routes extending into the Mediterranean as far as Alexandria. This was followed by a mail contract to India, which prior to the opening of the Suez Canal in 1869 required passengers and mail to take an overland route, joining a different ship in Aden. Eventually the ships were making regular line voyages as far as Japan and Australia. In the early days of steam navigation, and with the voyages getting ever longer, further shipwrecks were inevitable – all part of the risk associated with running a pioneering shipping company at this time. Often navigational errors and weather were the cause, and one particularly bizarre mishap occurred when the P&O vessels *Pacha* and *Erin* collided in the Malacca Strait, causing the former to sink. Interestingly, the *Erin* was herself wrecked just three years later.

In 1904 P&O suffered its only loss in Australian waters when the liner, coincidentally named *Australia* (2), grounded entering Port Phillip. No lives were lost, but the passengers of the *Oceana* were not so lucky when it collided with the sailing ship *Pisagua* in the English Channel in March 1912, just one month before the White Star Line's *Titanic* sailed on her fateful voyage.

When the First World War broke out in 1914 it had a devastating effect on the P&O fleet and twenty-two vessels were lost. The *Egypt* was the only interwar shipwreck, but history repeated itself again in the Second World War when a further nineteen ships were lost. As such, over half the vessels lost in the history of P&O have been due to acts of war and have also accounted for the highest loss of life; the *Rawalpindi* alone claimed 275 souls when it was sunk in 1939.

Just two shipwrecks occurred after the Second World War, the last being the cargo liner *Shillong* (2), which sank following a collision in the Red Sea on 22 October 1957.

Despite having such a long history, P&O did not suffer the high-profile losses of its contemporaries. White Star will be forever remembered for the *Titanic* disaster in 1912 and Cunard Line suffered its most infamous loss in 1915 when the *Lusitania* was torpedoed duing the First World War. This aspect of P&O's rich history can often be overlooked, but each one of the shipwrecks has a unique story to tell, not just of the ships but also of the countless lives that have been affected in a number of ways.

Unlike a ship which is sold for scrap, the life of a sunken vessel does not necessarily end on the day of the wreck, especially for those that lie within depths that are accessible by recreational scuba divers. From a total of seventy-eight losses since 1837, at least a third of the P&O wrecks can be explored by divers. Many lie in English coastal waters and classic wreck dives such as the *Salsette* (2), *Moldavia* (1), *Oceana* and *Somali* (2) are well-known names among the British diving community. There are also wrecks in warmer waters that are accessible to divers with an entry-level scuba-diving certification, such as the *Carnatic* in the Red Sea, probably the most visited and photographed of all P&O wrecks. At the other extreme is the wreck of the *Egypt*, which lies at a depth of over 100m in the cold, strong currents off Ushant, making it an advanced technical dive that can only be undertaken by highly qualified divers using specialised equipment. Unusually, however, it is possible for anyone to visit the wreck of the *Socotra* (1) in France, since it is exposed on the beach during periods of exceptionally low tides, at which point it can be accessed by foot.

The shipwreck stories that follow are presented in the order of sinking, commencing with the *Don Juan* in 1837 and ending with the *Shillong* (2) in 1957. Each chapter recounts the history of the ship, the circumstances of the loss and, where applicable, details of the wreck underwater. The scope has been restricted to the vessels that ended their career as a shipwreck while under P&O ownership. Ships wrecked but subsequently refloated or salvaged, such as the *Liverpool* and *China* (2), are not included. A summary of the vessels wrecked after being sold by P&O are listed in an appendix.

Authors' Note

Like many of their contemporary shipping lines, P&O frequently used the same ship name more than once. The convention adopted by many, and employed in this book, is to place a numeric suffix in brackets after the name. For example, the first ship to be called *Salsette* in 1868 is *Salsette* (1) and the second vessel constructed in 1908 is *Salsette* (2). Where tonnage is given, this is gross tons and typically at the time of the vessel's original construction, unless otherwise stated. In order to distinguish between First World War and Second World War U-boats, the former are given without a hyphen (i.e. *UB 40*) and the latter with a hyphen (*U-22*).

All illustrations are from the authors' combined collections, unless otherwise credited.

Disclaimer

The activity of recreational scuba diving, and in particular wreck diving, requires specialised training and instruction through study, education and in-water teaching. This book does not purport to offer any kind of substitute for seeking professional instruction through the established professional training agencies. The diving techniques and practices recounted are presented in their historical context and do not constitute, advocate or promote any given approach. It should also be noted that scuba diving is a constantly evolving pursuit and as such the equipment, technique and best practices adapt accordingly.

A BRIEF HISTORY OF THE P&O LINE

ALTHOUGH THE OFFICIAL beginning of the company that was to become known simply as 'the P&O' is regarded to be the inaugural mail-service sailing of the *Don Juan* in September 1837, the story originates in 1815, when Brodie McGhie Willcox commenced business as a London shipbroker. Willcox engaged the services of Arthur Anderson, a Scot from the Shetland Islands who had recently left the Royal Navy where he had served as captain's clerk during the Napoleonic wars. After seven years brokering trade to the Iberian Peninsula the two men entered into partnership under the name of Willcox & Anderson, acting as agents for sailing vessels to Spain and Portugal.

The paddle steamer *William Fawcett*, traditionally acknowledged as the first P&O ship, commenced regular sailings to the Peninsula in 1835. (Mick Lindsay)

In the early 1830s the business inevitably became embroiled in the Portuguese and Spanish civil wars, during which Willcox & Anderson actively supported both legitimist parties. Their involvement in the positive outcome earned the company the right to fly both sets of royal colours, leading to the creation of the legendary P&O house flag, which combines the blue and white of the Portuguese with the red and gold of the Spanish.

The first steamship sailing advertised by Willcox & Anderson was the paddle steamer *Royal Tar* (308 tons) of the Dublin & London Steam Packet Company and owned by Captain Richard Bourne RN and associates. The ship made two voyages to Lisbon in 1834 and was followed in March 1835 by a more permanent arrangement on the Peninsula route using the *William Fawcett* (206 tons), also owned by Bourne. Although neither vessel was actually owned by Willcox & Anderson, the *William Fawcett* is traditionally acknowledged as the first P&O ship. By this time Bourne had also become a partner in the company, which had begun trading under the name of the Peninsular Steam Navigation Company.

Towards the end of 1836 the company was advertising a fortnightly service from London and Falmouth to the Peninsula using a fleet of six paddle steamers. Despite an initial proposal to operate a mail service being turned down flat, Willcox & Anderson persisted and were rewarded for their efforts when the first contract was finally signed with the Peninsular Steam Navigation Company on 22 August 1837. The new contract got off to the worst possible start when the *Don Juan* was wrecked on the Spanish coast returning from the first voyage in the mail service. Although the ship was a total loss and not fully insured, there was no loss of life and all the mail was saved.

In 1840 the company was awarded a new mail contract to extend the service east to Egypt by offering a monthly sailing to Alexandria, which was successfully inaugurated by the *Oriental* (1) later the same year. On 31 December 1840 the company was formally incorporated by Royal Charter under the new name of the Peninsular and Oriental Steam Navigation Company, henceforth known as P&O. The new contract included the mandate that a mail service between Egypt and India be established within two years. The pioneering use of steamships on the route required significant investment in larger ships, along with supporting infrastructure such as coaling stations, docks and repair facilities. On 24 September 1842 the wooden paddle steamer *Hindostan* (1) sailed from Southampton for Calcutta via the Cape of Good Hope to commence the new service.

Although passengers could now travel all the way to India with P&O, it was necessary to disembark at Alexandria and take the arduous route overland to Port Suez in order to continue the onward journey. There were two established routes that had been in use since Biblical times: one crossed the desert to Suez, the other went up the River Nile to Luxor, via narrow-draft Egyptian boats, then across the desert to the Red Sea port of Cosseir. This was a distance of 250 miles from Suez and took eighty-eight hours. An advantage of the Cosseir route was that passengers could see the pyramids at Giza on their journey up the Nile.

Whilst the primary P&O trade at the time was in the conveyance of mail, passengers and cargo, the first advertisements for cruising began to appear as early as 1843 when a voyage to the Mediterranean on the *Tagus* was advertised as an 'interesting and classical excursion'. A year later the English novelist William Thackeray joined one of the voyages as a guest of P&O and wrote extensively about his experiences in his book *Notes of a Journey from Cornhill to Grand Cairo*.

By 1845 the P&O routes had extended to the Far East via Ceylon, Penang, Singapore and on to Hong Kong. A few years later the service was extended as far as Japan.

Advances in ship design led to P&O introducing their first sea-going iron-screw steamer to the fleet in 1851, the *Shanghai* (1) (546 tons). The following year the Admiralty accepted P&O's tender for a new Australian mail service, operating twice monthly from Singapore to Sydney. The contract was inaugurated by the iron screw *Chusan* (1) (700 tons), which sailed from Southampton on 15 May 1852 and arrived in Sydney on 3 August.

In 1853 the enterprising P&O managing director, Arthur Anderson, founded the Union Steam Collier Company (which in 1900 merged with the Castle Line to become Union-Castle) as a means of addressing the increasing demand for coal supplies at Southampton Docks. However, the Crimean War of 1854–56 found vessels from both company's fleets being requisitioned by the government for use as troop transports.

Over the years P&O had invested heavily in making improvements to the overland route in an effort to improve passenger comfort and the logistics of transferring mail and cargo. So when the Suez Canal

The iron-screw steamer *Chusan* (1) inaugurated the P&O mail service to Australia in 1852. (Oil painting by Charles Dickson-Gregory, State Library of Victoria)

opened on 17 November 1869 P&O suddenly found themselves with an outdated operation and under threat from new competition. This was further compounded by the passing of Arthur Anderson in 1868 and the earlier death of Willcox in 1862. The challenge was taken up by Thomas Sutherland, who had joined P&O as a young man in 1852 and risen steadily through the company until being appointed managing director in 1872, and, ultimately, chairman in 1881. Sutherland oversaw a drastic reorganisation programme that included cutting costs, rebuilding the fleet and relocating the home port from Southampton to London. He also managed to secure a place on the board of the Suez Canal Co., which helped protect the British shipping interests using the canal.

One of the highlights of the extensive shipbuilding programme that continued into the 1880s was the introduction of four 6,000-ton Jubilee-class passenger liners, *Victoria*, *Britannia*, *Oceana* and *Arcadia* (1), which coincided with Queen Victoria's Golden Jubilee in 1887. Towards the end of the nineteenth century the cargo-carrying capacity of new vessels entering the P&O fleet had steadily increased, and in 1896 *Candia* (2) became the first purpose-built cargo liner to enter service.

The passenger liner *China* (2) was built in 1896 and employed on the mail services to India and Australia. In March 1898 the ship was stranded on Perim Island and did not resume service for another two years. (Allan C. Green/State Library of Victoria)

During the Boer War of 1899–1902 a significant number of P&O liners were taken up by the government for trooping and were estimated to have carried over 150,000 personnel to and from South Africa.

In 1904 P&O used the word 'cruise' for the first time when they advertised a 'midsummer vacation cruise' on the 'Steam Yacht *Vectis* (3)', offering summer holidays to Norway, Baltic and northern capitals. The 5,010-ton *Vectis* (3) was built in 1881 as the *Rome* for the Australian service, but renamed *Vectis* (3) in May 1904 after being refitted as a cruise liner, providing accommodation for 150 first-class passengers only.

P&O had tried to introduce an intermediate service to Australia via the Cape in 1889 but it faced too much existing competition to be viable. However, when the Blue Anchor Line went into liquidation following the tragic disappearance of their flagship *Waratah* off the South African coast in 1909, P&O seized the opportunity to purchase the company.

The early twentieth century also saw the introduction of ten new M-class liners, commencing with the 9,500-ton *Moldavia* (1) in 1903. The impressive twin-screw passenger liners had a service speed in excess of 16 knots and were able to reduce the passage time to India to just two weeks. Many of the vessels also operated on the Australia service. The last M class was the *Medina*, which was commissioned as HMS *Medina* to convey King George V and Queen Mary to the Delhi Durbar in 1911 before entering P&O service in 1912.

In May 1914 P&O announced a merger with the complementary British India Line, after a lengthy period of negotiations between Sir Thomas Sutherland and the British India chairman, Sir James Lyle Mackay (later Lord Inchcape). Although both companies retained their own identities, Mackay took over as P&O chairman in 1915, following the retirement of Sutherland, who after sixty years with P&O was now in his eighties.

The outbreak of the First World War in 1914 had an immediate impact on the P&O fleet, since many of the fast passenger liners were ideally suited for use as Armed Merchant Cruisers (AMC) and troop transports, while many other ships could be employed as hospital ships and supply vessels. The *Mantua* (1) was one of the first ships to be taken up by the Admiralty for use as an AMC in August 1914 and managed to survive the war, eventually returning to active service in 1920. Other vessels were less fortunate, with nearly twenty being sunk as a direct result of enemy action and many others being badly damaged in attacks. During the hostilities many hundreds of officers, passengers and crew lost their lives.

Despite the war, Lord Inchcape was still able to continue expanding the P&O group and during this period the company took over the New Zealand Shipping Co. and Federal Steam Navigation Co., along with acquisition of interests in the Union Steamship Co. of New Zealand, Hain Steamship Co., and James Nourse. One of the most significant investments came in 1919 when it was announced that P&O had acquired a 51 per cent controlling interest in the Orient Steam Navigation Company. The years following the war saw an intense fleet rebuilding programme, during which many of the ships lost during the war were replaced with bigger and larger vessels, often using the same name, such as *Moldavia* (2) (1922, 16,449 tons) and *Maloja* (2) (1923, 20,837 tons).

The period of post-war optimism was marred by the tragic loss of the *Egypt* in a collision in thick fog off Ushant in May 1922, during which eighty-six lives were lost, including fifteen passengers. A cargo of bullion worth in excess of £1 million also went down with the ship, although it was later recovered by an audacious Italian salvage operation in the 1930s.

At the end of the decade the *Viceroy of India* entered service and was the first European passenger liner to adopt oil-fired turbo-electric propulsion machinery.

A highlight of the 1930s was the introduction of the celebrated Strath liners, the first being the *Strathnaver* (1) (22,547 tons), which sailed on her maiden voyage to Australia in October 1931. She was joined by *Strathaird* (1) (1932), *Strathmore* (1) (1935), *Stratheden* (1) (1937) and *Strathallan* (1938). All five vessels marked a departure from the traditional P&O livery, since they were painted with white hulls and buff funnels, earning them the nickname 'White Sisters'.

Despite the success of the new liners, the depression made it a difficult period and 1932 was the first year that a dividend had not been paid since 1867. Lord Inchcape died the same year and left a generous £40,000 legacy to the officers serving in the P&O and British India fleet. Each of the 202 captains received £100 and a further £50 was distributed to each of the 200 chief officers and 200 chief engineers. Inchcape was succeeded as chairman by his son-in-law Alexander Shaw (later Lord Craigmyle), who retired on health grounds in 1938 and was followed by Sir William Crawford Currie.

By 1936 P&O had returned to profitability and in 1937 the centenary was celebrated enthusiastically throughout the company. However, just two years later war intervened once more and many ships were quickly taken up by the Admiralty. The AMC *Rawalpindi* was the first vessel to be lost when she was sunk in a dramatic encounter with two German battlecruisers off Iceland on 23 November 1939 with a high loss of life. Many of the P&O ships were actively involved in the Operation Torch landings in North Africa in 1942, a year in which ten P&O ships were lost. By the end of the war P&O had lost nineteen ships, including the *Mata Hari* which been captured and sunk by the Japanese in February 1942. Although the ship was refloated and used by the Japanese, it was sunk permanently by US forces three years later. The collective P&O group of companies lost over 150 vessels, a third of which were from the British India fleet. The company lost many of their officers and crew, but many were praised for gallant conduct and by the end of the war seventy-nine staff, afloat and ashore, had been decorated.

In addition to having to replace vessels lost during the war, P&O not only faced renewed international competition from other shipping lines, but also the growing threat of commercial airline travel. For the first few years after the war the only new ships to enter the fleet were cargo liners, commencing with the *Perim* (2) in November 1945. It wasn't until 1949 that the first new passenger liner entered service, the 27,955-ton *Himalaya* (3), delivered eighteen months late and £1 million over budget. However, the liner's service speed of 22 knots reduced the passage time to India to fifteen days and Australia to four weeks. The *Himalaya* (3)

P&O passenger liners provided a fortnightly service from London to Australia.

Strathmore (1935, 23,428 tons) was the third of the five Strath liners. The ship was employed on the Australian service and served as a troop transport during the Second World War. (Mick Lindsay)

was followed by *Chusan* (3) one year later, then *Arcadia* (2) and *Iberia* (2) in 1954.

In 1958 *Himalaya* (3) made P&O's first trans-Pacific voyage from Sydney to San Francisco, and the following year inaugurated the new Orient and Pacific Line service. In 1960 P&O acquired the remaining shares in the Orient Steam Navigation Company and the two passenger fleets were consolidated under the name 'P&O-Orient Lines', but the Orient name was dropped altogether in 1966.

On 2 June 1961 the illustrious *Canberra* sailed on her maiden voyage from Southampton to Australia, New Zealand and the west coast of America. The 45,720-ton passenger liner was the largest ship ever built for the Australian service and had an impressive service speed of 27.5 knots. The *Canberra* was to be the last passenger liner built under the registration of the Peninsular and Oriental Steam Navigation Company.

The *Canberra* was the last passenger liner built under the registration of the Peninsular and Oriental Steam Navigation Company. (Richard de Jong)

The 141,000-ton *Britannia* joined the modern-day P&O Cruises fleet in March 2015. (Richard de Jong)

The *Ocean Dream* (ex-P&O Lines *Spirit of London*) capsized and sank at Laem Chabang in February 2016 after spending over a year abandoned at anchor. (Geir Vinnes)

Regular passenger services to the Far East were withdrawn in 1969 and as the passenger trade began to dwindle P&O started to place more emphasis on cruising. However, the group continued to invest in cargo services, including bulk carriers, oil tankers and a foray into containerisation.

In 1971 the entire P&O group underwent a radical reorganisation, during which more than 100 subsidiary companies were amalgamated into five new operational divisions: Bulk Shipping, General Cargo, Passenger, European and Air Transport, and General Holdings. Two British India educational cruise ships, *Uganda* and *Nevasa*, were transferred to the Passenger Division and re-registered under the ownership of Peninsular and Oriental Steam Navigation Company in 1972. The first new passenger ship to enter the fleet was the Italian-built *Spirit of London*, which had been bought on the stocks in 1971 by the new P&O Lines Ltd. The ship sailed from Southampton to the Caribbean in November 1972 and heralded the new P&O cruising era.

The American cruise operator Princess Cruises was acquired by P&O in 1974, along with their chartered Flagship Cruises vessel, *Island Princess*. The *Spirit of London* transferred to the fleet under the new name of *Sun Princess*, and the following year the *Sea Venture* was acquired and renamed *Pacific Princess*. In 1977 the Passenger Division was restyled as P&O Cruises Ltd, which, along with the *Canberra*, still included the ageing *Arcadia* (2) and ex-Orient Line *Oriana*. The fleet was bolstered by the purchase of the *Kungsholm*, which joined in 1979 as the renamed *Sea Princess*, but it was not until five years later that the first new purpose-built liner joined the fleet, the 45,000-ton *Royal Princess*, launched by HRH Diana, Princess of Wales.

The *Canberra* and *Uganda* were among several ships from the P&O group that were requisitioned by the government during the 1982 Falklands conflict. Fortunately none of the ships suffered any damage or loss of life. *Canberra* returned to service after a lengthy refit and spent many more years cruising out of Southampton until eventually being scrapped in September 1997.

In October 2000 the P&O group divested its cruise business, including P&O Cruises, under a new independent company, P&O Princess Cruises, which was acquired three years later by the American-owned Carnival Corporation. The Peninsular and Oriental Steam Navigation Company was acquired by DP World in 2006, who are now the custodians of P&O's rich history through the P&O Heritage Collection.

On 3 July 2012 P&O celebrated its 175th year when seven of its cruise ships – *Oceana*, *Adonia*, *Azura*, *Oriana*, *Aurora*, *Arcadia* and *Ventura* – arrived together in Southampton at dawn. They were reviewed by the Princess Royal before sailing together again that evening.

HRH Queen Elizabeth II officially named the 141,000-ton *Britannia*, the newest cruise ship to the P&O fleet on 10 March 2015.

Although the cruise ships of the modern-day P&O Cruises fleet are no longer registered or operating under the original company name, the P&O brand is still very much alive and the distinctive P&O flag is still instantly recognisable around the globe.

Sadly, even in recent times shipwrecks still occasionally happen and in February 2016 the *Ocean Dream* (ex-P&O Lines *Spirit of London* and Princess Cruises *Sun Princess*) came to grief. After lying abandoned at anchor at Laem Chabang for over a year the ship mysteriously capsized and sank in shallow water.

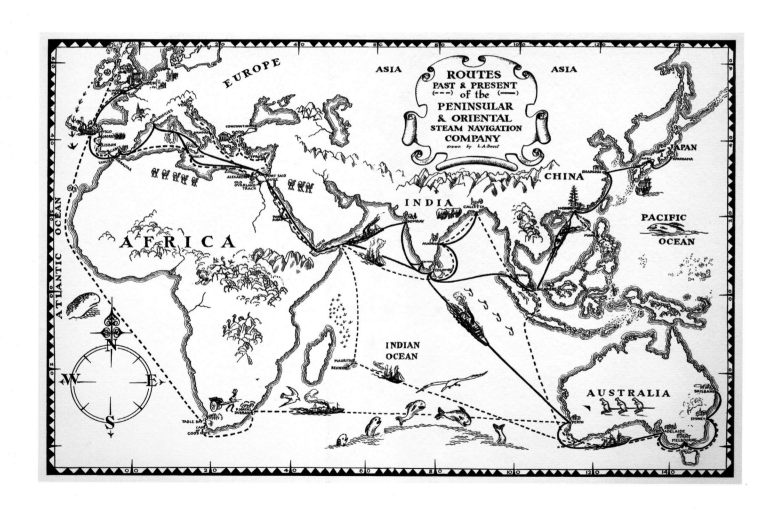

SHIPWRECKS

PART 1

1837–1868

– *Don Juan* –

1837, Spain

The wooden paddle steamer *Don Juan* (932 tons) was built by Fletcher, Son and Fearnall, Poplar, London. The length was 148ft (45.2m) and beam 24ft (7.1m). The paddles were powered by a 360hp two-cylinder direct-acting steam engine, giving a service speed of 7 knots. The passenger capacity was twenty-four.

The *Don Juan* was launched on 10 September 1836 at a ceremony attended by Baron de Moncorvo, the Portuguese ambassador, and his wife. The ship was named in honour of the late Spanish minister, Juan Mendizábal. After the launch *Don Juan* sailed for Glasgow where the steam engine was fitted by Claud, Girdwood and Co. With a cost of £43,000, the ship was claimed to be the largest and most powerful steam ship built. The *London Morning Post* was suitably impressed with the 'superb vessel' and reported:

> The cabin accommodations of the *Don Juan* are laid out on an entirely novel plan, parties wishing to be select will find in her separate cabins, with every convenience, adapted for families or parties, from two up to twenty in number. Indeed this plan, which has been too much neglected generally in passage-vessels, is, we understand, to be adopted in all the new vessels of this company.

The master of the *Don Juan* was Captain John Ralph Engledue, a 29-year-old former Royal Navy lieutenant and gunnery officer who had recently joined the company. The *Don Juan* sailed on her maiden voyage to Gibraltar on 20 July 1837 and just one month later on 22 August the Peninsular Steam Navigation Company signed the first mail contract with the Admiralty. The *Don Juan* was chosen to take the first weekly contract sailing to the Peninsula, departing London on 1 September and calling at Falmouth a few days later to collect the mails. Further calls were then made at Vigo, Oporto, Lisbon and Gibraltar. On board was Arthur Anderson, one of the company founders, along with his wife Mary and several businessmen. Although not mandated by the mail contract, the *Don Juan* continued to Malaga where cargo was loaded that included 25 tons of fruit, 25 tons of lead and $21,000 in specie.

On the return voyage the *Don Juan* called once more at Gibraltar, departing on the afternoon of 15 September. Within hours a thin mist had transformed to a thick fog and visibility had been reduced to less than 100m. Arthur Anderson recounted the events that followed in a letter written to the Lloyd's Agent at Gibraltar:

> About half past four I left Captain Engledue, with whom I had been conversing on the paddle boxes and quarter deck, and descended to my cabin, where I had only been a few minutes when I heard Captain Engledue calling out loudly,

The *Don Juan* badge on a ceramic shard recovered from the wreck bears the company's early name, Peninsular Steam Navigation Company.

'Hard a starboard. Stop her. Back her.' I immediately rushed on deck, and saw a ledge of rocks about 40 yards or so from the starboard bow, with Tarifa Lighthouse at a short distance. The wind was blowing rather fresh from the eastward. The vessel could neither be stopped nor veered round quickly enough to clear the rocks, but her speed was so far checked that she touched very gently forwards, carrying away, as she grazed the rocks, the starboard paddle boards. The fore part only appeared to be aground. The boats were immediately lowered away; a large kedge was carried out on the starboard quarter, a strong hawser passed from it abaft, a tackle put on, and everyone on board set on to endeavour to heave her off. These efforts were, however, in vain, and I learned with deep regret, from some Spanish fishermen who had come to see us, that the tide was still falling. It was now resolved to dispatch a messenger by land to Gibraltar for assistance, which was done, and for greater security I determined to proceed there by sea myself.

The *Don Juan* had grounded off Tarifa Point, which is the southernmost point of the Iberian Peninsula and approximately 20 miles due west of Gibraltar. The point is on a small island connected to the mainland via a causeway.

After much negotiation Anderson managed to charter a local Spanish fishing boat to take him and the mails back to Gibraltar. Also accompanying him was his wife, two gentleman passengers, and the Admiralty representative in charge of supervising the mails,

P&O co-founder Arthur Anderson was travelling on board the *Don Juan* when it was wrecked.

Lieutenant Roupel. After an exhausting passage in rough weather they arrived at 1 a.m. the following morning. Assistance was rendered by HMS *Medea*, which embarked the mails, carpenters and a party of Royal Marines from HMS *Asia*. The services of the Scilly Isles schooner *Lady Newman* were also engaged to board any cargo and stores that could be saved from the *Don Juan*. Within a couple of hours HMS *Medea* departed for Tarifa, taking the *Lady Newman* in tow, and by 6 a.m. they had arrived back at Tarifa.

Overnight it had become clear that there was no hope of saving the *Don Juan* and Captain Engledue saw to it that the specie was landed, along with some cabin furniture and stores. This was made all the more difficult by skirmishes with opportunistic locals who attempted to plunder the wreck. Securing the specie now became the first priority for the rescue party. But when Anderson and a group comprising six marines set about transporting it towards HMS *Medea*'s boats they found their way barred by Spanish soldiers. It transpired that the local governor had taken exception to the English presence, claiming an insult to the Spanish nation by 'bringing armed men ashore without permission, landing effects on the Spanish soil, and taking them away again without the licence of the Spanish authorities, breaking the sanitary regulations'.

Fortunately Anderson was fluent in Spanish and was able to explain to the governor that they had acted out of necessity and that no insult or hostility was intended. A tense situation was diffused and the governor eventually offered his assistance to help with the secure recovery of the remaining items of value from the wreck. The HMS *Medea* departed for England with the mails but the *Don Juan* ultimately became a complete loss. This was made worse for the fledgling Peninsular Steam Navigation Company, since the vessel was only partially insured. If the wreck had resulted in any loss of life, or if the mails had been lost, then the outcome for the company could have been very different. The same is also true for Captain Engledue, who was ultimately accountable for the loss of his ship. However, Anderson did not hesitate to present a positive case for the captain and in his letter to the Lloyd's Agent he wrote:

The active vigilance of Capt. Engledue as a seaman, and his frank kindness and gentlemanly attention to his passengers, have gained him the esteem of everyone who has the pleasure of knowing him. I have myself been a witness of his great diligence and attention to his duties, as well as the precision with which he usually estimated the ship's course and distance during the late voyage of the *Don Juan*. As a manager of the company, I have great reason to lament the unfortunate loss of so fine a vessel, a loss which, at this outset of enterprise, is irreparable, and must be productive of serious disadvantages to it, but, notwithstanding this feeling, I cannot attach blame to Captain Engledue.

Anderson concluded:

An error of this nature, even if there was one, surely ought to be judged with leniency, and whoever is aware of the nature of Captain Engledue's feelings under his misfortune will, if he have a spark of generosity in his bosom, be more disposed to administer the balm of sympathy and consolation that to aggravate his distress by thoughtless or illiberal censure.

After a full investigation Captain Engledue was fully exonerated of all blame and was soon given command of another vessel. A few years later he was promoted to superintendent of the P&O fleet and ultimately took a seat on the board of directors, remaining active in the role until his death in 1888.

Diving the Wreck

The remains of the *Don Juan* lie in a depth 30m off the south-east tip of Tarifa Point, in an area that is regularly frequented by scuba divers; it is considered the most popular dive in the area. However, in a case of mistaken identity the wreck is known locally as 'San Andrés'

A diver exploring the wreck of the wooden paddle steamer *Don Juan*. (Simon Bell/Simply Diving)

Parts of the *Don Juan* wreck, known locally as 'San Andrés', have been described as resembling a Greek temple. (Simon Bell/Simply Diving)

or sometimes 'Minho'. Early divers visiting the wreck site discovered lead ingots which were believed to have come from the San Andrés foundry in Malaga and whence named the wreck San Andrés. Partially as a result of the ingots it was later believed to be the *Mino*, which sank in a collision with the *Minden* in 1856. However, the *Mino* was an iron-screw steamship, not a wooden paddle steamer and therefore not consistent with the remains found on the seabed. The discovery of lead ingots ties in with the 25 tons of lead known to be loaded on board the *Don Juan* in Malaga. Consequently, few divers visiting the *Don Juan* fully appreciate the true historic significance of the wreck.

The wreck itself is a fantastic dive in an area of good visibility, populated with an abundant variety of marine life. Although possible as a shore dive, the *Don Juan* is best dived from a boat. Divers will typically drop in at a depth of a few metres and descend down the steep slope of the Point. The area is regularly visited by turtles and sunfish and provides an ideal cleaning station for pelagic species visiting from the Atlantic Ocean. At a depth of around 18m there are large sea fans and the wreck comes into view a further 10m below.

The most distinctive feature of the wreck is the engine that stands upright and several metres proud of the seabed. The rocker cover is easy to make out, along with connecting rods. It is possible to swim through the centre of the structure, which 'resembles a Greek temple'. On either side are the remains of the paddle wheels, each about 6m in diameter. Large eels are often found within the wreckage. One very large conger eel caught on video camera in 1995 was estimated to be 3.5m in length and around 70kg in weight! Beyond the main wreck the water very quickly descends to 45m and beyond so care should be taken not to venture too far. Had Captain Engledue not taken the precaution to secure the stricken ship by passing the chain cables around rocks then the *Don Juan* would almost certainly have slid off into deep water, never to be seen again.

– Great Liverpool –

1838–1846, Spain

The wooden paddle steamer *Great Liverpool* (1,382 tons) was originally built as the *Liverpool* (1,140 tons) for the Transatlantic Steamship Company at the Humble & Milcrest Yard, Liverpool, and launched on 10 October 1837. The length was 213.7ft (65.1m) and beam 25.5ft (7.8m). The paddles were powered by direct-acting side-lever steam engines, giving a service speed of 9 knots. Passenger capacity was ninety-eight.

On 20 October 1838 the *Liverpool* set sail on her maiden voyage from Liverpool to New York under the command of Captain Fayrer. Despite making reasonable progress against severe weather conditions it soon became apparent that the ship was consuming coal at more than double the rate anticipated. Six days into the voyage and with insufficient coal to complete the crossing, Captain Fayrer decided to put about and make for Cork. After taking on more coal and completing a short two-day voyage to reassess the consumption rate, the *Liverpool* proceeded to New York, completing the voyage in a little less than seventeen days.

One of the passengers destined to cross the Atlantic on the *Liverpool* was Samuel Cunard, who was awarded the first British trans-atlantic steamship mail contract in 1939 and founded the famous Cunard Line the year after.

Despite successfully completing six further transatlantic crossings in 1839, the *Liverpool* operated at a considerable financial loss and early the following year the Transatlantic Steamship Company assets were absorbed by P&O. In addition to the *Liverpool* this included the unfinished *United States*, which was renamed *Oriental*. Because the P&O fleet already included a vessel named *Liverpool* (1830, 330 tons) the new addition was renamed *Great Liverpool* and the older vessel acquired the nickname 'Little Liverpool'. After an extensive refit, during which time the boilers were replaced, the *Great Liverpool* made a short trial voyage to the Isle of Man before being placed on the mail service to Alexandria in October 1840.

On 1 February 1843 the *Great Liverpool* sailed from Southampton with a full complement of passengers to inaugurate P&O's first interconnecting service through to India. After disembarking in Alexandria the passengers travelled to Suez via the overland route where they joined the newly instated *Hindostan* (1) for the second leg of the voyage to Calcutta.

The *Great Liverpool* suffered a mechanical failure in the Mediterranean Sea in November 1843 when the intermediate shaft broke and the vessel was forced to proceed under the power of a single paddle wheel. To ensure that the mails were not held up HMS *Alecto* carried them to Malta, from where they were taken on to Gibraltar by HMS *Geyser*. Apparently a lengthy financial dispute ensued between the Royal Navy and P&O over payment for the naval vessels' assistance.

At the beginning of 1845 the *Great Liverpool* inaugurated twice-monthly sailings to Egypt and was fitted with new boilers that had been originally intended for the *Braganza*, one of the older ships in the P&O fleet.

The wooden paddle steamer *Great Liverpool* operated as the *Liverpool* for the Transatlantic Steamship Company prior to joining the P&O fleet in 1840. (© P&O Heritage Collection www.poheritage.com)

On the afternoon of 21 February 1846 the *Great Liverpool* sailed from Gibraltar on the final leg of another routine voyage from Alexandria. The ship was under the command of Captain McLeod, one of the P&O company's most experienced and popular masters. In the early hours of 24 February the *Great Liverpool* was about 7 to 10 miles off Cape Finisterre, steaming at full speed. It was a pitch-black, hazy night with a heavy sea running when at 3.50 a.m. the ship suddenly struck a submerged rock. Within minutes, water rushed into the lower-deck cabins and engine room. Captain McLeod immediately set course for land with the hope of getting the stricken ship aground on a beach, but within just fifteen minutes the water had extinguished the engine room fires and the *Great Liverpool* began to drift towards the shore, at the mercy of wind and tide. An hour later the ship grounded on a small sandy shoal at Gures, just a short distance off the beach where a heavy surf was breaking.

The captain gave the order for the boats to be readied to land the passengers and crew and an advance party of seamen were dispatched to secure a rope ashore. One of the passengers later recalled the drama that unfolded:

A boat was at length lowered, and chiefly laden with ladies and children; long did they sit in it by the vessel's side, waiting the chance that the surge might abate, even but a little: at last it set out – every heart beat high, and every eye was strained to see it as it slowly advanced in its perilous way. It reached the beach – the breakers dashed full on it – it was swamped – we saw the ladies and children struggling and dragged through the foaming waters by the sailors. One lady, however, was carried out by the retiring wave and disappeared; another, a child, was carried away, and a female Indian servant swam long, but she

Passengers and crew took to the boats in heavy surf when the *Great Liverpool* was wrecked off Cape Finisterre in February 1846.

too sank at last. One woman and a child were recovered, and carried back to the ship by another ship's boat nearly lifeless. The boat floated out and turned keel up, and as there was no other that could live in such a sea, we had no hope but the feeble one that the wind might lull, and the sea become a little calmer, before the ship broke up.

For a while, however, the gale increased, and the sea too, and we were drenched with rain and spray, the ship's timbers ever and anon yielding with a crashing sound, whilst the water kept rising higher and higher within her, and our eyes kept continually straining towards the shore. Thus were we in awful uncertainty for hours, yet hope still lived on feebly. At length the voice of Captain Bowen, of the merchant service, a passenger, was heard. The boat was righted, baled out, and another cargo of living beings was seated in it. Bowen accompanied them; and we cheered loudly as we saw her return to the beach. She was hauled back by the hands on board the ship; and three times did Bowen safely, by his able directions and exertions, take a boat-load of his fellow creatures to land. He slackened not until exhausted, and the last boat brought off the few remaining, including the captain. All now were safe, save the unfortunate three lost from the first boat.

Captain John Bowen was from the P&O ship *Hindostan* (1) and was returning from Ceylon as a passenger. He was later presented with a silver breakfast platter by the passengers of the *Great Liverpool* in recognition of his gallant conduct. The three unfortunate people who lost their lives were Mrs Archer, wife of Dr Archer from HM 17th Foot; 7-year-old Rebecca Morris, who was travelling with her mother and two siblings; and an Indian female servant.

Captain McLeod was the last to leave the ship at around 11 a.m., after assuring himself that no one else remained on board. Upon reaching the shore he found that many items had already washed up on the beach and were now being plundered by the local people. The purser, Mr Lane, was swiftly dispatched to the nearby town of Corcubión to seek assistance, but the Spanish consular agent could not speak any English and failed to help. Lane was left with no alternative but to proceed to Corunna, which was over 50 miles away. Meanwhile, Captain McLeod continued to oversee recovery of mail, cargo and passenger luggage but was helpless to prevent continued systematic pillaging from the wreck. His efforts were further thwarted by officialdom, since the local customs officer refused to permit items to be removed without written consent from the Minister of Customs.

In the early hours of Friday 27 February, the *Great Liverpool* finally succumbed to the elements and broke up. When morning came help finally arrived from Corunna. The remaining property was loaded into ox-drawn carts and arrangements were made to repatriate the passengers to England. The officers and crew were found temporary accommodation in a large storeroom. The next day Captain McLeod composed a letter addressed to James Allan, secretary of the Peninsular and Oriental Steam Navigation Company, detailing a full account of the circumstances surrounding the loss of the *Great Liverpool*.

Captain McLeod remained in nearby lodgings for another week in an effort to salvage further cargo and effects from the wreck. By this time the stress of recent events had taken a noticeable toll and his demeanour 'appeared to be labouring under great depression of spirits'. The lives lost in the tragedy clearly weighed heavily on his mind and idle gossip even suggested that he may have been romantically involved with one of the deceased. On the morning of 8 March the Spanish consul's party called for Captain McLeod at his lodgings. A heavy fall was heard from within the room and upon entering they were horrified to discover the captain's body lying on the floor, evidently having just taken his own life. Captain McLeod was buried the same afternoon in the garden of an old store on the beach at Fornelo, leaving behind a widow and two children in England.

A full inquiry into the loss of the *Great Liverpool* was held at the P&O offices on 7 April 1846 where Captain McLeod was exonerated of any blame, the board concluding:

An extensive archaeological survey recorded the remains of the *Great Liverpool*, which lies in a maximum depth of just 7m. (Miguel San Claudio/Archeonauta SL)

A gold brooch and gemstones resting on one of the *Great Liverpool*'s timbers most probably belonged to one of the ships more affluent passengers. (Miguel San Claudio/Archeonauta SL)

Silver plate egg cup from the wreck of the *Great Liverpool*. (Victoria Folgueira)

Silver inkwell from one of the stationery sets found on the wreck. (Victoria Folgueira)

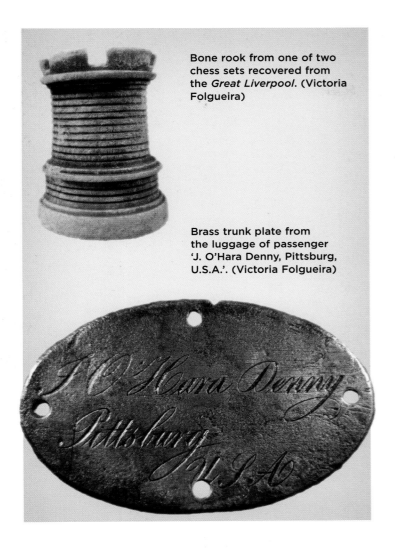

Bone rook from one of two chess sets recovered from the *Great Liverpool*. (Victoria Folgueira)

Brass trunk plate from the luggage of passenger 'J. O'Hara Denny, Pittsburg, U.S.A.'. (Victoria Folgueira)

Diving the Wreck

Cape Finisterre is positioned on the north-west tip of the Iberian Peninsula where it reaches out into the cold North Atlantic. This dangerous, exposed and rocky coastline is known in Spain as La Costa de la Muerte (the Coast of Death) and has claimed many lives and vessels. On the night of 28 October 1596 one of the worst maritime disasters in the area took place when a storm caused the loss of twenty-five ships belonging to an armed Spanish fleet. Over 2,000 men were drowned.

In 2007 a wreck was discovered in the area that was believed to be the remains of one of the lost fleet. As a result of this the regional government of Galicia initiated an extensive underwater survey of the area. The survey revealed several more wrecks from the 1596 fleet and also led to the discovery of further shipwrecks, one of which was the *Great Liverpool*. In 2012 a comprehensive archaeological survey of the *Great Liverpool* was carried out under the auspices of the newly formed Finisterre Project, supported by numerous organisations, including the Institute of Nautical Archaeology, and led by Spanish archaeologist Miguel San Claudio.

The wreck of the *Great Liverpool* rests parallel to Gures Beach in shallow water where the depth ranges between just 3m and 7m. The steam engine, boilers and other valuable materials have long since been salvaged over the course of the intervening years since the disaster but the remaining wooden hull planking has been found to conceal a fascinating time capsule from a bygone era. Of most significance are the multitude of small personal effects, many of which would have belonged to the complement of affluent first-class passengers returning from the Far East. Recoveries have included coins from a multitude of periods and denominations, gemstones, jewellery including a gold ring and brooch, combs and buttons. According to local folklore the unfortunate passenger Mrs Archer had drowned because of the weight of jewels carried within her robes!

Some of the more unusual items raised included two chess sets (one bone, one ivory) and Victorian travellers' stationary sets, the latter including inkwells consisting of a cut-glass silver body and silver lid. Many brass padlocks, keys and engraved nameplates from the trunks containing passenger belongings have been found. On one such plate the passenger's name was still clearly legible, reading 'J. O'Hara Denny, Pittsburg, U.S.A.'. This appears to have belonged to James O'Hara Denny, a young, recently married man in his mid twenties.

A diverse range of items from the *Great Liverpool*'s table service has been recovered, including crockery, hallmarked silver and cutlery.

The committee deem it due to the character of the late commander of the *Great Liverpool*, to state that the utmost vigilance and care for the safety of the vessel and those on board committed to his charge have been uniformly manifested by that lamented officer; and the committee, after mature deliberation on the whole evidence adduced, are unanimously of opinion that the loss of the *Great Liverpool* was occasioned by a very unusual inset from the ocean, which had never been met with in any of her former voyages, or in the experience of the several commanders and officers whose evidence has been taken.

These have been found to bare the identification marks of both P&O and the ship's previous owners, the Transatlantic Steamship Co. There is an abundant range of glass bottles for beverages such as beer, wine, port and soda, along with distinctive 'torpedo' bottles. The *Great Liverpool* was carrying ivory tusks in the cargo and many of these have been recorded on the seabed. Navigational equipment was represented by the viewer from a sextant, complete with intact optics, and a compass.

All of the recovered artefacts have been professionally conserved and are now held at Museo do Mar de Galicia (Museum of the Sea of Galicia) in Vigo. However, the final resting place of the *Great Liverpool* remains under constant threat from the environment as erosion removes the protective sediment, further exposing wood and artefacts.

– Frederick VI –

1785–1846, near Singapore

The *Frederick VI* (755 tons) was an old sailing ship that was originally built in 1785 as the *Fort William* for David Mitchell and chartered to the East India Company. The ship was sold to Robert Donald in 1790, then again in 1803 to the Danish East India Company when it was renamed *Frederik Den Sjette*. In 1845 P&O purchased the vessel with the intention of using it as a coal-storage hulk in Hong Kong and the name was anglicised to *Frederick VI*.

The *Frederick VI* set sail on the long voyage from London on 27 February 1846 under the command of Captain Robert Leisk. At daybreak on 31 July within just 90 miles of Singapore the ship struck an uncharted coral reef and immediately started taking on water. With little hope of saving the vessel the captain immediately dispatched a boat to Singapore to request assistance. HMS *Spiteful* arrived at the scene two days later with the brig *John Bagshaw* and schooner *Buffalo* in tow. The remaining officers and crew of *Frederick VI* were taken off safely and HMS *Spiteful* remained on site for several days to salvage as much as possible from the wreck. Sadly, Captain Maitland of HMS *Spiteful* contracted a fever brought on by the 'excitement arising from the operations at the wreck' and died a few days later.

– Tiber –

1846–1847, Portugal

The iron paddle steamer *Tiber* (764 tons) was built for P&O by Caird & Co., Greenock, and originally laid down as *Ceylon* but was renamed before delivery. The length was 183.8ft (56m) and beam 26.7ft (8.1m). The *Tiber*'s paddles were powered by oscillating steam engines, giving a service speed of 9 knots.

The *Tiber* sailed on her maiden voyage from Southampton to Linorvo, Italy, on 31 October 1846 under the command of Captain Thomas Russell, late of the P&O chartered steamer *Queen*. A few months later the *Tiber* was placed on the Peninsula route to Gibraltar, calling at Vigo, Oporto and Lisbon. A typical cargo manifest for the return voyage included items such as oranges, dates, eggs, casks of wine and leeches (the use of leeches for bloodletting reached its peak in mid-nineteenth-century Britain when an estimated 6 million were imported annually).

In February 1847 Captain Russell transferred to the *Erin* and was succeeded in the *Tiber* by Captain Bingham. The *Tiber* was already proving to be a very successful and much-admired vessel, but its promising career was soon brought to an abrupt and premature end.

On 20 February 1847 the *Tiber* sailed from Lisbon on the homeward voyage from the Peninsula. The ship was carrying twelve cabin passengers, a few from second class and some local Gallegos who were travelling on deck to Vigo. The next day, while making the difficult approach to Oporto, the *Tiber* encountered a very thick fog, which had been lingering over the coast for the last few days. Captain Bingham kept a diligent lookout and fired guns at regular intervals. The lead was cast and the depth was shown to be an ample 17 fathoms, but at noon the *Tiber* suddenly struck a reef while still some distance offshore. Within just twenty minutes the vessel parted midships and quickly became a total wreck. The Gallegos made a clumsy bid to lower the lifeboats, which resulted in them all being stove-in. Fortunately some local fishermen arrived at the scene and rescued the majority of those on board. However, several lives were lost, including the cook, a Spanish general named Lecarte and a number of deck passengers, one of whom one was a young Spanish boy.

A small quantity of the mail was saved and dispatched to England by HMS *Bloodhound*, but there had not been any time to save the passenger luggage or other items of value. Trunks and remnants of the cargo were soon found washed-up along the local coastline whereupon they were rapidly seized by the local people. No blame was apportioned to anyone over the loss of the *Tiber*, which despite costing £28,600 to build was only insured for £20,000.

By unusual coincidence Captain John Bowen (praised for saving lives in the *Great Liverpool* wreck a year earlier) was once more sailing as a passenger. All his nautical instruments went down with the *Tiber*.

Diving the Wreck

Just north of the small Portuguese village of Angerias, 2 miles due west in a depth of 33m, lies the wreck of an old paddle steamer. When it was first discovered by local fisherman they simply named it 'Navio do Norte' or 'North Wreck'. Although the identity of the wreck has never been positively identified, it is widely accepted to be the remains of the *Tiber*.

Resting in open sea on a flat, sandy seabed the *Tiber* attracts an amazing variety of marine life including shoals of pouting, conger eels, octopus, lobsters, crabs and starfish. Unfortunately the exposed location means that fishing lines and nets frequently get caught on the wreck, causing damage and imposing a hazard to visiting divers.

Despite the age of the wreck a significant amount of structure exists to be explored, which sometimes includes exposed timbers

Exploring the scattered remains of the short-lived iron paddle steamer. (Zé Beto Miranda)

that have been preserved by the shifting sands. Ballast stones are littered amongst the tangled iron debris, along with batches of copper sheets that probably formed part of the cargo. Unusual and distinctive features on this wreck are the iron cannons complete with gun carriages and accompanying cannon balls.

Underwater visibility is often good in the area and the *Tiber* has become a popular dive site.

A cannon on the wreck of the *Tiber* which is known locally as the 'North Wreck'. (Zé Beto Miranda)

– *Ariel* –

1846–1848, Italy

The iron paddle steamer *Ariel* (709 tons) was built for P&O by Ditchburn & Mare, Blackwell, and launched on 28 February 1846. The length was 194ft (59.1m) and beam 28.3ft (8.6m). The *Ariel* was powered by two-cylinder oscillating steam engines, giving a service speed of 9 knots. The vessel was also one of the first merchant ships to be constructed with watertight compartments.

The *Ariel* was destined to be employed in the Mediterranean on the Malta–Alexandria mail service. Captain Caldbeck was clearly pleased with his new ship when he recalled the maiden voyage:

The *Ariel* left Southampton Sept. 26, four p.m.; arrived at Malta October 5, at eleven a.m.; being eight days eleven hours on the passage, exclusive of a stay of eight hours at Gibraltar. I think the *Ariel* a most perfect vessel. She is a very fast ship, and an excellent sea-boat, as she fully proved herself in the rough weather we encountered in crossing the Bay of Biscay.

The ship soon established an excellent reputation for speed and reliability and it was not uncommon for the *Ariel* to make record-breaking passages, reaching speeds in excess of 10 knots. The directors of P&O were understandably very pleased and used the *Ariel* as a model for building larger vessels in the future.

In 1848 the British government decided to withdraw the mail service between Malta and Alexandria and the *Ariel* was recalled to England, departing Malta for the final time on 28 May 1848. After calling at Civitavecchia the *Ariel* made for Livorno, Italy, in order to embark further passengers, but never reached her destination. On 2 June the *Ariel* became stranded on the dangerous rocky shoals of Mal di Vetro, some 13 miles south of the Livorno lighthouse. The vessel stuck fast on the reef and water immediately started to enter the holds. Fortunately the weather was favourable, enabling all the lifeboats to be launched without incident. There was no loss of life and the passengers were safely landed at nearby Vada.

When news of the wreck reached London, P&O immediately dispatched a representative to the scene to see if the *Ariel* could be saved. With the assistance of steam frigate HM *Sidon* several attempts were made to get the ship off the rocks but the *Ariel* remained stuck fast. On 1 July the weather took a turn for the worse and the *Ariel* broke up overnight.

The cause of the accident was deemed to be due to magnetic deviation of the ship's compass and Captain Caldbeck was treated sympathetically by the public.

– *Pacha* –

1843–1851, Malacca Strait

The iron paddle steamer *Pacha* (548 tons) was built for P&O by Tod & McGregor, Glasgow, launched on 22 September 1842 and completed in 1843. Length 160ft (48.8m) and beam 26ft (7.9m). The *Pacha* was powered by direct-acting steam engines, giving a service speed of 9 knots. She carried fifty-five passengers and cargo capacity was 5,898 cubic feet (167 cubic metres).

For the first few years of her career the *Pacha* operated on the Peninsula route. In July 1847 the ship was re-registered with an increased tonnage of 590 tons and sailed on the Southampton–Genoa service for the following year. After reverting to the Peninsula itinerary for another two years the *Pacha* was repositioned to India in 1851 in order to commence regular sailings to China.

On 21 July 1851 the *Pacha* was involved in a fatal collision with the P&O paddle steamer *Erin* (1846, 798 tons) in the Malacca Strait. The *Pacha* was commanded by Captain Miller and his counterpart on the *Erin* was Captain Tronson. Captain Miller was an experienced navigator but had only recently been given command of the *Pacha*, having joined the vessel in Hong Kong on 10 July.

The *Pacha* sailed from Singapore shortly after noon on the fateful day and proceeded north-west-by-west up the strait. There were only a small number of passengers on board but the ship was carrying a very valuable cargo, which included twelve boxes of gold bars, forty-seven boxes of dollar coins, nine boxes of gold dust and six boxes of *sycee* (a form of Chinese currency). At 11.30 p.m. the officer of the watch on the *Pacha* sighted the light of another vessel about 9 miles ahead. This was the *Erin* on her voyage from Calcutta to Hong Kong, having last called at Penang. The *Erin* had likewise observed the lights on the approaching *Pacha*. In such a situation the Trinity regulations for avoidance of collisions at sea dictate that both vessels put their helm to port, which Captain Tronson duly did. However, Captain Miller, concerned over the proximity of the Formosa Shoal, did not believe he could safely pass to port and turned to starboard instead. Neither vessel reduced speed and shortly after midnight the vessels collided with great force.

The *Pacha* went down within a matter of minutes, leaving no time to launch the boats or get all the sleeping passengers up on deck. Although the *Erin* sustained considerable damage, the vessel remained afloat, almost certainly preserved by her watertight compartments. The *Erin* picked up the survivors and proceeded the

96 miles to Singapore for repairs. A total of sixteen lives were lost, four of whom were passengers.

In July 1855 word reached the P&O board that the wreck had been discovered by a Mr Lovi. By June the following year over half the treasure had been raised and Lovi was confident in recovering the remainder, but he sadly lost his life soon after, 'owing to exposure and fatigue just as success had crowned his exertions'. The legal disputes in respect of salvage rights and claims for lost or damaged cargo dragged on for several years.

The wreck of the *Pacha* is believed to lie in around 45m but it is not clear whether it has ever been relocated, or if there is any treasure remaining. The Formosa Shoal (or Formosa Bank) is located near the mouth of the Batu Pahat river and stretches for about 6 miles.

– *Douro* –

1853–1854, Paracel Islands, South China Sea

Douro (810 tons) was built for P&O by Tod & McGregor, Glasgow, and launched on 25 June 1853. The length was 226.4ft (70m) and beam 28.3ft (8.6m). The *Douro* was of iron construction and her single screw was powered by a steeple-geared steam engine, giving a service speed of 10 knots.

The *Douro* left Southampton on 27 August 1853 for her maiden voyage, which was a round-trip to Constantinople. At the end of the year the *Douro* left for India to sail on the Bombay–Singapore–Hong Kong service.

On the night of 24 May 1854 the *Douro* encountered a severe typhoon in the South China Sea while en route from Hong Kong to Singapore under the command of Captain Hederstedt. The ship took such a heavy pounding that the lifeboats and funnel were washed overboard and the engines were disabled. When morning broke the gale was moderating and the captain decided to return to Hong Kong under sail. All was going well until midnight when the *Douro* struck fast on the northern shoal off the Paracel Islands. A lascar seaman fell overboard and drowned but fortunately no further lives were lost.

Finding themselves in such an isolated location the decision was made to dispatch the small jollyboat to the island of Hainan to seek assistance. The boat left under the charge of second officer Charles Baker, along with a crew of five and two passengers. Following an altercation with pirates off Hainan the jollyboat eventually arrived in Hong Kong after an exhausting eight days at sea and having sailed over 500 miles. The P&O steamers *Malta* (1) and *Tartar* immediately set sail to find the *Douro*. One of the passengers left behind on the *Douro* later described the agonising wait for help:

We remained in this helpless condition for ten days, constructing rafts, building a boat, and making preparations in case the ship should break up but the weather remained beautifully fine and the sea smooth during the whole time, a thing very unusual in the China Sea, particularly during the change of the monsoon. We were much cheered and comforted by the prayers offered at morning and evening by the Rev. Mr. Young, a missionary, and which all Europeans, without exception, attended. Two Chinese junks were seen at different times. With one we succeeded in communicating, but her captain refused to take anybody on board, and would not go to Hong Kong, though offered 1000 dollars. We could not catch her, or under those circumstances we should have taken her by force, and sent a part of the passengers and crew to Hong Kong.

On 5 June the *Malta* (1) arrived at the wreck, followed by the *Tartar* the next day. All the passengers, mail and baggage were safely recovered.

The *Douro* was less than a year old when she was wrecked off the Paracel Islands in 1854 after encountering a severe typhoon in the South China Sea.

– Madrid –

1845–1857, Spain

The paddle steamer *Madrid* (479 tons) was built for P&O by Miller, Ravenhill & Company, Blackwell, and registered in November 1845. The length was 163ft (49.7m) and beam 23.5ft (7.2m). The ship was of iron construction and her paddles were powered by side-lever steam engines, giving a service speed of 10 knots.

The *Madrid*'s maiden voyage sailed on 17 November 1845 and the ship was primarily employed on the Peninsular service.

On 17 February 1857 the *Madrid* sailed from Southampton under the command of Captain G. Bradshaw, bound for Gibraltar and carrying the mails, eleven first- and eight second-class passengers, a full general cargo and specie valued at £26,857. The *Madrid* was rounding Point Hombre at the entrance to Vigo Bay in the afternoon of 20 February when the ship struck a submerged rock. The engines were immediately stopped, the boats swiftly lowered, and the passengers, mails and specie safely got away. The *Madrid* was taking in water fast but Captain Bradshaw managed to get the ship off the rock with the rising tide. The vessel was then beached in a nearby sandy bay where it was later broken up by the elements.

A Board of Trade inquiry was held into the loss of the *Madrid* and Captain Bradshaw was exonerated from blame, since the rocks were not marked on the Admiralty chart.

In the 1980s a series of underwater archaeological excavations took place around the entrance to Vigo Bay. The remains of the *Madrid* were found close to those of a nineteenth-century armed sailing ship, believed to be HMS *Stag*, wrecked in a storm in 1800.

– Erin –

1846–1857, Sri Lanka

The paddle steamer *Erin* (798 tons) was originally given the name *Erin-go-Bragh* when launched on 26 May 1845, but this was changed before the vessel was finally completed in 1846. The *Erin* was built for P&O by Ditchburn & Mare, Blackwall, London. The length was 199ft (60.6m) and beam 27.5ft (8.4m). The vessel was of iron construction and powered by a two-cylinder steam engine.

The *Erin* was initially employed on the Southampton–Black Sea route but transferred to the new India–China service in 1851. She was the first P&O ship to carry a cargo of Malwa opium. On the night of 21 July 1851 the *Erin* collided with the P&O paddle steamer *Pacha* in the Malacca Strait. The incident proved fatal for the *Pacha*, which sank within minutes, claiming the lives of sixteen of her passengers and crew.

On 1 June 1857 the *Erin* sailed from Bombay under the command of Captain Francis Bayley. Among the small group of passengers on board were several British Army officers, including William Johnson who had been serving in the Persian campaign. A few days into the voyage Johnson summarised his first impressions of the *Erin* in a letter written to his brother:

The *Erin* is tolerably comfortable: commissariat very good, except the tea, which is a go between that article and coffee. However, as much good claret as you can drink supplies the deficiency without grumbling. Such curious critters by way of servants – Chinese without eyes, and with most glorious pigtails, down to the bottom of the calf of the leg; they are very clean, and make excellent servants.

Not long after midnight on 6 June, Johnson was awakened by a violent bumping sensation. He rushed on deck to find that the *Erin* had run aground about 200yd from shore, just off Kalutara, north of Galle on the south-west coast of Ceylon.

A squall had blown-up and with a heavy sea running it was not possible for Captain Bayley to get the boats lowered. Distress rockets were fired and blue signal lights were lit, attracting the attention of the natives onshore. With their assistance, lines were got ashore and the ship was made fast. As soon as it was daylight all the passengers were safely landed, along with the mails, specie and most of the baggage. The *Erin* began to rapidly fill with water and much of the cargo was washed ashore, along with various livestock carried on board. Only a third of the 1,200 cases of opium being carried was recovered. Unfortunately, William Johnson was not able to save all his possessions from the wreck:

I lost some of my silver kit and camp kit on board the *Erin*, which will put me to some inconvenience. It was down in the hold, and they could not get it out. Such a dirty steamer this, and cockroaches as big as young rabbits.

Captain Bayley was very upset over the loss of the *Erin*, especially since he had only been in command for six months. He was admonished at the resulting Board of Trade inquiry for not taking sufficient soundings when close to land, but did not lose his certificate. The board also expressed their disappointment in the officer of the watch, John Gregory, for failing to call the captain when the weather thickened, despite being given orders by Captain Bayley to do so.

Captain Bayley went on to become the P&O agent in Galle and later in Colombo. While in Galle he built a mansion on Closenburg Island called Villa Marina, which is now the heritage Closenburg Hotel.

In August 1883 Ceylon experienced a huge tsunami wave. The residents of Kalutara reported that the sea receded from the shore by over 100m, briefly exposing the entire wreck of the *Erin*.

– *Ava* –

1855–1858, Sri Lanka

Ava (1,620 tons) was built for P&O by Tod & McGregor, Glasgow, and launched on 3 May 1855. The length was 267.8ft (81.6m) and beam 35.2ft (10.7m). The *Ava* was of iron construction and her single screw was powered by trunk-geared steam engines, giving a service speed of 12 knots. She had capacity for ninety-seven first- and thirty second-class passengers.

The *Ava* sailed on her maiden voyage from Southampton on 20 August 1855, under the command of Captain Field. While off Lisbon, and just a few days into the voyage, the ship's three-bladed propeller sustained some serious damage. The *Ava* was forced to proceed under sail to Gibraltar, where she was taken in tow to Malta by HMS *Medusa*. The passengers and mails were then transferred to the P&O paddle steamer *Valetta* (1) for the remainder of the voyage to Alexandria.

After a year operating on the Southampton–Alexandria service, the *Ava* sailed for Calcutta, from where the ship began regular sailings to Suez.

On 10 February 1858 the *Ava* sailed from Calcutta bound for Suez under the command of Captain Cooper Kirton. The 30-year-old captain had been with P&O for eleven years and been given his first command the previous year. This, however, was his first voyage as master of the *Ava*. Although Trincomalee, Ceylon, was not a regular port on the mail service, on this occasion Captain Kirton had been given instructions to land a consignment of government specie there.

Despite losing the *Ava* in 1858, Captain Cooper Kirton remained in the service of P&O until his retirement in 1902 as superintendent in Malta. (Paul Allen Kirton & Miriam Ruth Kirton Macdonald)

Captain Kirton recorded the 'death' of the *Ava* alongside other family events inside his book of scripture readings. (Paul Allen Kirton & Miriam Ruth Kirton Macdonald)

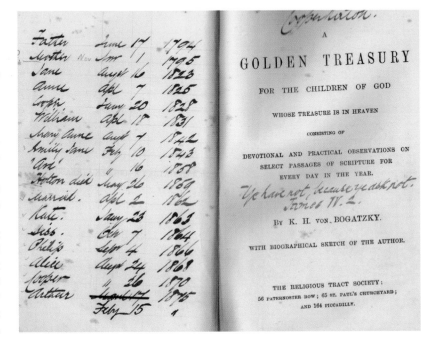

The *Ava* called at Madras on 15 February, where Captain Kirton applied for permission to depart at 2 p.m. in order to reach Trincomalee before nightfall on the 16th, but this was refused based on an objection by the post-office authorities. When the sun went down at 6 p.m. the captain hauled in the sails but continued steaming at full speed in the darkness. At 7.55 p.m. the *Ava* struck a rock near the Pigeon Islands, 12 miles north of Trincomalee, and some distance from the captain's expected position.

One of the passengers on board was Lady Julia Inglis, who was returning to England with her three children following the retreat from the siege of Lucknow. Lady Inglis was on deck with another passenger when the *Ava* struck and described the moment in her diary:

Mrs. Case and I, finding it very hot in the saloon after tea, had come on deck, and were sitting on the bulwarks behind the wheel. Suddenly we were startled by a loud grating sound something like the letting down of an anchor, and just then saw a large rock close to us. I said, 'We must have touched that.' Several men rushed to the wheel, and then again we heard the same sound, only louder, and a quivering of the whole ship. She then remained stationary, only heaving backwards and forwards.

The first boat was launched within twenty minutes, swiftly followed by six more. The passengers spent a long, uncomfortable night in the open boats, staying in the vicinity of the wreck until making for shore the next morning. Captain Kirton and the crew remained on board overnight but the passengers were reassured by the presence in the boats of Captain Haswell RN of the *Himalaya* (1), whose 'quiet self-possession and power of commanding had made him of great use since our disaster occurred'.

Fortunately no lives were lost, but there was little chance of saving the *Ava*, which soon broke in two and sank, taking the valuable cargo with her. The *Ava* was the first P&O screw steamer to be lost.

An inquiry was held into the loss of the *Ava* where Captain Kirton was asked to give his explanation of how he lost his ship. He cited the reasons as being underestimating the strength of the west-north-west current and an unreliable navigation light onshore. The Board of Trade concluded that neither cause 'would have occasioned the loss of the ship, if the ordinary precaution of soundings had been adopted', whereupon Captain Kirton's certificate was suspended for six months.

Despite the mishap with the *Ava*, Captain Kirton remained in the service of the P&O and went on to become the superintendent in Malta, a position he held until his retirement in 1902, after fifty-five years in the company. Captain Kirton possessed a small leather-bound book of scripture readings, where within the front cover he recorded family births, marriages and deaths. He must have considered the *Ava* part of his family since the vessel was listed as a death on 16 February 1858.

Salvaging the Wreck

In December 1857 the P&O *Alma* broke her propeller shaft and had been laid-up in Aden, causing considerable inconvenience to her owners. The replacement shaft had been put aboard the *Ava* in Calcutta and consequently had gone down with the ship. With recovery of the shaft and cargo a matter of urgency, HMS *Chesapeake* was sent to the wreck and diving operations commenced in March. On 25 March 1858 one of the salvage crew wrote a letter where he described the progress made in the first twelve days. In an extract from the letter published in *The Times* on 13 May 1858, he wrote:

The first thing to recover was an iron engine shaft intended for another of the Company's steamers, which is quite useless until it arrives; its value, therefore, to the Peninsular and Oriental Company is immense, though its intrinsic value does not exceed £2,000 or £3,000. Our boat's crews worked away most manfully, diving down and putting lashings around it, and eventually hoisting it up to the surface. It was then made fast to a pontoon of boats and empty casks, and towed alongside the ship, where we rigged heavy purchases, and hoisted in the mass of 10 tons weight like a plaything. We are now busy getting at the rupees in the after holds, and great interest is excited as box after box comes in, each of them worth £500, but stinking awfully of bilge. If we can get the whole of the boxes (worth about £250,000), we flatter ourselves that the East India Government will scarcely begrudge us a few boxes to divide among ourselves for our trouble.

The shaft eventually made it to Aden via the P&O steamer *Bentinck* and the *Alma* resumed service, but unfortunately became the next P&O shipwreck, just over a year later. A large quantity of the mail was also recovered from the *Ava* by divers and had to be carefully dried-out by post-office officials. Each item was stamped 'Saved from the wreck of the *Ava*' before being dispatched to its intended destination. These are now highly prized by collectors.

Diving the Wreck

Although it hasn't been conclusively identified as such, all the evidence would seem to suggest that the popular wreck known locally as the 'Irrakandy Shipwreck' is that of the *Ava*. The dive site lies in a maximum depth of just 12m, a forty-minute boat ride from Nilaveli Beach. Despite the shallow depth, a significant amount of the hull remains intact, standing several metres proud of the seabed in places and exposing a latticework of iron frames. The propeller and remnants of the engines are consistent with a coal-fired steamer of British origin. The wreck is covered in colourful coral and has become home to an abundance of marine life, including batfish, grouper, shoals of snapper, trevally and glassfish, moray eels and octopus.

– *Alma* –

1855–1859, Hanish Islands, Red Sea

Alma (2,165 tons) was the first ship to be built for P&O by John Laird, Sons & Co., Birkenhead. The *Alma* was originally named *Pera* when launched on 12 July 1854, but this was changed in recognition of the Anglo-French victory in the Battle of Alma during the Crimean War when the ship was completed the following year. The length was 288.2ft (87.8m) and beam 37.3ft (11.4m). The vessel was of iron construction and her single screw was powered by an oscillating geared steam engine, giving a service speed of 11 knots.

After completing trials in March 1855 the *Alma* was called up for troopship duties, transporting sixty officers and 1,390 men to Crimea on her maiden voyage. In December 1855 the *Alma* began commercial voyages, operating on the mail service from Southampton to Alexandria. Six months later the *Alma* transferred to the Suez–Calcutta service.

The *Alma* broke her propeller shaft on 14 December 1857 while en route from Calcutta to Suez and was laid up in Aden until April the following year awaiting a replacement. The lengthy delay was due to the new shaft being lost (and subsequently salvaged) in the wreck of the *Ava* in February 1858.

On 18 May 1859 the *Alma* set sail from Calcutta on one of her regular voyages to Suez. The ship was under the command of Captain George Henry, an experienced P&O master who had made the passage dozens of times. When the ship reached Aden on 10 June, Captain Henry became very ill, confining himself to his cabin and placing Chief Officer William Davis in command. Davis possessed a master's certificate and was familiar with the *Alma* and the current passage.

The *Alma* sailed from Aden on 11 June with the mail, valuable cargo and a complement of nearly 200 passengers. One of the passengers was Sir John Bowring, who had recently retired from his five-year position as 4th Governor of Hong Kong. As the ship proceeded northwards through the Red Sea the weather remained calm and favourable, and it was a beautiful moonlit night when Bowring retired to his cabin. Then at 3 a.m. the *Alma* inexplicably struck a reef on the eastern fringe of the Hanish Islands. The dramatic and unexpected events that followed were described by Bowring in his memoir, *The Autobiographical Recollections of Sir John Bowring*:

> In June 1859, I left Aden in the *Alma*, with my daughter, and on the 12th we heard *crash*, CRASH, CRASH. The ship was wrecked. The water rushed in like a flood through the ports, and there were horrible shrieks, 'we are lost! we are lost!' prayers, and invocations. The vessel was almost on her beam-ends, and it was difficult to hold on but I endeavoured to escape through the port. There was neither rope, however, nor chain, nor hand to help, nor ear to hear, so I returned and tried to get to the door of the saloon, but it was underwater, and out of my depth.

When the *Alma* was wrecked near the Hanish Islands in the Red Sea in 1859 sails from the wreck were used to shade the survivors from the burning sun. (© P&O Heritage Collection www.poheritage.com)

Then the sea broke in and extinguished the lights, and all was darkness, the water still rising and rising, till we thought there was little hope, and committed ourselves to Him who wisely ruleth all. Those around us thought that nothing remained but calmly to die, but at this moment a rope descended, friendly hands were stretched out, and we were dragged, one after another, through the skylight.

We had nothing on but our night garments. We were helped to crawl up the deck, and get over the bulwarks to the outside of the ship, and were then lowered into a boat which was full of water. We were rowed to a coral reef, where we landed, barefooted, the coral tearing our feet like jagged knives, but we were delighted to see, from the deposits of the birds, that the sea did not ordinarily wash the higher parts of the island. Arrangements were made to save what could be saved, to organize, to arm, to bring sails for shade against the burning sun, and spars, and stores, and liquids. There was no water for the men, for this, brackish though as it was, was kept for the women and children and the sick. The men took their posts gallantly, keeping watch by night, for we did not know whether the Arabs might not attack us, and we could not trust the crew, who were clamorous for water which we could not give, and who began to break open and plunder the baggage. We constantly bathed our heads with seawater, and though there were many sad cases of sunstroke, there was only one death, that of the purser, who was killed by over-exertion and anxiety the first day. An officer left for Mocha to send us water, and to communicate with Her Majesty's ships of war at Aden. On the fourth day the *Cyclops* appeared, and well did the brave captain and crew exert themselves, conveying all the passengers to that place, where we were hospitably received by Colonel Coghlan. We had some first-rate men among the Indian officers, who exhibited presence of mind, a calm foresight, and a disposition to make the best of and to do the best in everything.

After landing the passengers at Aden, HMS *Cyclops* returned to the *Alma* to salvage as much as possible from the wreck. Arab divers were enlisted to help with the challenging work of recovering the submerged cargo. There were cases of men fainting from overexertion in diving and from the effects of noxious gases; the cargo contained a large quantity of indigo and silk which gave off an 'offensive and sickening smell' as it decomposed in the salt water.

The following October a comprehensive inquiry was instituted by the Board of Trade where Sir John Bowring was among several passengers that gave evidence. Captain Henry and the chief officer were examined at great length over the inexplicable loss of the ship, an answer being sought to the key question:

Here is a ship which takes twelve months in building her. The company to which she belongs goes to a heavy expense in sending her to India; she is well manned, and well found; she is running with government mails and is carrying a valuable cargo, as also numerous passengers, consisting of ladies, gentlemen, and children, with fine, beautiful weather, and the ship is lost. I will ask whether under these circumstances a ship can be lost without carelessness?

The Board of Trade came to the conclusion that Chief Officer Davies was to blame, citing his considerable carelessness, in particular for failing to consult the chart and not reducing speed when unsure of his position. His certificate was suspended for twelve months.

Diving the Wreck

The Hanish Islands are situated in the middle of the narrow southern end of the Red Sea, with Eritrea to the west and Yemen to the east. Sovereignty of the Hanish Islands has been a frequent source of conflict between the two countries but the majority of the island group has officially been part of Yemen since 1998. The diving around the islands is excellent but the geographical location, combined with political unrest, has meant that the area is much less dived than the northern Red Sea.

In 1991 underwater photographer Erik Bjurström described the wreck and its marine life in an article published in *Aramco World* magazine:

The steamer was very much broken down, but the stem [*sic*] was beautifully intact, with a huge bronze propeller. Under the overhang of the stern we found a big nurse shark lying on the bottom. Nurse sharks are docile creatures and we were able to study this one at close range, but his patience was not limitless: After too many strobe flashes in his face he swung around violently, pushed the divers aside and swam away looking insulted.

For a while, we were puzzled by a strange noise in the water around the wreck. We kept hearing a sharp crack, like the snapping of a tree branch. The mystery was solved when we surprised a huge jewfish – a giant species of the grouper family – on the wreck. The fish shot away from us, making that distinctive cracking sound by closing its gill-covers quickly, perhaps intending the noise as a warning. There were many of these huge groupers around, but they fled as soon as they noticed our presence.

The divers also found fragments of P&O porcelain on the wreck, with the company motto 'Quis Separabit' (from the Latin 'Who shall separate us?') still clearly legible.

– *Canton* (1) –

1848–1859, China

The paddle steamer *Canton* (1) (400 tons) was built for P&O by Tod & McGregor, Glasgow, and launched on 28 March 1848. The length was 172.7ft (52.6m) with a beam of 21.4ft (6.5m). The iron vessel was powered by side-lever steam engines, giving a service speed of 8 knots.

The *Canton* (1) was employed on the unsubsidised Hong Kong–Canton and Macao branch service. Due to the constant threat from Chinese pirates the ship was fitted with guns and muskets, and cutlasses and pistols were provided for the crew, some of

whom were ex-naval gunners. One notable incident occurred in 1849 when *Canton* (1) rendered assistance to HMS *Columbine*, which was becalmed during an engagement with pirate junks. The *Canton* (1) was able to tow the sailing brig into enemy range and a comprehensive victory followed.

In 1856 the *Canton* (1) ran aground on an uncharted rock and was stuck fast for eight weeks. Fortunately the ship was successfully salvaged and repaired, remaining in service for the next three years.

On 5 October 1859 the *Canton* (1) met her end when the ship encountered a typhoon and was driven ashore at Macao. Luckily there was no loss of life, but the ship broke in two and had to be abandoned.

– *Malabar* –

1858–1860, Sri Lanka

Malabar (917 tons) was built for P&O by William Denny & Brothers, Dumbarton. The ship was originally laid down as *Semiramis* for the European and Australian Royal Mail Steam Packet Company, but was purchased and renamed by P&O in December 1857 when the owners went into liquidation. The length was 224.8ft (68.5m) and beam 31.3ft (9.5m). The single-screw iron ship was powered by direct-acting inverted steam engines, giving a service speed of 11 knots. There was passenger capacity for twenty-one first class.

A few months after entering service, the *Malabar* sailed out to India where the ship was employed on the Bombay–Hong Kong route.

The *Malabar*'s career came to a premature end in Galle Harbour, Ceylon, on 22 May 1860. The ship had lain at anchor for a couple of days and was preparing to depart for China. At about 2.30 p.m. the *Malabar*'s master, Captain Grainger, went to his cabin for a change of clothes when, without warning, a terrific squall blew up from the north-east. The *Malabar* keeled over with such force that one of the moorings parted and within minutes the ship swung around onto a reef. The main anchor held and the squall abated but by then the *Malabar* was rapidly taking on water. Captain Grainger ordered the chief engineer to get the steam up as soon as possible so that the pumps could be put to use, but for the pumps to work effectively the ship would have to steam ahead out of the harbour. The idea of putting to sea in such a state horrified the chief engineer, who pleaded, 'In the name of God, Captain, don't proceed to sea.'

In 1849 the iron paddle steamer *Canton* (1) towed HMS *Columbine* into action against pirate junks.

A sudden squall resulted in the *Malabar* being shipwrecked in Galle Harbour in May 1860. (Marzolino/Shutterstock)

When the passengers got wind of the plan they petitioned the captain, who by then had abandoned the idea, responding, 'Going to sea! We are going down.' The engines were put astern but the broken hawser fouled the screw, bringing the engines to a sudden halt. The boats were lowered and two other vessels in the harbour rendered assistance. All the passengers and crew were saved but the *Malabar* went aground and broke up on Hospital Reef.

Although a good proportion of the cargo was salvaged, the passengers lost most of their possessions. This caused considerable inconvenience for two ambassadors, Lord Elgin and Baron Gros, who lost state dresses, credentials, important papers and insignia of their honours.

– *Colombo* –

1853–1862, Indian Ocean

Colombo (1,865 tons) was built for P&O by R. Napier & Sons, Govan, and launched on 9 July 1853. The length was 286.5ft (87.3m) and beam 35.9ft (10.9m). The vessel was of iron construction and her single screw was powered by beam-geared steam engines, giving a

service speed of 10 knots. The *Colombo*'s maiden voyage sailed from Southampton to Alexandria on 20 December 1853.

On 16 July 1854 the *Colombo* was requisitioned by the Admiralty for service as a transport ship during the Crimean War. The ship became affectionately known as 'Santa Claus' when she delivered her cargo and Christmas mail to Balaclava. Two years later *Colombo* was released from all military duties and returned to P&O where she recommenced her commercial service.

In August 1858 the *Colombo* lost her screw 20 miles East of Cabo de Gata while sailing from Malta to Gibraltar. She was taken in tow by the Spanish warship *Castilla* and arrived first at Gibraltar, where the tug HM *Redpole* took over and towed her to Vigo. From there she was towed by *Benares* to Liverpool where John Laird and Sons replaced her screw. At this time the *Colombo* was also lengthened and given a second funnel.

The *Colombo*'s eventful career came to an end at the Laccadive Islands on 19 November 1862 while en route from Galle to Aden under the command of Captain Farquhar. Owing to heavy weather no observations had been taken since leaving Galle and by the morning on the 19th visibility was reduced to no more than a ship's length. Speed was reduced to 'full slow', but two hours later breakers were reported a short distance ahead. The engines were immediately

The *Colombo* was wrecked on a reef near the Laccadive Islands in the Indian Ocean as a result of encountering exceptionally bad weather.

reversed, but it was too late to prevent the vessel from being driven forcefully onto Minicoy Reef. Nothing could be done to save the ship and by 8 a.m. all the passengers and crew were safely landed at a nearby island.

For the first few days everyone was accommodated in a makeshift camp, but better arrangements were soon provided by a local rajah. Meanwhile, the fourth officer took command of a local boat that sailed for Galle to seek assistance. Fortunately there were several other P&O vessels in the vicinity and on 30 November the passengers were taken off by the *Ottawa*. A couple of days later the cargo and lascar crew were taken off by *Azof*, and the following day the remainder of the crew boarded the *Nemesis*.

It transpired that the *Colombo* had drifted 32 miles northward from her intended course, a fact which was later attributed to exceptionally strong currents caused by cyclonic weather. Captain Farquhar's handling of the disaster was highly praised by the passengers and he was exonerated of all blame by the Board of Trade.

In 2010 an Indian television documentary team visited Minicoy to film three wrecks, one of which is believed to be the *Colombo*.

In 1843 the *Hindostan* (1) inaugurated the new service from Suez, allowing P&O passengers to travel all the way to India from the UK via the overland route. (Mick Lindsay)

– *Hindostan* (1) –

1842–1864, India

The wooden paddle steamer *Hindostan* (1) (1,800 tons) was built for P&O by Thomas Wilson & Co., Liverpool, and launched on 24 April 1842. The length was 217.6ft (66.3m) and beam 35.8ft (10.9m). The vessel was powered by direct-acting steam engines, giving a service speed of 10 knots. There was a crew of fifty-three and capacity for 102 first- and fifty second-class passengers. The *Hindostan* (1) was employed primarily on the India–Suez service.

The *Hindostan* (1) made her maiden sailing from Southampton on 24 September 1842, bound for Calcutta via the Cape of Good Hope with a full complement of passengers. One of the passengers on board was Captain Engledue, former master of the *Great Liverpool*, on his way to take up a new position as the P&O superintendent in Calcutta.

On 17 January 1843 *Hindostan* (1) sailed from Calcutta with the first passengers to travel all the way to the UK by P&O. After calls at Galle and Aden the passengers disembarked at Suez for the overland route, completing the voyage in *Great Liverpool* and ultimately arriving in Southampton on 16 March 1843.

A highlight of the ship's career was a royal visit from Queen Victoria and Prince Albert at the Cowes Roads mooring off Osborne on 16 July 1849. The royal party were greeted at the gangway by Sir John Pirie, vice-chairman of P&O, and were given a comprehensive tour of the *Hindostan* (1), expressing that they were 'highly pleased with this noble vessel'.

After eighteen years of service the ageing *Hindostan* (1) was withdrawn and reduced to a hulk in Calcutta, where she took on a new role as a store ship. On 5 October 1864 *Calcutta* was caught in the midst of a great cyclone. The *Hindostan* (1) was one of 195 ships in the port at the time, most of which broke loose from their moorings and were driven ashore. The *Hindostan* (1) drifted out of control down the River Hooghly, snagging the P&O ship *Nemesis*, which in turn parted her anchor and struck the company's *Nubia* (1). Although the *Nubia* (1) and *Nemesis* escaped with minor damage the *Hindostan* (1) was driven ashore and wrecked on 6 October.

– Corea –

1864–1865, South China Sea

Corea (610 tons) was originally built for Mr Cohen of Moulmein by Gourlay Brothers, Dundee, and named *The Cohen* when launched on 19 December 1863. When the ship was completed in April 1864 it was purchased by P&O and renamed *Corea*. The length was 226.8ft (69.1m) and beam 27ft (8.2m). The vessel was of iron construction and her single screw was powered by an inverted direct-acting steam engine, giving a service speed of 13 knots. There was passenger capacity for 140, and she was employed on the China coastal and Japanese branch services.

On 29 June 1865 the *Corea* sailed from Hong Kong on a typical east coast voyage, with calls scheduled for Swatow, Amoy and Foo-chow. The weather upon departure was very unsettled and there had been a prolonged period of low pressure. However, Captain Bird did not anticipate that he would encounter anything more severe than a monsoon breeze. As the evening wore on the weather took a rapid turn for the worse and soon broke into a fearful typhoon.

The steamer *Oriflamme* had left Hong Kong a couple of hours before the *Corea* and narrowly escaped foundering, reporting losing three of her boats. During her voyage the *Oriflamme* encountered three dismasted junks, five wrecked fishing boats and large quantities of floating wreckage. A week later word reached the P&O agent in Hong Kong that the *Corea* was reported overdue at Swatow, so the P&O *Azof* was dispatched to search for any sign of the missing ship. Sadly, no trace of the ship was ever found.

The *Corea* was carrying a small cargo and just three European passengers: Mr Noble of the Agra Bank, one Portuguese and one German. Captain Bird's wife had also been travelling on board, on her way to Swatow to visit some friends. There were ten officers on board, among a crew totalling 100.

– Jeddo –

1859–1866, India

Jeddo (1,631 tons) was built for P&O by John Laird, Birkenhead, launched on 22 December 1858 and completed in March 1859. The length was 277.2ft (84.5m) and beam 35.6ft (10.9m). The ship was constructed of iron, with a single screw powered by a direct-action inverted steam engine, giving a service speed of 11.5 knots. The *Jeddo* was employed on services from Bombay to Suez, Hong Kong and Sydney.

Before leaving England for India, *Jeddo* completed a return voyage to Alexandria, which set a new passage record between Southampton and Gibraltar. The positioning voyage out to Bombay was made in fifty-seven days, another record.

On 14 July 1860 the *Jeddo* left Bombay on her first voyage to Sydney, with calls at Galle and King George Sound (Albany, Australia). On another trip to Sydney five years later, *Jeddo* accidently collided with the barque *Ada* (307 tons) off Bradleys Head in Sydney Harbour. Although the *Ada* sank instantly, all lives were saved by the *Jeddo*'s boats with the exception of a crew member named Codling,

The *Jeddo* was wrecked off the Indian coast in 1866 after striking a rock during a voyage from Hong Kong to Bombay.

who was in the forecastle 'under the influence of liquor' at the time of the collision. The *Ada* was later refloated.

On 15 January 1866 the *Jeddo* sailed from Hong Kong, bound for Bombay, under the command of her experienced master, Captain George Grainger. On the night of 2 February the *Jeddo* was less than a day from reaching her final destination when the ship struck a rock, 3 miles off the coast, near the Bancote (Savitri) river. No lives were lost and the passengers and mail were taken off by the P&O ship *Salsette* (1).

A week after the wreck, over 100 members of the *Jeddo*'s native engine room crew appeared before the bar in Bombay charged with refusing to do their duty. Initially the men had co-operated with Captain Grainger in his efforts to salvage the ship but by the fourth day two-thirds of the crew decided to refuse to take further orders. When called to make their defence they said that it was because their clothes were wet. The appalled magistrate sentenced each offender to twelve weeks in the house of correction.

Captain Grainger later admitted to being aware of a discrepancy of 12 miles longitude between the morning and afternoon observations, placing the ship much further east than expected, and closer to shore. Since the captain had not taken any remedial action, the Board of Trade inquiry into the loss concluded that: 'every available precaution should have been taken to ascertain the steamer's true position; that Captain Grainger ought to have stopped his ship and have taken soundings; and that the loss of the *Jeddo* was caused by his omission to adopt that simple precaution.' As a consequence of the verdict Captain Grainger's certificate was suspended for six months.

– *Singapore* (1) –

1850–1867, Japan

The iron paddle steamer *Singapore* (1) (1,300 tons) was built for P&O by Tod & McGregor, Glasgow, and launched on 24 September 1850. The length was 253.3ft (77.2m) and beam 29.3ft (8.9m). The ship was powered by direct-acting oscillating steam engines, giving a service speed of 11.5 knots. A sister ship, *Ganges* (1), had been launched earlier the same year. *Singapore* (1) carried a crew of ninety-six and was employed on the Bombay–Hong Kong and Hong Kong–Shanghai services.

The *Singapore* (1) completed one round-trip voyage from Southampton to Constantinople before being prepared for relocation to India. Within days of her intended departure, last-minute orders were received for the ship to assist in conveying troops to the war in Kaffraria. After undergoing some modifications, which included the addition of an orlop deck, the *Singapore* (1) sailed for the Cape on 17 March under the command of Captain Robert Evans.

After five years in service, P&O considered a proposal to fit the *Singapore* (1) with new boilers and convert the paddles to screw propulsion, but the plan was dropped. In 1860 the ship was laid up in Bombay for a while before undergoing an extensive refit and resuming service in 1862. In March 1867 the ageing paddle steamer inaugurated the new Shanghai–Yokohama service.

Shortly after noon on 20 August 1867, while on a passage from Yokohama to Hakodate, the *Singapore* (1) struck an uncharted rock

Passengers preparing to board a P&O steamer at Southampton Docks in the 1850s.

within just a few miles of her destination. The ship was travelling at full speed and the weather was calm and clear. The force of the impact tore the side of the ship open and water immediately rushed into the engine room. Without hesitation, Captain Wilkinson ordered the boats to be lowered and the passengers placed in them. The exercise was carried out with utmost efficiency and the first boat was away within six minutes. The captain stayed on board with a few men for as long as he could, saving passenger baggage, provisions and his navigational instruments. By now the *Singapore* (1) had drifted about 5 miles out into deeper water and, with the stern ports just a few inches above the waterline, Captain Wilkinson finally abandoned ship. His recollections of the vessel's last moments were reported in the *Japan Times Overland Mail*:

> She turned as if upon a pivot, the stern disappeared, her forefoot rose 30 feet out of the water, and she sank at once. And then occurred a curious incident, which would almost seem to show that, after she had so long 'walked the waters like a thing of life,' the sentiment principle only deserted her as she went down to her grave. The last thing one of the quartermasters had done before he left the ship was to run up the flags, and the well-known colours of the company were flying at the main as the last boat left her side. But when she took her final plunge the main signal halyards broke, and the flag slowly dipped as she disappeared, as if to bid her crew a mute farewell.

All the boats made it to shore settlements where their occupants passed a sleepless night, being plagued by mosquitoes and other strange insects, including 'one particularly venomous little black creature' whose bite left very unpleasant after-effects. The passengers and crew were soon taken on board the Prussian steam frigate *Vineta* where they were very well attended to. The *Vineta* transported them as far as Hakodate, from where they completed the rest of the voyage to Yokohama aboard the chartered Japanese steamer *Taipangyo*.

Captain Wilkinson was highly praised for his handling of the incident and averting any loss of life, the *Japan Times Overland Mail* concluding:

> This happy result is in great measure due most certainly to Captain Wilkinson, whose care of and pride in his boats has constantly been the subject of remark.

The cargo lost with the *Singapore* (1) included sugar and $47,000 of Japanese coin.

– Niphon –

1865–1868, China

Niphon (695 tons) was built by John Key at Kinghorn, Kirkcaldy, for the builders themselves, and named *Kinghorn* when launched on 12 April 1865. A few months later the ship was purchased by P&O and renamed *Niphon*. The length was 223.7ft (68.2m) and beam 26.6ft (8.1m). The ship was iron with a single screw, powered by direct-acting horizontal steam engines, giving a service speed of 10 knots.

The *Niphon* sailed on her maiden voyage from Southampton to Alexandria on 1 November 1865, after which the ship was placed on the China Coast service.

During the early evening of 23 January 1868, the *Niphon* was proceeding up the Chinese inner coastal passage in a heavy sea with the wind blowing fresh from the north-east when her master, Captain Peake, was surprised to find the ship strike a reef. The position was estimated to be just eastward of House Hill, some 25 miles south of Amoy (modern-day Xiamen). With the vessel rapidly filling with water and two boats already washed away, the captain ordered the remaining boats to be lowered as quickly as possible. One lifeboat was stove-in but there was just enough time to transfer the occupants to the remaining boats. Before everyone could be taken off, the *Niphon* suddenly shipped a heavy sea and rolled violently, taking the lives of boilermaker William Truscott, gunner Charles Parker, five Chinese crew and four Chinese passengers. The remaining Chinese passengers were reluctant to leave the sinking vessel and one man refused to go, clinging steadfastly to the mizzenmast, which soon fell, taking the man with it. Just as the last boat was leaving, the *Niphon* split in two and rapidly broke up. When all the surviving passengers and crew were mustered on shore a total of thirteen were confirmed missing. Only one bag of mail was saved.

An official inquiry into the loss of the *Niphon* was convened at Amoy the week after the wreck. The cause was found to be primarily due to an 'unusually strong indraught' and 'the existence of an uncharted reef projecting from House Hill'. Captain Peake was exonerated of all blame and acknowledged for doing everything within his power to save the lives of passengers and crew. The court also singled out a passenger for praise, Lieutenant Anson RN, 'who at great personal risk made many and successful attempts to save the lives of the people on board'.

– Benares –

1858–1868, Fisherman's Islands, China Sea

Benares (1,491 tons) was built for P&O by Tod & McGregor, Glasgow, and launched on 1 February 1858. The length was 293.7ft (89.5m) and beam 38.5ft (11.7m). The ship was constructed of iron, with a single screw powered by direct-acting inverted steam engines, giving a service speed of 12 knots. There was accommodation for ninety first- and thirty second-class passengers.

The Benares sailed on her maiden voyage from Gravesend on 3 April 1858 under the command of Captain Joy. The ship was bound for Alexandria and was carrying 600 troops on board, whose final destination was India.

In August 1858 Queen Victoria and Prince Albert received an invitation to the opening of a new port at Cherbourg where Napoleon III was keen to reassure Britain that his improvements to the naval base did not pose a threat. The Benares took part in celebrations, along with P&O's Pera (2) and Salsette (1).

The Benares was involved in several incidents that required her to tow other P&O vessels: in August 1858 Colombo was towed from Vigo to Spain, in February 1864 Candia (1) was towed from

Officers and crew on board the Benares. The ship was wrecked in 1868 after striking an uncharted rock off the coast of Taiwan.

Sandheads to Calcutta, and in March the same year the tug *Colabah* was towed from Sandheads to Bombay.

In April 1865 the *Benares* narrowly escaped being wrecked when the vessel briefly grounded leaving Hong Kong. This was followed a couple of months later by another incident at Hong Kong when the *Benares* collided with the Holt Line steamer *Agamemnon* (2,270 tons). The vessel's luck finally ran out on 23 May 1868 when she struck an uncharted rock off the Fisherman's Islands while en route from Shanghai to Hong Kong.

The *Benares* sailed from Shanghai at noon on a hot and humid day, with Captain McCulloch in command. All was going well on board until 11.15 p.m. when the passengers were aroused from their sleep by a heavy rumbling noise followed by a severe shock. Upon rushing on deck they were astonished at the site of the steamer's bowsprit almost touching a headland. The engines were put full astern in an effort to get the vessel off, but the *Benares* was stuck fast. Over an hour passed before orders were finally given to get the boats away, but by then the ship had started to list heavily on account of the falling tide, making it difficult to lower the boats on the port side. Fortunately all the passengers and crew were able to get away safely and were soon picked up by the Prussian steamer *China*.

A couple of days later Captain McCulloch and some officers returned to the wreck to salvage as much as they could, only to find it being ransacked by the locals, who soon ran away. A good proportion of the cargo was subsequently recovered, but most of the silk was badly damaged by the salt water. The blame for the loss of the *Benares* was apportioned to the two officers on watch, who failed to alert the captain when they sighted land.

PART 2
1869–1912

– *Carnatic* –

1863–1869, Sha'ab Abu Nuhâs, Red Sea

Carnatic (2,014 tons) was built for P&O by Samuda Brothers, London, and launched on 6 December 1862. The length was 294.7ft (89.8m) and beam 38.1ft (11.6m). The ship was constructed of iron, with a single screw powered by tandem compound inverted direct-acting steam engines, giving a service speed of 12 knots.

Carnatic was intended to be based in India, where the ship would initially provide the mail service from Calcutta to Suez. As with many of her predecessors, the *Carnatic*'s maiden voyage was from Southampton to Alexandria, which allowed the vessel's seaworthiness to be fully tested prior to the lengthy voyage around the Cape. The *Carnatic* sailed from Southampton on 27 April 1863 under the command of Captain Burne and made calls at Gibraltar and Malta before arriving in Alexandria on 9 May. On the final leg of the return voyage, passenger Mrs Louise Boyd, wife of Major Daniel Boyd, HM Bombay Army, died at sea and her body was committed to the deep.

On 27 June 1863 the *Carnatic* set sail for India under the command of Captain Purchase. After arriving safely in Calcutta, the *Carnatic* spent the following year making regular sailings to Suez. The ship then repositioned to Bombay, from where she made a number of voyages to Hong Kong before settling permanently on the Bombay–Suez route. The *Carnatic* proved to be a reliable and successful ship, never in the news for the wrong reasons, but her career came to an abrupt and premature end on a fateful night in the Red Sea on 13 September 1869.

On Sunday 12 September 1869 the *Carnatic* set sail from Suez, bound for Bombay, with Captain Philip Button Jones in command. In her six years since entering service, the *Carnatic* had sailed under thirteen different captains, of which Captain Jones became the eleventh during a brief spell between May and August 1868, returning once more in June 1869. There was a complement of thirty-four passengers on board, comprising twenty-three from first class and eleven from second class, amongst which were three female passengers, a child and a stewardess. The mixed-race crew totalled 176. The *Carnatic* was in excellent condition and well equipped with three compasses and seven boats.

The weather throughout the day was fine and calm with a light northerly breeze. As day gave way to a clear and moonlit night, the *Carnatic* continued at full speed on the usual course that Captain Jones had set many times before. The captain was still on the bridge at 1 a.m. when the lookouts sighted the Shadwan light appearing in the distance. At that point he ordered a slight course alteration to the east, but just as the manoeuvre was being completed breakers were sighted off the bow. The master cried out, 'Hard a starboard,' but it was too late and the *Carnatic* struck hard and fast upon a coral reef.

Despite the force of impact an inspection of the ship revealed that the *Carnatic*'s hull had not been breached. Throughout the night the crew tried everything they could think of to get the ship off the reef. The passengers also leant assistance wherever they could, working capstans and throwing cargo overboard in an effort to lighten the vessel. But by 8 a.m. the next morning, a night of bumping and scraping against the hard coral had taken its toll and the *Carnatic* started to take on water. At noon the lifeboats were lowered and made ready for service but Captain Jones still chose not to abandon ship, somewhat to the bemusement of the passengers who continued to be served their meals at the regular times. Some of the passengers even resorted to fishing while they anxiously awaited instructions from the captain.

At 5.30 p.m. the captain finally came and addressed the passengers, thanking them for their behaviour and asking them to form a small committee to act on their behalf. Major John Champain was one of the three chosen, a first-class passenger who was travelling out from

The *Carnatic* moored at Garden Reach, Calcutta. The ship was primarily
employed on the Suez–India mail service. (© P&O Heritage Collection
www.poheritage.com)

The *Carnatic* aground on a coral reef at Sha'ab Abu Nuhâs in the Red Sea in September 1869.

England to superintend the laying of a second telegraph cable from Bushahr to Jashk. When the committee met with Captain Jones they agreed with his proposal to remain on board for the night, his rationale being that since it was already getting dark and the weather was calm, it would be preferable to go ashore in the morning. The captain was also aware that the P&O *Sumatra* (1) was due to pass northbound imminently and would therefore be able to render assistance.

The passengers retired to bed, only to be awoken once more in the early hours of the morning. The pumps had not been able to keep up with the rising water levels, which had extinguished the fires and stopped the engines. The passengers were ordered to muster at the forecastle, where they spent a very anxious and uncomfortable night. By daybreak the *Carnatic* was listing to starboard at an increasingly alarming rate, and the rising tide was washing over the quarterdeck.

Major Champain described the moments of *Carnatic*'s inevitable demise in an account published in the *Illustrated London News*:

Some of us, after waiting hours for orders to take to the boats, went below out of curiosity, and were witnesses of a very remarkable sight. The saloon was full of water, which poured in with amazing violence through the shattered skylights, every advancing wave threatening to carry away the whole after part of the ship. Tables, chairs, and benches were careering about, washed hither and thither by the swirling water. On returning to the fore part of the ship, a climb of some difficulty, we found that the only women on board (two passengers and the stewardess), with a little girl about three years old, had just been placed in the life-boat and some of the passengers were on the point of following. It was ten minutes before eleven in the forenoon. At this instant the vessel suddenly fell back, a frightful crash told us that she had parted amid-ships, and we were all plunged with terrific force into a whirlpool.

At this point the *Carnatic* rolled over on her portside and luggage, cargo, mailbags, men and an 18-pounder gun came tumbling down the deck. Major Champain continued:

Bruised, bleeding, half stunned, and battered by the luggage, we were carried under till all seemed dark. On coming to the surface the sight that presented itself was one which I shall never forget, but which I find it absolutely impossible to describe. Heads, arms, and legs, bales of merchandise, boxes, sheep, fowls, and things of all sorts were being tossed backwards and forwards, up and down, by the rushing water. Drowning men were clutching at each other in their frantic struggles to reach a resting-place, which too many found only at the bottom of the sea. I myself was thus dragged under three times, but, being a good swimmer, I finally got hold of the foretop, which was half above water, and crawled up into the crosstrees, to take breath. In a short time, mutually assisting each other, all the men that could be seen in the water were hauled up. Being now in a safe position, we could look about us; but the foretopsail prevented our seeing the boats, or the men who had escaped direct to the reef, from the starboard side of the ship, as she went under, and for about two hours we knew not the state of affairs on the other side. At length a boat came off to us; we fastened those who could not swim and those half-stunned by a rope about their waists, and let them down. We were all taken off in three or four trips.

The survivors decided to make for the nearest point of land, which was Shadwan Island about 3 miles away. First this required the exhausting task of dragging the boats across the reef in order to reach the deep-water channel on the southern side. By early evening everyone had finally made it to the island where thoughts turned to rescue. Several hundred large bales of Manchester cotton that had been thrown overboard from the *Carnatic* were washed up along the shoreline and were found to be dry inside. These were soon put to good use building a signal fire and fashioning hats, bedding and clothing. The blazing fire soon appeared to have caught the attention of a passing steamer and the survivors fired their single distress rocket to make sure. It turned out to be the passing *Sumatra* (1), which hove to overnight and took everyone off the next morning.

P&O officially declared the number of lives lost in the wreck of the *Carnatic* to be thirty, which included five first-class passengers (Captain Pope, RA, Mr Cuppage, 35th Regiment, Mr Warren, Dr Thomson and Mr Pidding), the ship's purser, Mr Gardner, and his clerk Mr Mackintosh, the doctor Mr Ransford, two engineers and a steward.

A very thorough official inquiry into the loss of the *Carnatic* took place over three days in November 1869, where judgement was made over two key issues: the conduct of Captain Jones leading up to the stranding of the *Carnatic* on the reef and his decision to remain on the ship for so long. Captain Jones was not able to offer a convincing explanation for the first point, simply stating that he steered the same course as all his previous voyages and that an unknown current may have caused him to drift to the west. But since no bearings had been taken to confirm this, he was deemed 'guilty of a grave default'. The court found it harder to reach a consensus on the second issue, especially in light of conflicting evidence between the officers and passengers. The final verdict delivered was for the suspension of Captain Jones' certificate for nine months.

Diving the Wreck

The first diving activity on the *Carnatic* took place just a few weeks after the ship was lost when Lloyd's engaged Captain Henry Grant to facilitate salvage of the mail and the highly valuable gold specie. Despite initial reports that the *Carnatic* had sunk in deep water, Captain Grant was relieved to discover that the vessel was resting on a shallow reef with some parts still protruding from the surface. After several days making daily dives to the wreck, English hard-hat diver Stephen Saffrey eventually managed to penetrate the mail room, recovering decaying mail bags, gold and silver watches and valuable jewellery. A few days later he managed to cut his way into the adjacent room and within three days twenty-two boxes of specie had been sent to the surface. Captain Grant also enlisted local Arab free divers to salvage copper cargo from the wreck and several hundred pieces were soon recovered. By mid November the operation drew to a close and it was officially reported that all the cases of specie had been salvaged, with a total value in excess of £40,000, the equivalent of several million pounds in modern-day currency.

In modern times the Egyptian Red Sea has become one of the most popular scuba-diving destinations in the world. Visiting divers are attracted by clear blue warm water, excellent visibility, abundant marine life, colourful reefs and a diverse range of interesting shipwrecks. The diving offers something to suit all levels of certification, supported by a diving tourism infrastructure offering everything from casual shore-based diving to luxury live-aboard dive safaris.

The wreck of the *Carnatic* lies in a maximum depth of 27m on the northern side of the Sha'ab Abu Nuhâs coral reef, north of Shadwan Island. Loosely translated from the Arabic, *Sha'ab Abu Nuhâs* means 'reef of father of copper', leaving little doubt this was named after the *Carnatic*'s cargo. Despite the presence of three other much more recent shipwrecks at Sha'ab Abu Nuhâs and the clue given by the location's name, the *Carnatic* was not rediscovered by recreational divers until the 1980s. Since then it has become one of the most popular wreck dives in the Red Sea and is probably the most frequently dived of all P&O shipwrecks.

Although the *Carnatic* broke in two when it went down, the two halves have settled together and the wreck lies straight and parallel to the reef with the bow pointing east, canted over at a 45-degree angle to port. The shallowest part of the wreck is at 17m along the starboard side of the hull. The bow and stern sections are the most intact, with both offering opportunities to safely penetrate into the interiors, whereas the midships area is very broken up.

A typical dive on the *Carnatic* will start by descending the sloping reef to the bow. At the very tip of the bow is the mounting that once bore the *Carnatic*'s distinctive bearded male figurehead. Set back a few metres from this is a circular fixture about half a metre in diameter which once secured the wooden bowsprit. This can also be reached from inside the wreck and the view looking forward is very photogenic, although this can sometimes be obscured by the shoals of tiny glassfish that inhabit the wreck.

The exterior of the *Carnatic*'s hull is adorned with all manner of marine life, including hard and soft corals and there is an abundance of varied fish species. At the deepest point the reef gives way to a flat, sandy seabed, further enhancing the excellent visibility, which often reaches in excess of 20m. When exploring the exterior of the wreck it can be worth swimming off a short distance and looking back to gain a greater appreciation of its features. Amazingly for a wreck of this age, several pairs of lifeboat davits still stand proud in their original positions. Good places to see these are along the starboard side and portside stern quarter.

A shoal of glassfish and colourful corals inside the wreck of the *Carnatic*. (Paul Vinten/Shutterstock)

Above left: The light and open interiors allow divers to safely penetrate the *Carnatic*. (Paul Vinten/Shutterstock)

Above right: The intact bow section of the *Carnatic*. (Paul Vinten/Shutterstock)

Although the midships section is less defined than the rest of the wreck it should not be overlooked. In amongst the confused mass of metal there are various engine parts and a boiler. This is also a good place to spot moray eels. The two masts lie flat on the seabed and extend 20m out at right angles to the port side.

At the stern it is possible to penetrate several decks. The wooden decking has long since rotted away and the gaps in the exposed iron frames afford plenty of ambient light. Inside the stern one of the more unusual features that can be found are the expansive wine racks, which housed hundreds of wine bottles. The exterior is also particularly impressive, highlighted by the rudder, three-bladed propeller and distinctive rectangular windows.

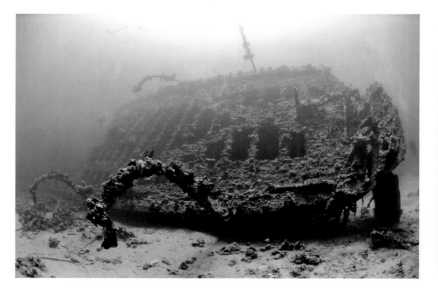

Lifeboat davits are still in position at the stern of the *Carnatic*. (Paul Vinten/Shutterstock)

For a wreck that is 150 yearls old, the *Carnatic* still remains in remarkably good condition, but sadly the hull has been stripped of all non-ferrous fixtures and fittings, along with most artefacts of historical and archaeological interest, now lost forever. Janelle Harrison researched and dived the *Carnatic* while studying for a masters degree in maritime archaeology at the University of Bristol and carried out a non-intrusive survey of the wreck in 2007. In her dissertation, Harrison concluded the site to be 'a valuable source of underwater cultural heritage, and should be fully surveyed and promoted as one of the leading sites for a submerged cultural resource management plan in the Red Sea'. Unfortunately with the absence of funding and an on-going conflict of interests with the Egyptian tourism industry there is little likelihood of this ever happening. In the meantime it is fortunate that affordable modern technology has at least meant that visiting divers have been able to share extensive photographic and video records of the *Carnatic* online.

– *Rangoon* –

1863–1871, Sri Lanka

The *Rangoon* (1,776 tons) was built for P&O in 1863 by Samuda Brothers, London – the same yard that had completed the *Carnatic* just a few months earlier. The length was 294.9ft (89.9m) and beam 38.1ft (11.6m). The ship was of iron construction, with a single screw powered by a tandem compound inverted direct-acting steam engine, giving a service speed of 12 knots.

The *Rangoon* was launched on Saturday afternoon on 4 April 1863 amid the cheers of spectators lining the Thames. When the ship reached mid channel the anchor was let go but would not hold the vessel, and before tugs could get hold of her the *Rangoon* ran stern-first on to the riverbank at East Greenwich on the opposite side of the river. When the tide lowered, gangs of labourers were employed to clear away the mud around the stern and the ship was floated off undamaged at 1 a.m. the next day. The cause of the accident was found to be a faulty 2-ton anchor, its shank broken.

After successfully completing trials in Stokes Bay, the *Rangoon* sailed on her maiden voyage from Southampton on 31 August 1863, calling at Galle and arriving in Calcutta on 4 November. A few weeks later the *Rangoon* left Calcutta on her first voyage to Suez but met with disaster in the early hours of 10 December when the ship grounded a short distance from Aden. The ship was reported to be in a very critical condition but not taking on any water. After an anxious wait of two weeks, on Christmas Day P&O were relieved to receive a telegram from one of their assistant managers in Aden, Mr H. Bayley:

The unceasing exertions of the last fourteen days were this morning rewarded with success, and the *Rangoon* is now safely moored in this harbour. She came in under her own steam. The ship is apparently uninjured, and will be despatched to Calcutta in a few days. I shall proceed in her. The *Norna*, with the outward Mauritius mail of the 20th–26th November, which has been detained here to assist the *Rangoon*, will leave for Mauritius early tomorrow.

A year later, the *Rangoon* found herself in the news once more when a fatal explosion occurred several days out from Bombay on 18 January 1865. Shortly after 3 p.m. the contents of the powder magazine ignited, completely blowing away the hatch cover and setting fire to the saloon. Tragically, a young European boy, the son of Mr Steel from Bombay, was seated at the spot, in the company of his *ayah* (native nurse). The boy died shortly afterwards from severe burns and the *ayah* was in a critical condition and not expected to survive. At great risk to his own life, the chief engineer retrieved the remaining copper kegs of gunpowder from the magazine and the fire was soon extinguished. By 5 p.m. the worst of the incident appeared to be over, but the death of the little boy cast a gloom over all on board.

Then just half an hour later it was revealed that another fire had broken out on board, this time among the cotton bales in the cargo hold. The passengers rallied with the crew to extract the bales and even assisted manning the pumps for the fire hoses. It wasn't until midnight that Captain Coleman was finally able to declare the threat to be over and the *Rangoon* resumed her usual course.

For the next six years the *Rangoon* continued to operate successfully on the Bombay–Suez service without any major incidents. In early 1871 the ship transferred to the Galle–Sydney mail service where she made some of the fastest trips on record, on one occasion arriving in Sydney six days ahead of the contracted date. The *Rangoon*'s regular master during this period was Captain Nicholas Skottowe, one of the most experienced officers in P&O's service.

On Saturday 28 October 1871 the *Rangoon* was anchored in Galle Harbour, making preparations for another voyage to Sydney, which on this occasion was to be Captain Skottowe's last before

All the passengers and crew managed to get off safely before the *Rangoon* sank a short distance from Galle Harbour.

so they were ignored. With water flooding the engine room and the situation now becoming critical, the *Rangoon* made for two large sailing vessels anchored a few miles off the harbour – *Bernice* and *Sydenham*. The passengers were quickly transferred and a boat was dispatched to shore to seek assistance.

It wasn't until around 10 p.m. that two small steamers finally arrived on the scene, with the hope of taking the *Rangoon* in tow, but by then the stricken ship was settling fast and it was too late to save her. However, this didn't deter the local natives from coming alongside in canoes and plundering whatever they could. The *Rangoon* held out longer than expected, but shortly after midnight the ship suddenly plunged stern first, taking several of the natives to their deaths. Eventually all the passengers and crew were safely returned to shore, where they were put up in the Oriental Hotel.

Not only had the *Rangoon* been the next ship built for P&O after the *Carnatic*, but she now followed as the next to be lost – the *Carnatic* herself having been wrecked on 3 September 1869. The loss of the *Rangoon* was discussed at the thirty-first annual general meeting of the Peninsular and Oriental Steam Navigation Company, held in London the month after the disaster. It was recorded that the result of the official investigation 'entirely cleared Captain Skottowe and all the officers of the *Rangoon*, but blamed the pilot'.

his retirement. By Monday the ship was ready to sail, but was held up awaiting the arrival of the China mails with the *Travancore*. By early evening on Wednesday 1 October the *Travancore* had still not arrived so the P&O agent had no alternative but to let the *Rangoon* sail, since the contracted departure date was now up. It was hoped that the *Rangoon* might sight the *Travancore* outside the harbour entrance and arrange a transfer of the mails. For some reason the local mails had not been put aboard either, but in order to clear the harbour in daylight the *Rangoon* weighed anchor at 6 p.m. prompt and set sail under charge of the local pilot.

As the *Rangoon* arrived at the harbour entrance the vessel slowed right down so that a boat carrying the local mails could come alongside. At that point the *Rangoon* was caught by a strong current, causing the ship to drift out from the main channel and perilously close to Kadir Rock. But before evasive action could be taken the *Rangoon* struck the rock violently, breaching the hull plates aft and letting in water at an alarming rate. The pumps were immediately started and every effort was made to signal the other vessels in the harbour and the authorities ashore of the emergency. The distress rockets were seen from ashore, but were mistakenly thought to be the *Rangoon* in communication with the *Travancore* regarding mails,

Diving the Wreck

The wreck of the *Rangoon* is not as intact as her sister ship, the *Carnatic*, but considering how old it is there is still a considerable amount left to explore. The wreck lies a short distance from Galle Harbour, within view of the historic Galle fort, and is just one of many popular dive sites in the area. The highlight of any dive on the *Rangoon* is definitely the varied and prolific marine life. It is not unusual to descend through a thick layer of tiny pulsating jellyfish before the old iron steamer reveals itself 30m below.

The wreck lies on a seabed of white sand and the visibility in the warm 28°C water is usually excellent. On bright, sunny days it can be just like diving in a tropical aquarium; at times the large shoals of bluestripe snapper can be so dense that they obscure the wreck completely. The *Rangoon* is also home to species such as rabbitfish, bluefin trevally, red soldierfish, bullseyes, lionfish and puffer fish. These are complemented by a diverse range of colourful anemones and soft corals that cover much of the metal structures.

The bow of the *Rangoon* stands upright, several metres proud of the seabed, and has been described as being reminiscent of 'an ancient Viking ship'. Part of the midships section has collapsed, allowing the sand to encroach on the wreck but it is still possible to determine the

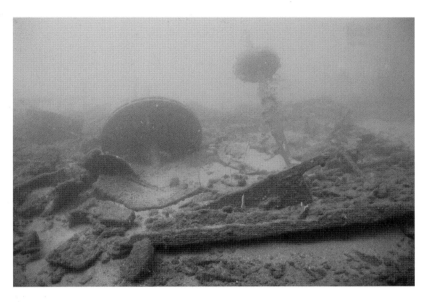

Two of the *Rangoon*'s masts. (Dharshana Jayawardena)

Sections of the *Rangoon*'s iron hull are still intact. (Dharshana Jayawardena)

The wreck of the *Rangoon* rests on a sandy seabed at a depth of 30m. (Dharshana Jayawardena)

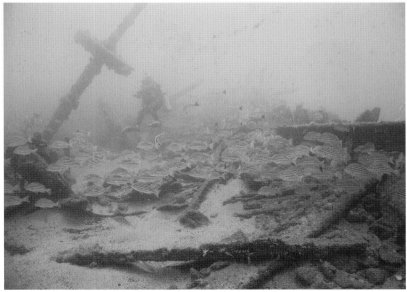

Shoals of bluestripe snapper are common on the wreck. (Dharshana Jayawardena)

The P&O rising sun emblem and motto '*Quis Separabit*' on an ironstone china dinner plate recovered from the *Rangoon*. (Dr Malik Fernando)

A small brass porthole from the *Rangoon* – the diameter of the glass is just 15cm. (Dr Malik Fernando)

outline of the hull. A distinctive and unexpected feature in the centre of the wreck is the remains of two of the *Rangoon*'s masts. Instead of lying flat across the seabed as is typically the case they angle up towards the surface. Both masts are complete with their circular masthead platforms, giving them the appearance of giant sewing spindles. Towards the stern the *Rangoon* starts to rise up again out of the sand with the highest point being the tip of the sternpost.

– Hindostan (2) –

1869–1879, India

Hindostan (2) (3,113 tons) was built for P&O by C.A. Day & Co at the Northam yard, Southampton, and launched on 12 June 1869. The length was 353.9ft (107.8m) and beam 43ft (13.1m). The hull was constructed mainly of iron, but some steel was used above the waterline. The single screw was powered by direct-action horizontal steam engines, giving a service speed of 14.5 knots. The capacity was for 175 first- and fifty-two second-class passengers.

The *Hindostan* (2) sailed on her maiden voyage from Southampton on 3 November 1869, via the Cape to Calcutta. In doing so she became the last P&O vessel to be sent out to India via this route. The ship reached Galle in forty-eight days, but when the *Australia* (1) went out via the Suez Canal ten months later the passage was reduced to thirty days.

On the night of 24 June 1873 the *Hindostan* (2) was involved in a minor collision with the French barque *Alcinous* while off the east coast of Ceylon. The *Alcinous* suffered some minor damage and the *Hindostan* (2) was later held responsible.

P&O had enjoyed a run of eight years without losing a ship, but this came to an end in the early hours of 21 October 1879 when the *Hindostan* (2) ran aground on a reef near Sadras, about 40 miles south of Madras. The ship was on a voyage from Southampton to Calcutta under the command of Captain Haselwood, carrying a general cargo and thirty-five passengers. All the mail was saved and the passengers were landed safely at Sadras. Although much of the cargo was recovered, all hope of salvaging the wreck was given up a month later and the *Hindostan* (2) was left to the mercy of the monsoon weather.

At the subsequent court of inquiry the captain was found at fault for the loss of the ship but, 'in consideration of the anxiety and suffering which the commander has already undergone', had his certificate returned.

– Travancore –

1868–1880, Italy

Travancore (1,900 tons) was built by John Key & Sons at Kinghorn, Scotland, and launched on 29 August 1867 as the *Sultana*. The ship was purchased by P&O a few months later and completed as *Travancore*. The length was 281.6ft (85.8m) and beam 35.5ft (10.8m). The *Travancore* was of iron construction with a single screw powered by direct-acting horizontal steam engines, giving a service speed of 12 knots. The vessel had capacity for eighty-five first- and thirty-four second-class passengers.

After completing trials in Stokes Bay and a circumnavigation of the Isle of Wight, the *Travancore* sailed on her maiden voyage to Alexandria under the command of Captain Methven, departing Southampton on 13 June 1868. The vessel was then repositioned

Launched in 1867 as *Sultana*, the ship was purchased by P&O and renamed *Travancore* prior to her completion in 1868. (Newall Dunn Collection)

The *Travancore* was shipwrecked in March 1880 at the entrance to the Acquaviva inlet, near Castro, Italy.

to India, arriving in Bombay on 19 November. In October 1875 the *Travancore*'s engines were upgraded, after which the ship operated on the Venice–Alexandria and Bombay services.

In April 1877 the *Travancore* made one round-trip voyage from Bombay to Melbourne, calling at Galle, King George Sound and Glenelg. On the first leg of the return voyage the *Travancore* was delayed by extremely rough weather, during which a heavy sea swept over the steamer, breaking a lascar's leg. A handsome bay racehorse named Sultan was also very badly injured and died before it could be landed at Adelaide. A few days later police were patrolling the beach near the south Australian town of Millicent and were surprised to find a large quantity of debris washed ashore from the *Travancore*, which included chicken coops and chairs.

On 5 March 1880 the *Travancore* sailed from Alexandria for Brindisi, Italy, under the command of Captain Robert Scott. The ship was carrying fifty-seven passengers and 1,000 tons of cargo, consisting mainly of cotton. By the morning of 7 March the *Travancore* was abreast of the Greek island of Stamphani. The weather remained clear and fine throughout the day, with very little wind and a perfectly smooth sea. At midnight the second officer, Melbourne Blott, came on watch and about forty minutes later reported sighting Santa Maria Light to the captain. By 2.30 a.m. a thick fog had developed and the light was no longer visible. Captain Scott came on deck and made a couple of small course corrections before returning below to check his charts. In the meantime the *Travancore* continued at full speed, making around 11 knots. Shortly after 3 a.m. the captain returned to the bridge to adjust the course once more, but on sighting land he immediately ordered the helm hard aport. But before the *Travancore* could respond, the ship grounded on a rock in the Bight of Castro, inside Point Maccarone.

With the vessel making water fast, Captain Scott wasted no time in getting the boats ready and at around 4 a.m. he gave the order to land the passengers and mail. While the passengers were being cared for by the local people of Acquaviva, the master and crew remained on board and spent the following day trying everything possible to get the ship off the rocks. By 5 p.m. there was 17ft of water in the hold, so the ship was abandoned and all the remaining officers and crew went ashore. They returned the next morning and salvaged some of the cargo, but the *Travancore* became a total wreck.

At the Board of Trade inquiry into the loss, it transpired that there had been some confusion over the bearing on the Santa Maria Light reported by the second officer to the captain, with the captain thinking it was the compass bearing when it was in fact the true bearing. It also emerged that the second officer was not very experienced, having recently joined the *Travancore* in Bombay and possessing only a second mate's certificate. In conclusion it was deemed that 'the vessel was not navigated with proper and seamanlike care' and Captain Scott and Second Officer Blott shared the blame, both having their certificates suspended for three months.

Diving the Wreck

The *Travancore* remained largely forgotten for over a century until the municipal administration of Diso, whose territory includes the hamlet of Marittima and Acquaviva, decided to place a plaque in commemoration of the tragedy on 8 March 2005. The inscription reads: '*A ricordo del 125 anniversario del naufragio della nave Travancore*' ('In memory of the 125th anniversary of the *Travancore* ship sinking').

The wreck of the *Travancore* lies 15m deep at the northern tip of the picturesque Acquaviva inlet and is just a short swim from the shore. Despite the passing years it still has interesting features to show scuba divers, who have reported finding glass, pottery, household utensils and minor non-ferrous fixtures amongst the iron wreckage. Very little of the superstructure itself remains, most of which is fused into a rocky reef and covered in a light growth of flora.

– *Indus* (2) –

1871–1885, Sri Lanka

Indus (2) (3,462 tons) was laid down as *Timsah* by William Denny & Brothers, Dumbarton. The ship had originally been ordered by Cunard Line as the sister ship to *Parthia* (1) but P&O took over the contract and the vessel was launched as *Indus* (2) on 20 February 1871. The length was 360.4ft (109.8m) and beam 40.4ft (12.3m). The ship was made of iron, with a straight stem (a first for P&O), and driven by a single screw powered by compound inverted direct-acting steam engines, giving a service speed of 13 knots. There was capacity for 129 first- and fifty second-class passengers. The *Indus* (2) sailed on her maiden voyage from Southampton to Bombay on 3 June 1871.

In 1874 the *Indus* (2) was involved in two collisions with other vessels. The first incident occurred on the morning of 17 March when the *Indus* (2) was steaming up the Thames and had to alter course in order to avoid a small schooner. Before the ship could resume her intended course she struck a 1,000-ton barque that was anchored off the Ship and Lobster pub, Gravesend. The barque sank within ten minutes but the crew and single passenger were all rescued in time. The second accident took place on 24 November off Dover, shortly after *Indus* (2) had sailed from London. The *Indus* (2) was steaming at full speed in clear weather when the Red Star Line

Abbotsford, outward-bound from Dover with emigrants, struck the *Indus* (2) on her starboard quarter. Neither ship was fatally damaged and both were able to proceed, but when the *Indus* (2) arrived in Southampton three large holes were found in the hull, requiring the ship to be docked for a full survey and repairs.

On 8 November 1885 the *Indus* (2) was stranded on a shoal off Mullaitivu, about 60 miles north of Trincomalee, Ceylon. The ship was on a voyage from Calcutta to London carrying a cargo of wheat, indigo and tea. The *Indus* (2) was also believed to be carrying a valuable collection of sculptures from Bharhut, a third-century Buddhist monastery in India. There were just twenty-two passengers on board.

The *Indus* (2) had not been holed by the impact so Captain Breeze and his crew tried throughout the day to get the ship off the reef. Towards the afternoon the anchor was let go and an attempt made to warp the vessel off into deeper water. At high tide on the morning of 9 November the *Indus* (2) was worked off the shoal but the main hatch was found to be full of water; it appeared the vessel had somehow gone ahead over it's own anchor and driven the fluke right into the hull! With water coming in fast, the ship was abandoned and soon sank. The passengers and mails were landed at Trincomalee by the gunboat HMS *Ranger*, and from there taken on board the P&O *Clyde*.

Captain Breeze was found at fault for the loss of the *Indus* (2), on account of failing to use the lead when in sight of land and not making allowance for the set of the current. His certificate was suspended for twelve months. It was also revealed that the ship's chart of the area was out of date.

Diving the Wreck

In 2014 the Maritime Archaeology Unit of Sri Lanka published a paper announcing that they had located the possible remains of the *Indus* (2) off Mullaitivu during an expedition in August 2013:

The site is fully covered in fishing nets and it would be a risk to dive there before clearing the nets. Due to its age, the wreck must be in a fragile condition. We observed that it rests on a sandy bottom in water at a depth of around 8–10 m. The wreck is some two miles away from the location marked on the nautical chart. The location is matching with data collected from archived [*sic*] in terms of distance from land and seascape. It is resting in less than 10m of water. There is no other record of a similar ship being lost in this area.

The evidence on site suggested that it was unlikely that any previous attempts had been made to excavate the wreck and there was therefore a strong possibility that the priceless sculptures could be recovered by a future expedition.

– *Tasmania* –

1884–1887, Corsica

Tasmania (4,488 tons) was built for P&O by Caird & Co., Greenock, and launched on 17 May 1884. The length was 400.3ft (122m) and beam 45.2ft (13.8m). The steel passenger liner's single screw was powered by compound inverted direct-acting steam engines, giving a service speed of 14 knots. There was capacity for 107 first- and forty-four second-class passengers.

The *Tasmania* sailed on her maiden voyage from London to Calcutta on 30 July 1884. She was soon followed by three similar sister ships: *Chusan* (2), *Coromandel* (1) and *Bengal* (2).

On 1 April 1887 the *Tasmania* sailed from Bombay, bound for London via Marseilles, under the command of Captain Charles Grigg Perrins, an experienced 52-year-old man who had been in P&O service for thirty years, twenty of those as master. The crew of 161 was made up of fifty-five Europeans and 106 lascars, seedie boys (unskilled African sailors) and natives. The navigation and deck department comprised sixteen Europeans and forty lascars, the Europeans consisting of the master, five officers, a boatswain, seven quartermasters, a carpenter and a joiner. In the engine room department there were six Europeans, comprising five engineers and a boilermaker, and forty-six natives of India and seedie boys. In the passenger and steward departments there were thirty-three Europeans and twenty natives, including a doctor, writer, electrician, refrigerating engineer, mechanics and others. There were 144 passengers on board, some of whom were excited to be travelling to England in order to attend the Golden Jubilee ceremonies for Queen Victoria. One such passenger was Maharajah Sir Pertab Singh, who had brought his best jewels with him for the occasion, said to be valued at £40,000.

After transiting the Suez Canal, the *Tasmania* sailed into the Mediterranean, on through the Straits of Messina, and set course for the Straits of Bonifacio, which separate the islands of Sardinia to the south and Corsica to the north. As the ship passed through the Straits of Bonifacio at full speed on the night of 16 April, the weather became dark and threatening, with a fresh breeze blowing from the south-west. Multiple lookouts were stationed and at midnight Second Officer John Richard Blood Curtis came on watch. Captain Perrins remained on the bridge and eventually retired to his cabin shortly after 3 a.m., having set the course for Marseilles. An hour later the forward lookout sighted breakers dead ahead but before any evasive action could be taken the *Tasmania* struck upon Monachi Rocks. The captain immediately rushed up on deck and ordered the engines full astern, but the ship was making water fast and in imminent danger of sinking.

The *Tasmania* was built in 1884 and employed on services to India and the Far East. (Henderson & Cremer Collection)

Captain Charles Grigg Perrins was one of many people who lost their lives when the *Tasmania* was wrecked off Corsica in April 1887. (K&A Gibbney Collection)

The surviving passengers and crew from the *Tasmania* were rescued the morning after the wreck.

Captain Perrins ordered the boats to be swung out but the vessel had developed a strong list and three out of the four boats on the portside were smashed, along with one of the starboard boats. The women and children were sent to the boats first and were away by 9 a.m., but two ladies, Mrs Walker and Mrs Piggot, refused to leave their husband's sides. After the boats had left, the remaining people on board set to constructing life rafts from whatever materials they could find. One raft had been completed and was lashed alongside in readiness for use when it was seized by a group of native firemen. In defiance of the orders issued by the chief officer they cut the rope and made for land, but only one of the occupants reached shore alive.

The captain thought it would be prudent to save the ship's papers from the chart room, but in doing so he was struck down by the wreckage of a falling skylight. He was heard to cry out, 'For God's sake take this thing off my chest.' Several men rushed to his assistance but they were too late, for a heavy sea broke over the vessel and he was washed away into the submerged forepart of the ship, never to be seen again.

By nightfall many of the exhausted passengers and crew had congregated at the stern where they took refuge in the smoking room, which one surviving passenger later described as resembling 'the black hole of Calcutta', it being a cabin just 12ft by 16ft with seventy people crammed inside. Others took to the rigging, where several perished from the cold.

On the morning of 18 April the weather finally began to improve and the survivors were greeted by the welcome site of the steam yacht *Norseman*, followed not long after by the French vessel *Perseverance*. The shipwrecked passengers and crew were taken off, furnished with 'hot coffee and other restoratives' and taken to Ajaccio, where they were later joined by the other passengers who had been landed in the boats at Roccapina Cove. Two days later everyone embarked on P&O's *Chusan* (2) to continue their onward journey. Although all the passengers survived, there were thirty-five fatalities comprising the captain, fifth officer, quartermaster and thirty-two lascars, mostly from the engine room crew.

The Maharajah was very distressed over the loss of his valuable jewellery but was relieved to receive news via the Foreign Office not long after that it had been recovered by divers. Captain Yates of the Afghan Frontier Commission was not so fortunate. Although he had disembarked the *Tasmania* in Suez, all his luggage had remained on board. Many of his possessions were irreplaceable and included valuable specimens of Central Asian antiquities and natural history and a recently completed manuscript for an important work on Central Asia.

A lengthy Board of Trade inquiry into the loss of the *Tasmania* concluded that the second officer was at fault for the wreck, since he had sole responsibility for the safe navigation of the vessel during his watch. It was alleged by some witnesses that he had not even kept his station on the bridge, having gone below shortly before the ship struck the rocks. In their final summing up, the court condemned his conduct, stating, 'More reckless navigation it has seldom been the lot of this Court to see.' It further stressed his responsibility for the lives and safety of such a large and valuable passenger vessel: 'In this case the second officer has shown less care than would be required from the master of a small trading vessel.' As a consequence John Curtis had his master's certificate suspended for two years, but was permitted a first mate's certificate in the interim. On a more positive note, the court singled out Chief Officer Watkins for special praise:

It appears to us that he is deserving of the highest praise, for although the only officer left on board, after the captain and fifth officer had been drowned, and with only two quartermasters to carry out his orders, he seems to have done his duty throughout as a gallant and experienced officer, taking the lead in the construction of the rafts, and doing everything for the safety of the passengers and crew who remained on the wreck. All indeed speak well of him.

The passengers were also keen to show their appreciation for the chief officer. During the return voyage on the *Chusan* (2) on 20 April they composed a memorial with forty-nine signatures which was delivered to the directors of P&O, along with a purse of 50 guineas: 'The undersigned will ever bear in mind the coolness Mr Watkins displayed in the time of danger, and the undeviating courtesy he showed throughout to all.'

Following the loss of the *Tasmania* the wreck and cargo were auctioned off and treasure hunting, both official and clandestine, began. Furniture and effects from the wreck can still be found in local houses today.

Diving the Wreck

At the peak of the steep hillside overlooking Roccapina, the rock formation 'Lion de Roccapina' gazes out across the clear turquoise sea to Les Moines Rocks and the distinctive yellow lighthouse erected in 1911. The location falls within the boundary of the Réserve Naturelle des Bouches de Bonifacio marine nature reserve where scuba diving has been prohibited since 1999.

The wreck of the *Tasmania* rests in a sandy depression among outcrops of rock in a maximum depth of 25m, with the shallowest part just 10m below the surface. Much of the wreckage is covered in a light growth of seaweed that sways gently in the current. The stern section is the most recognisable part of the ship and lies on its starboard side with the rudder still in place. The large propeller is a few metres away and the tips of two blades have broken off.

The most intact and striking parts of the wreck are the large boilers that have tumbled out across the seabed. With some of these it is even possible for a careful diver to swim into the stoke holes and peer out through the other side. The remainder of the *Tasmania*'s flattened hull is spread out over a large area and heavily concreted. However, it is still possible to make out some of the typical features, such as winch gear and mooring bollards. For a detailed history on the *Tasmania*, including many underwater and artefact photographs, the French book *Le Tasmania* by Charles Finidori is highly recommended.

– *Hong Kong* –

1889–1890, Red Sea

Hong Kong (3,174 tons) was built for P&O by Caird & Co., Greenock, and launched on 15 April 1889. The length was 349.4ft (106.5m) and beam 42.1ft (12.8m). The single screw was powered by a triple-expansion steam engine, giving a service speed of 12 knots. There was accommodation for twenty-six first-class passengers but the vessel's primary purpose was cargo, having a capacity of 214,419 cubic feet (6,071 cubic metres).

The *Hong Kong* sailed on her maiden voyage from London on 1 June 1889, bound for Shanghai via the Suez Canal, with calls at Colombo, Singapore and Hong Kong.

The *Hong Kong* had been in service for little over a year when the ship was wrecked in the Red Sea on 5 December 1890. The ship set sail from Shanghai on 28 October 1890 on a voyage to London under the command of Captain W.J.B. Watkins. On 4 December the *Hong Kong* sailed out of the Gulf of Aden and into the southern approaches to the Red Sea. The captain initially set a course to pass through the Mandeb Strait, with the island of Perim to the east. But at 4.15 a.m. on 5 December he changed his mind and decided instead to pass through the much narrower strait, with Perim to the west. The captain did not take any further soundings or bearings, choosing to navigate only by eye, and neither did he make any consideration for the direction and strength of the irregular tides in the area. As a consequence, the *Hong Kong* stranded on Azalia Rock, on the south-east tip of Perim Island, at 5.10 a.m. The P&O ships *Ballaarat* and *Shannon* both arrived at the scene on the day of the wreck and fortunately there was no loss of life. The following day another P&O vessel, the *Assam*, arrived and took off a large amount of the cargo. On 15 December the *Hong Kong* broke in two and all hope of salvaging the ship was abandoned.

Captain Watkins was found at fault for the loss of the *Hong Kong*, for which his certificate was suspended for six months. The chief officer was also held partially to blame for not taking more frequent bearings and for not suggesting to the master that the courses steered 'were too fine and dangerous'. However, credit was given to the captain, officers and crew for using every possible means to save cargo, stores and fittings.

Eight years later an almost identical incident happened to another P&O ship when the *China* (2) ran aground at Azalea Point on 24 March 1898. After a lengthy salvage operation the vessel was eventually refloated and repaired, finally returning to service two years later.

The master, Captain Morris de Horne, was also suspended for six months, having failed to heed warnings from the second officer.

– *Nepaul* (2) –

1876–1890, England

Nepaul (2) (3,536 tons) was built by Alexander Stephan and Sons, Glasgow, and originally laid down as *Theodor Korner* for the short-lived German Transatlantic Steam Navigation Line. The unfinished vessel was purchased on the stocks by P&O, renamed *Nepaul* (2) and launched on 30 March 1876. The length was 375.2ft (114.3m) and beam 40.1ft (12.2m). The ship was constructed of iron with a single screw powered by compound inverted direct-acting steam engines, giving a service speed of 14 knots. There was accommodation for 117 first- and thirty-eight second-class passengers and a cargo capacity of 111,900 cubic feet (3,168 cubic metres).

The *Nepaul* (2) sailed on her maiden voyage from London to Calcutta on 29 May 1876 under the experienced command of Captain Methven, and from then on the ship commenced regular services to India and the Far East.

In November 1879 the *Nepaul* (2) spent several weeks in attendance to the wreck of *Hindostan* (2), which had been wrecked off the Indian coast on 21 October 1879.

In the aftermath of the Bombardment of Alexandria in July 1882, in which the Anglo-French defeated Egypt, the *Nepaul* (2) was taken up as a troop transport. The vessel embarked 831 officers and men of the York and Lancaster Regiment, many of them wounded, and landed them safely at Portsmouth in October. The following month the *Nepaul* (2) was required for further trooping duties, sailing with Vice Admiral Sir John Commerell, VC, the new commander-in-chief of the North American and West Indian station, together with fresh crews for HMS *Northampton* and HMS *Tenedos*. This was an unusual voyage for a P&O ship since it required crossing the Atlantic to Antigua and Barbados in the West Indies. The Admiralty charter continued well into the new year and the *Nepaul* (2) eventually resumed commercial service for P&O in March 1883.

A tragic incident took place on the morning of 20 January 1887 when the *Nepaul* (2) was inbound to Shanghai in a thick fog. Captain Alderton was on the bridge and ordered the speed to be reduced to 'half-slow', the foghorn was sounded regularly and a good lookout was being kept. Then just as the *Nepaul* (2) was approaching the outer reaches of the Yangtze river, the whistle from another steamer was heard close by. The engines were immediately reversed, but it was too late to prevent the *Nepaul* (2) from colliding with the Chinese man-of-war *Wan Nien Ching*, which was anchored in the river mouth waiting for the fog to clear. The *Wan Nien Ching* was carrying close to 300 Chinese passengers, many of whom were travelling to the Spring Festival. Their ship holed and, sinking, the panic-stricken passengers swarmed onto the decks, some taking to the rigging, others desperately scrambling on board the *Nepaul* (2). After some initial difficulty most of the *Nepaul* (2)'s lifeboats were launched and the ship's crew did everything within their power to save as many lives as possible. Some of the *Wan Nien Ching*'s passengers were frozen with fear and had to be forcefully pushed into the boats. Sadly, despite all their best efforts, nearly 100 lives were lost.

A Supreme Court inquiry was held in Shanghai where the Swedish master of the *Wan Nien Ching*, Captain Damström, made the negligent admission that he had 'made no effort to get out our boats, because I saw it was completely useless as they were completely crowded with Chinese'. However, the *Wan Nien Ching*'s owners were represented by a particularly ruthless lawyer, William Drummond, and the case ultimately ruled against P&O, primarily on the grounds of navigating with excessive speed in fog.

On 13 September 1888 the *Nepaul* (2) ran aground off Marseilles in an incident that proved fatal for the master, Captain Samuel Frederick Cole. The *Nepaul* (2) sailed from Marseilles in fading moonlight but the night had become pitch black by the time the

During her fourteen-year career the *Nepaul* (2) established a reputation as being an 'unfortunate ship'. (Roy Roseveare)

pilot disembarked. Not long after the engines had picked-up full speed, the ship struck upon shelving rocks off Batoneau Island. With the forward part of the ship taking on water it was decided to beach the vessel at a nearby shallow creek. By the early hours of the morning all the passengers had been landed safely, but on seeing the hold full of water, Captain Cole was heard to groan, 'God help me!' He then staggered, gasped for breath and fell down dead. Some early newspaper reports cruelly suggested that he had taken his own life, but the cause was later said to be 'cerebral congestion, brought on by the shock and the painful apprehension which he experienced'. He was described as 'a most popular officer, one of the best men in the P. & O. Company's service, and reputed a good and painstaking seaman'. The day after the accident the *Nepaul* (2) was safely towed stern-first back to Marseilles by a flotilla of tugs and the damage was fully repaired.

The collision and grounding incidents had earned the *Nepaul* (2) a reputation for being an 'unfortunate ship' so it was no great surprise when the next accident to befall the ship proved terminal. The end came just five days after P&O had suffered the loss of the *Hong Kong* in the Red Sea on 5 December 1890. The final voyage of *Nepaul* (2) commenced in Calcutta under the command of her experienced master, Captain George Westrop Brady. The ship sailed on 7 November 1890, bound for London with a general cargo that included tea, wheat, rice and indigo. After making calls at Colombo, Aden, Suez and Port Said, the *Nepaul* (2) arrived in Marseilles, where the majority of the passengers disembarked. On 4 December the ship sailed from Marseilles, intending to make one final call at Plymouth before continuing up the English Channel towards London.

At 5.10 p.m. on 10 December the *Nepaul* (2) sighted the Eddystone Light. As the vessel began its final approach towards Plymouth Sound the weather and visibility began to deteriorate, so the speed was gradually reduced. Captain Brady signalled for a pilot, but with none forthcoming he proceeded cautiously ahead. At 7.20 p.m. a light was observed off the port bow, which both the captain and chief officer believed to be the breakwater light, then fifteen minutes later a flashing light was seen on the starboard bow, so the helm was put over hard-a-port. Captain Brady also claimed to have ordered the engines stopped at this point, but the engineers later denied receiving any such order. After another fifteen minutes had passed a buoy was sighted just off the port bow and only 80yd off. Then just a few minutes later, with the vessel still slowing turning, the *Nepaul* (2) struck fast on a rock close to the Shagstone, swinging right around and coming to rest with the stern facing ashore.

With the vessel taking water fast, the boats were swung out and distress rockets fired. The passengers were taken off and soon

The *Nepaul* (2) struck a rock near the Shagstone whilst approaching Plymouth Harbour on the evening of 10 December 1890.

The wreck of the *Nepaul* (2) as seen from Plymouth Hoe. Local boatmen made a lucrative trade taking spectators out to view the wreck.

afterwards transferred to a pilot cutter. A tug arrived shortly after 10 p.m. and all hands worked into the night trying to salvage as much as they could from the vessel. All the specie, silver plate and navigational instruments were saved and the cook even managed to pack up all his copper pans and utensils. Eventually the rising tide and incoming water extinguished the fires, which stopped the pumps, and all hope of saving the *Nepaul* (2) was abandoned.

The following morning over 100 men from Plymouth descended on the *Nepaul* (2). Salvage operations commenced in earnest and

The distinctive Shagstone rock near the Eastern entrance to Plymouth Sound.

the ship was systematically stripped of all fixtures, fittings, furniture and equipment. The livestock, which consisted of sheep, poultry and a cow, were also placed in lighters and taken ashore. As much of the cargo as possible was saved, but most of the tea in the waterlogged holds was found to have spoiled. The presence of the wrecked liner so close to shore attracted a great deal of interest from local residents, and several boatmen made a lucrative trade taking large numbers of visitors out to the wreck over the weekend.

It was later speculated that the light that led Captain Brady onto the Shagstone was that of the small trawler *Baroda*, which grounded within 100yd of the *Nepaul* (2) on the same rock. However, the subsequent Board of Trade investigation found Captain Brady at fault for losing the ship and ruled that:

the stranding of the said ship was caused by the master, Mr George Westrop Brady, continuing to proceed on in very dark and misty weather in the direction of the shore after the soundings obtained had warned him of the ship's proximity to danger, and by his not promptly and completely stopping the headway of the ship when a buoy was sighted on the port bow. The Court therefore finds the master in default for such stranding, and also for the loss of the said ship consequent on such stranding, and suspends his certificate for six months.

Diving the Wreck

With an average depth of less than 10m the *Nepaul* (2) is both the oldest and the shallowest P&O wreck dive in UK waters. Lying just a short distance from the coastal path at Renney Point it can even be undertaken as a shore dive, sometimes even a freedive.

Unfortunately, after being submerged for well over a century the elements have severely taken their toll on this historic liner. The wreck has become very broken-up and what little remains has been scattered over the reef to the east of the Shagstone and to the north of Renney Rocks. Kelp grows in abundance on the rocks and boulders, which rise up from the gravel seabed. In fact, the kelp becomes so dense that any attempt to locate the wreck in the summer is fruitless, so the *Nepaul* (2) is best dived during winter months. Just 100m to the east, at the foot of the Shagstone, lies the wreck of the smaller *Constance*, wrecked two years earlier. The remains of the little *Baroda* are also in the same general area. Being the larger of the three vessels, it can be assumed that much of the wreckage belongs to the *Nepaul* (2).

Even when the kelp has died back the wreck is still heavily camouflaged and it can be all too easy to completely miss some parts of it. An observant diver can hope to find sections of the hull, ribs, derricks, winches and possibly even the donkey boiler. Part of the bow is believed to lie on the southern side of the Shagstone reef. The *Nepaul* (2) is a good wreck site to rummage for smaller, everyday artefacts. Some of the items that have been found over the years include shards of P&O china, cutlery, ceramic inkpots and tiles.

Visibility is usually very good and the lack of much significant wreckage is compensated for by some colourful and varied marine life. However, divers do need to be aware that there is a lot of ordnance scattered over the seabed in this area.

– *Bokhara* –

1873–1892, Pescadore Islands, Taiwan

Bokhara (2,932 tons) was built for P&O by Caird & Co., Greenock, and launched on 18 December 1872. The length was 361.5ft (110.2m) and beam 39ft (11.9m). The ship was of iron construction with a single screw powered by a two-cylinder compound inverted direct-acting steam engine, giving a service speed of 12 knots. There was capacity for 133 first- and fifty-five second-class passengers.

The *Bokhara* sailed on her maiden voyage from Southampton on 10 April 1873, bound for Bombay, with calls at Alexandria, Suez and Aden. Just two months later on 21 June the ship struck a rock while leaving Hong Kong, requiring her to be beached at Kowloon then dry-docked in Hong Kong for repairs.

The *Bokhara* made a number of voyages from Bombay to Sydney between 1882 and 1883 before transferring to the Bombay–Trieste service for the next couple of years. In February 1885 the ship was taken up as a troop transport, along with the P&O *Thibet*, for service in the Egyptian War. Both vessels underwent rapid modifications so that 1,500 troops could be embarked for Souakim.

On 8 October 1892 the *Bokhara* sailed from Shanghai for Hong Kong under the command of Captain Charles Dawson Sams. The passengers included thirteen members of the Hong Kong cricket team, who were returning from a match in Shanghai. The ship also carried $200,000 in specie, 1,300 bales of silk, 800 tins of tea and other general cargo. Just a day after leaving port the *Bokhara* ran into a typhoon. After consultation with his officers, Captain Sams made the decision of 'laying to', whereupon the sails were furled and the engines reduced to dead slow. The next day the conditions worsened considerably and the *Bokhara* was exposed to tremendously strong winds and high seas. Shortly before noon all the boats on the port side were washed away, along with gangways and bulwarks. During the afternoon the rest of the boats were lost overboard and the ship suffered further damage. The onslaught continued into the evening and at around 9.45 p.m. the engine room skylights were stove-in, putting out the fires and disabling the engines. Meanwhile the ship was drifting perilously close to the Pescadore Islands and at 11.30 p.m. a grounding seemed inevitable. Captain Sams said goodbye to his officers on the bridge and informed them that all possible steps had been taken to save the ship. He then went below and was never seen again. A few minutes later the *Bokhara* struck violently on Sand Island, rebounded, struck once more and sank instantly.

The chief officer, third and fourth officers, two quartermasters, sixteen lascar seamen and two saloon passengers were washed overboard and managed to reach the shore alive. Everyone else on board perished. The survivors spent a difficult night on the island, where they sought refuge in a ruined hut. They were later found by local fishermen who took them to the nearby island of Pehoe, and then on to Makung where they were received and cared for by the local mandarin. Eventually they were all rescued by the Douglas Line steamer *Thales*.

Over 100 lives were lost in the wreck and just two members of the Hong Kong cricket team survived – Dr James Lowson and Lieutenant Markham. Lowson had to have a lung removed but continued to play cricket for Hong Kong until 1898. At the investigation into the loss of the *Bokhara* the surviving passengers testified to the 'gallant conduct of the captain and officers', who were not attached any blame for the wreck. However, the chief officer, Giles Prickett, was so traumatised by the events of the shipwreck that he retired from the sea.

To this day the Hong Kong and Shanghai cricket clubs continue to play regular matches in which they compete for the Bokhara Bell Memorial Trophy. In Hong Kong the bell is used to announce start of play, lunch, tea and end of play.

– *Aden* (2) –

1892–1897, Socotra

Aden (2) (3,925 tons) was ordered by P&O as a replacement for the *Hong Kong*, which had been wrecked in 1890. The ship was built by Sir Raylton Dixon, Middlesbrough, and launched on 5 October 1891. The length was 366ft (111.5m) and beam 46.1ft (14.1m). A single screw was powered by a triple-expansion steam engine, giving a service speed of 12 knots. There was capacity for just thirty-six first-class passengers but the ship had a cargo capacity of 252,970 cubic feet (7,162 cubic metres).

The *Aden* (2) incurred some damage during her launch, which caused the vessel to be delivered later than planned, in February 1892. The first few years of the ship's career passed fairly uneventfully. However, there was one minor mishap in December 1894 on the Thames when the *Aden* (2), outbound for Antwerp, collided with the inbound P&O steamer *Malacca* (2). Fortunately neither vessel incurred any significant damage.

In April 1897 the *Aden* (2) sailed from Yokohama for London under the command of Captain R.E. Hill, carrying a cargo of silk, tea and tin. After making calls to several ports in China and the Straits the ship arrived at Colombo where the bunkers were fully loaded with coal, along with an additional 75 tons, which was stowed on deck. When the ship left Colombo on 2 June there were thirty-four passengers on board, which included fourteen children and three native nurses.

On the morning of 8 June 1897, with a monsoon starting to blow, Captain Hill decided to lay the ship off the island of Socotra so that coal on deck could be shifted down into the bunkers. But in the early hours of the following morning the ship drifted and struck rocks

The *Aden* (2) survivors were rescued eighteen days after the wreck by the Indian Marine steamer *Mayo*.

1 mile south-east of Ras Radressa, causing the engine room to flood and power to be lost. The captain ordered distress rockets to be fired and the starboard boats prepared, but since it was a pitch-black night lowering did not commence until daybreak.

The seas were still heavy when the first boat was lowered and a large wave caused it to break adrift with three men it. Chief Officer Carden jumped overboard with a line to attempt to recover the boat and was quickly followed by the second officer in the cutter, but both boats were swept away, along with the men, never to be seen again. The one remaining, usable lifeboat was lowered to the rail to embark the passengers but a heavy sea carried away one of the falls, causing all the occupants to be thrown into the water. Two officers managed to recover the boat, which was loaded with the women and children, along with a few crew members. Captain Hill ordered the boat to make for shore, but despite land being in view the boat was carried away by the bad weather and vanished without trace.

The weather deteriorated even further and mountainous waves incessantly washed over the ship, one of which caught the captain, breaking his leg in two places. Before anyone could help him, another big wave washed him overboard to a watery grave.

The *Aden* (2) remained stuck fast to the rocks and although the P&O ships *Rohilla* and *Hydaspes* took part in a search for the overdue

ship, it wasn't until eighteen days later that the survivors were eventually rescued by the Indian Marine steamer *Mayo*. Three other ships had reportedly sighted the wreck and had they investigated further, help may have arrived sooner. A total of seventy-eight lives were lost, which included over twenty passengers.

– *Ganges* (3) –

1882–1898, India

Ganges (3) (4,196 tons) was built for P&O by Barrow Shipbuilding Co. Ltd, Cumbria, launched on 26 October 1881 and completed in early 1882. The length was 390ft (118.8m) and beam 42.2ft (12.9m). The single screw was powered by compound inverted direct-acting steam engines, giving a service speed of 14 knots. There was capacity for 120 first- and forty-six second-class passengers.

In 1885 the *Ganges* (3) was called up for the Egyptian War for use as a hospital ship at the port of Suakin, where some 13,000 British and imperial troops were concentrated under the command of Major General Sir Gerald Graham. A row of planking was removed along the entire length of both sides of the ship to allow better ventilation between the lower decks. There were 193 beds, supported by a medical staff of sixty-seven.

In January 1898 the *Ganges* (3) was responsible for a unique rescue in the Red Sea. The ship was bound for Colombo under the command of Captain Falck when distress signals were observed, emanating from the New York-bound *Fernfield* (1895, 3,142 tons). The main steam pipe on the *Fernfield* had broken the previous day and her captain requested a tow to the nearest port, Perim, a distance of over 200 miles. The tow was going well until just 6 miles from the destination when the hawser broke in a high sea. In a determined effort to get the *Fernfield* safely back to port, Captain Falck brought the *Ganges* (3) alongside and had the two vessels lashed together. After a little over two days at sea, the two vessels eventually arrived abreast in Perim, providing a novel sight for the local residents.

The end came for the *Ganges* (3) six months later while the vessel was lying in Bombay Harbour. After disembarking the passengers and unloading the cargo, the ship had been taken to a mooring in order for routine maintenance to be carried out. Captain Creery had already proceeded ashore, leaving the chief officer in charge of the vessel. At 5 p.m. on 30 June 1898 the dockyard hands finished work for the day and went ashore. Towards the end of the evening, at the standard hour of 10 p.m., the electrician shut down the ship's electric lighting and all hands except the anchor-watch turned in. In the early hours of the morning the chief officer was roused by the quartermaster, who had seen smoke while carrying out his rounds. Rushing up on deck, he saw flames shooting across the spar deck and he immediately ordered the quartermaster to ring the firebell. The crew battled to contain the blaze but it was soon raging out of control, so the first of the crew, commencing with the stewardesses, were disembarked in the P&O tender *Bandora*. At this point the second saloon stewardess, Mrs Atkins, was reported missing. A second P&O tender, *Sewree*, arrived on the scene and attempted to help fight the fire with her hoses. Captain Creery returned swiftly to his ship, but soon determined that it was too dangerous for anyone else to remain on board. After consultation with the P&O marine superintendent, the captain also concluded that by remaining at her moorings the *Ganges* (3) posed a serious risk to other vessels, so the ship was taken in tow by the P&O tug *Timsah* and beached nearby. The fire was finally extinguished on 2 July but by then the *Ganges* (3) was beyond repair and the ship had to be sold for scrap.

Although the exact cause of the fire was never determined, an inquiry into the loss concluded that it must have originated in Atkins' cabin. She was the only fatality and there was further speculation that she may have been smoking beneath her mosquito net.

Unfortunately the *Sobraon* became P&O's first loss of the twentieth century when the ship was wrecked after just one year in service. In the early hours of 23 April 1901 the *Sobraon* sailed from Shanghai, bound for London, under the command of her regular master, Captain Lewis Wibmer RNR. The ship was carrying seventy passengers, the mails and a general cargo of about 800 tons. At 8 a.m. the *Sobraon* rounded Elgar Island, having already made a good run of 140 miles. The ship continued to make good progress throughout the day, proceeding at full speed and further aided by a favourable current. By the time night fell the weather had become dark and cloudy. At 10.30 p.m. the captain retired to his cabin, leaving instructions in the night order book for the officer of the watch to take regular soundings and call him in the event of thickening weather, course deviation or sighting of land. At 2 a.m. the third officer took the second sounding of the night and after examining the chart concluded the vessel to be about 1½ miles inside her intended course. He duly reported to Captain Wibmer, who chose to remain below and the *Sobraon* continued at full speed on the same course. At 3.18 a.m. the ship struck on Tung Yung Island, which had been enveloped in thick fog and unseen by the lookouts.

The captain came on deck at once and ordered the engines to be stopped. The passengers were mustered on deck and provided with coffee, biscuits and blankets while the boats were swung out. Distress signals were fired and two boats were dispatched to locate possible landing places or any means of assistance. With

– *Sobraon* –

1900–1901, Taiwan

Sobraon (7,382 tons) was built for P&O by Caird & Co. Ltd, Greenock, and launched on 17 February 1900. The length was 450ft (137.1m) and beam 54.2ft (16.5m). Twin screws were powered by triple-expansion steam engines, giving a service speed of 16 knots. There was accommodation for 114 first- and fifty-seven second-class passengers, and a significant cargo capacity of 318,939 cubic feet (9,030 cubic metres).

The *Sobraon* had two sister ships, the earlier *Assaye* (1899, 7,396 tons) and the later *Plassy* (1900, 7,405 tons). All three vessels were designed to be capable of government trooping duties, should the need arise. The maiden voyage of the *Sobraon* sailed from Gravesend on 26 April 1900, bound for Bombay.

The twin-screw passenger/cargo liner *Sobraon* was completed in April 1900 but wrecked just one year later.

The *Sobraon* struck Tung Yung Island, Taiwan, during a night of thick fog.

Diving the Wreck

The wreck of the *Sobraon* is one of the most recent P&O shipwrecks to be discovered and dived.

In modern times Tungyin Island has become a heavily fortified outpost of Taiwan, located 90 miles north-west of the Taiwanese port of Keelung but only 25 miles from the coast of China. It is a site of missile batteries and early warning radar facilities, so for decades tight security has limited recreational diving off the island. Expressing a desire to protect and preserve their island's cultural heritage the local Tung Chung Community Development Association requested an official search for the *Sobraon*. A wreck thought to be the *Sobraon* was eventually located in 2013 by members of the Taiwan Ocean Security Conserve Association (TOSCA) and positively identified as the *Sobraon* in 2014 following further dives and recovery of artefacts from the wreck.

Diving conditions at the site were found to be challenging, with local tides and weather patterns meaning that diving could only take place between the months of June and September. This was further compounded by poor visibility of often less than a metre. The TOSCA divers found the wreck lying at a maximum depth of 30m – in two halves and badly broken up. They identified sections of hull plating, a mast and one of the twin propellers. Some of the items raised included metal taps, a fire hose nozzle, part of a hatch cover and railings.

There is particular interest in locating the *Sobraon*'s cargo since there have been suggestions that the ship may have been carrying the spoils of the British military intervention in Beijing to lift the siege of eleven foreign legations during the recent Boxer Rebellion. If this is true then the wreck could potentially reveal priceless items of China's cultural heritage.

the *Sobraon* starting to list heavily the passengers were ordered to the boats, but after determining his exact position Captain Wibmer changed his mind and they were brought back on board for a meal. After a while the passengers and the mails were taken off by three junks which made for Foo Chow on the mainland. However, two of the junks failed to make headway in the rough sea, so they turned back and landed the passengers on the island instead. On 29 April the P&O *Coromandel* (1) arrived and took the remaining passengers to Hong Kong. There were no casualties. The captain and crew remained on board to save what they could and prevent looting, but the vessel was abandoned after a couple of weeks.

After reviewing all the facts leading up to the wreck of the *Sobraon*, the inquiry into the loss concluded the cause to be 'that the course set by the master when off Hieshan to pass 10 miles eastward of Tung Yung was not made good, and that Tung Yung, being hidden by a fog and the night dark, that island was not seen till the vessel struck'. However, the court did not find any 'wrongful act of default' on the part of Captain Wibmer or any of his officers, who were exonerated of any blame.

The following year the British government commissioned the construction of a lighthouse on the islands, a direct consequence of the loss of the *Sobraon*.

– *Australia* (2) –

1892–1904, Australia

Australia (2) (6,901 tons) was built for P&O by Caird & Co., Greenock, and launched on 29 July 1892. The length was 465.6ft (139.1m) and beam 52.2ft (15.9m). A single screw was powered by triple-expansion steam engines, giving a service speed of 17 knots. There was accommodation for 265 first- and 144 second-class passengers.

Unsurprisingly, given her name, the *Australia* (2) was destined for use on the Australia service, for which she was joined by her sister ship, *Himalaya* (2), launched earlier the same year. Both vessels were an improvement on P&O's popular Jubilee class of 1887–88 and included a first-class dining room, which ran the full width of the main deck. The week before departing on her maiden voyage to Australia on 25 November 1892, the *Illustrated London News* commented on the well-appointed interiors:

> She is elaborately fitted up, and the different saloons, library, music-room, drawing-room, and smoking-room are ornamented with beautiful carvings by Signor Cambi, of Siena, from designs by Mr. T.E. Collcutt, the architect of the Imperial Institute ... A special feature in her arrangement is the large number of deck cabins. The bathrooms, which are fitted with douche, spray, wave, and needle baths, will prove a great luxury in the tropics.

Having reached speeds of up to 19 knots on trials, the *Australia* (2) soon proved to be a record breaker. In spring 1893 the ship set a record passage from London to Adelaide of twenty-six days and sixteen hours. In November the same year the *Australia* (2) was engaged in an unofficial race from Sydney to Melbourne with the French liner *Armand Béhic* (1892, 6,467 tons), as reported in the *Sydney Morning Herald*:

> According to the log books of the steamers *Australia* and *Armand Béhic*, which arrived from Sydney last night, the *Australia* did the voyage from heads to heads in two minutes less than the *Armand Béhic*. Commander Delacroix, of the

Armand Béhic, acknowledges that he started from Sydney with the intention of testing the speed of his vessel alongside the *Australia*. The officers of the latter boat do not admit that there was any racing so far as their boat was concerned. The chief officer explained that she 'merely maintained sufficient speed to prevent the *Armand Béhic* from passing her'. The *Australia* entered the heads at quarter-past 9 last night, and anchored at 11.45. The *Armand Béhic* entered the heads at 9.20, and brought up below the lightship at midnight. The net result was an advantage by the *Australia* over the *Armand Béhic* of two minutes at the Heads and 15 minutes in coming to anchor. Each vessel logged 576 miles, the average speed being 10.46 knots per hour. The actual steaming time of the *Australia* was 35 hours, being a record trip.

The *Australia* (2) continued to provide a fast and reliable service to Australia that lasted for over a decade. But when the vessel's career came to a dramatic end on 20 June 1904, a typically suspicious sailor later pointed out that the ship had since sailed on Friday 13th, thirteen years since her launch – 'What else could you expect?'

On Friday 13 May 1904 the *Australia* (2) sailed from England under the command of Captain Francis Cole, a highly experienced master who had been with P&O for nearly twenty years. His elder brother, Samuel Cole, had also been a captain with P&O up until his death in September 1888, when he died following the grounding of the *Nepaul* (2) off Marseilles.

The voyage to Australia had been another typically good one for the *Australia* (2). After leaving Fremantle, Captain Cole 'had had a splendid run across the Bight', covering the distance to Largs Bay, Adelaide,

Far left: The 'elaborately fitted up' *Australia* (2) was built in 1892 and employed on the UK–Australia service.

Left: A mistake by the pilot resulted in the *Australia* (2) grounding in the narrow entrance to Port Phillip in June 1904.

in record time. At 6 p.m. on Saturday 18 June the *Australia* (2) sailed from Largs Bay, arriving off Port Phillip Heads, Melbourne, shortly after midnight on the morning of 20 June. The compulsory local pilot embarked 5 miles outside the Heads at 1.05 a.m. and promptly ordered 'full speed ahead' towards the entrance to Port Phillip. As the *Australia* (2) was passing Point Lonsdale to port, Captain Cole went to the starboard side of the bridge to check for any obstructions. The captain immediately noticed that Point Nepean was far too close and just as he turned to order evasive action the vessel struck Corsair Rock. He then heard the pilot order 'full speed astern', at which point the master seized command and ordered, 'No! Slow ahead!', quickly followed by 'Stop her!' Aghast, Captain Cole turned to the pilot and exclaimed, 'You have run the ship ashore!'

When the vessel struck, the bottom 'crashed in like an egg shell' and water poured into the engine room. Within minutes the fires were quenched, the electric lights went out and the vessel was enveloped in darkness. The firemen were submerged up to their shoulders but the third engineer managed to bravely make his way to the boilers where he was able to blow off the steam and avoid a potential explosion. Captain Cole wasted no time in getting the lifeboats ready and within ten minutes the second officer was dispatched in a boat to search for the pilot steamer.

It was 1.45 a.m. when the *Australia* (2) hit the rocks, but despite the force of the ship striking at over 14 knots, very few passengers were awakened from their deep slumber. Orders were given for all the portholes to be closed and for the stewards to rouse the passengers from their cabins. Even then, many of them were reluctant to believe the surprising news. On being told the ship had struck, one man responded, 'Well, let it strike,' and another responded that to be awoken in the middle of the night was 'preposterous'. Many of the

sleeping crew members reacted in a similar way, with remarks such as 'Oh, she'll be alright' before turning over and trying to get back to sleep.

Eventually all the passengers were calmly mustered on deck, emerging out into a bitterly cold and drizzly morning, where they were all served with hot coffee and biscuits and issued with lifebelts, rugs and blankets. With the vessel listing precariously to starboard, four boats were quickly launched and embarked, ladies and children first. The Queenscliff lifeboat also arrived alongside to lend assistance, and by 5 a.m. all the passengers had been safely landed and made comfortable at the nearby Esplanade Hotel. Most of the crew were taken off by the pilot boat, *Victoria*, and there was no loss of life.

A full inquiry into the stranding of the *Australia* (2) commenced in Melbourne on 29 June, where close attention was paid to the conduct of the pilot, George Dennis, a man of over twenty years' experience. When questioned about making the approach to the Queenscliff navigation lights he described them as appearing very differently to how he had always observed them before – 'bushy, like two huge stars, almost touching each other'. He stated that he accepted full responsibility for the loss of the ship, but could not offer any further explanation, adding that he had no recollection of what took place after the ship struck. Focus turned to the pilot's questionable medical condition and a subsequent examination by his family physician the night after the wreck revealed multiple issues symptomatic of diabetes, most significant of which was severely impaired vision. Pilot Dennis had been totally unaware of his condition and the inquiry was startled to learn that there was no statutory requirement for pilots to undergo regular medical examinations. The court concluded that the accident was caused entirely by pilot error and that neither the master nor any of his officers were to blame.

Far left: Spectators gathered at Point Nepean to view the stranded liner.

Left: Passengers and officers from the wrecked *Australia* (2).

Diver George Beckett prepares for a dive on the *Australia* (2) during the lucrative salvage operation that commenced soon after the shipwreck.

Porthole from the wreck of the *Australia* (2). (Don Love)

local draper and businessman Mr John George Aikman, who was extremely surprised to secure the ship for a paltry £290, along with the remaining cargo for a further £60. Fortunately for Aikman, the weather remained fair and he retained the services of Beckett, who salvaged the manganese bronze propeller and stripped the engine room. Through a series of public auctions, it was said that Aikman returned a profit in excess of £180,000, a considerable sum in 1904.

Eventually the bow section broke off the *Australia* (2) and slid into deep water. Two years passed before the rest of the wreck finally broke up, and the remains were eventually dispersed by explosives in 1911.

Diving the Wreck

The wreck of the *Australia* (2) lies in a gutter just on the outside of the reef separating Port Phillip Bay and the ocean on the Nepean side. In the 1960s it came to the attention of local divers who saw an opportunity to salvage some of the remaining non-ferrous metals. Rather than using self-contained underwater breathing apparatus (scuba), the preferred technique was to employ a hookah line to deliver air from a compressor on board the boat anchored above. Although this gave a theoretical advantage of an unlimited air supply, there was always the risk of the line getting caught in the wreckage, especially when the tide started to pick up.

Often removing materials from the wreck would require the use of explosives to free them from the wreckage or to disperse them into more manageable pieces for raising. First the diver would descend to lay the explosive charges, then ascend to the safety of the boat where the charges were detonated remotely. He would then return to the wreck and survey the results, now facing the additional hazards of reduced visibility and razor-sharp metal edges of newly exposed steel plates.

Today the wreck of the *Australia* (2) lies scattered and broken across a wide area in a general depth of 5–7m. A substantial amount of the wreck still remains and makes for an interesting dive. The most significant features include the propeller shaft, boilers and parts of the engine. There is a lot of tangled and twisted metal providing lots of nooks and crannies to investigate. Several varieties of seaweed and kelp grow abundantly in the area but not sufficiently so as to obscure the wreck completely. Visibility can vary but is enhanced by the shallow depth and sandy seabed. The marine life is plentiful and may include an occasional appearance by a shovelnose ray.

Despite the shallow depth, diving in the area can be difficult and dangerous. The dive can only be undertaken on a slack tide and with consideration for passing vessels in the busy shipping lane.

Salvaging the Wreck

A detailed inspection of the hull revealed the *Australia* (2) to have a substantial split running alongside the keel, rendering it impossible to refloat the vessel. Over the weeks following the wreck, salvage teams worked hard on behalf of the Underwriters' Association to recover as much of value as possible, and a significant amount of the cargo and fittings were brought ashore. Divers were also engaged under the direction of George Beckett, Australia's leading hard-hat diver. The work was progressing well until one morning the salvage crew arrived to find that a mysterious fire had broken out on board. The heat from the blaze was so intense that it could be felt several hundred metres from the vessel and the hull was so hot that boarding was impossible. The fire continued to burn out of control for several days, entirely gutting the vessel and destroying valuable salvage equipment.

With the threat of bad weather, the underwriters decided to auction off the ship and remaining cargo. The successful bidder was

– *Delhi* (3) –

1905–1911, Morocco

Delhi (3) (8,090 tons) was built for P&O by Caird & Co., Greenock, and launched on 14 October 1905. The length was 470ft (143.2m) and beam 56.2ft (17.1m). Twin screws were powered by two quadruple-expansion steam engines, giving a service speed of 15.5 knots. There was accommodation for 160 first- and eighty second-class passengers. The *Delhi* (3) was primarily employed on the UK to India and China mail services.

On 24 August 1906 the *Delhi* (3) sailed from London with the mails and arrived in Hong Kong on 18 September, completing a record passage of twenty-four and three-quarter days, and in doing so P&O beat the rival Canadian Pacific 'westabout' route by five days. The competing westward route entailed sailing across the Atlantic from Liverpool to Quebec, traversing Canada by rail, and completing the final leg of the voyage from Vancouver to Hong Kong by ship. Both routes required travelling a distance of over 12,000 miles and it was said that by combining the two it would be possible to go around the world in fifty-five and three-quarter days.

The last voyage of the *Delhi* (3) sailed from London on 10 December 1911 under the command of Captain William Hayward, an experienced master with twenty-nine years' service with P&O. Amongst the complement of eighty-six passengers was a royal party bound for Egypt, comprising HRH Princess Royal Louise Victoria, her husband the Duke of Fife and their two daughters. The weather was poor from the outset, with strong winds, squalls and a rough sea. At 9 p.m. on 12 December, Captain Hayward

retired to his cabin, but was called to the bridge at 11.20 p.m. by the supernumerary second officer amid concerns that the expected Trafalgar Light had not yet been sighted. Two hours later, as a result of fog and some incorrect assumptions made by the master regarding his speed and position, the *Delhi* (3) grounded 2 miles south of Cape Spartel, Morocco.

At about 8 a.m. the French cruiser *Friant* arrived at the scene and dispatched her steam cutter, which took off some of the women and children. An hour later HMS *Duke of Edinburgh* appeared and the French cutter was able to tow one of the *Delhi* (3) lifeboats out to her. Tragically, on the return journey the cutter was turned over by the surf and three of her crew perished. These were to be the only casualties resulting from the disaster. The British battleship HMS *London* was also in attendance and at 11.30 a.m. the royal party were taken on board one of her large rowing boats, but had a very narrow escape when it also capsized in the surf. The rescue operations continued throughout the day and all passengers were landed, bar eleven who came off the next morning.

Although Captain Hayward was later found at fault for losing the ship, the court showed leniency in light of his unblemished career and the 'able manner in which he conducted operations after the casualty, thus ensuring the rescue of the whole of the crew and passengers'.

– *Oceana* –

1888–1912, England

Oceana (6,610 tons) was built for P&O by Harland & Wolff, Belfast, and launched on 17 September 1887. The length was 468.4ft (142.7m) and beam 52ft (15.8m). A single screw was powered by triple-expansion steam engines, giving a service speed of 16.5 knots. There was accommodation for 250 first- and 159 second-class passengers.

The *Oceana* was the third of four new Jubilee-class vessels built to commemorate fifty years of P&O and Queen Victoria's Golden Jubilee. The other ships were *Victoria* and *Britannia*, both completed in 1887, and *Arcadia* (1), which was completed a few months after *Oceana*. At the time of her construction the *Oceana* was the largest ship to have been built in Ireland and was the only one of the four ships to become wrecked. All four ships were heavily subsidised by the government, who required the design to incorporate features necessary for use as auxiliary cruisers, should the need ever arise.

HRH Princess Royal Louise Victoria and her two daughters, Princesses Alexandra and Maude, were among the passengers when the *Delhi* (3) was wrecked on the Moroccan coast in December 1911.

The Jubilee-class *Oceana* was launched in 1887, the year of Queen Victoria's Golden Jubilee, and made her maiden voyage to Australia the following year.

The maiden voyage from London to Australia was advertised in the *Morning Post* on 5 March 1888:

AUSTRALIA, NEW ZEALAND.TASMANIA.— By the P. and O. Company's Steamers (carrying her Majesty's Mails) from London. Departures every Fortnight. Electric lighting ; music and smoking saloons, very superior cuisine. The Company's fine Steamer OCEANA, 6.500 tons, 7.000-horse power, Captain G. N. HECTOR, will LEAVE LONDON for SYDNEY, MELBOURNE. ADELAIDE, and ALBANY, on FRIDAY, March 9, and will be followed by the Britannia, 6,257 tons, on March 23. These fine ships are fitted with all the latest improvements, and have accommodation for first and second saloon passengers equal to any afloat; fares from £30 to £70 : Return Tickets, £65 to £105. First and second class passengers only carried.

The *Oceana* arrived in Sydney on 20 April 1888 where the impressive new vessel was described as 'nothing short of a large floating hotel of the most sumptuous description'.

In October 1889 HRH Prince Albert Victor embarked on a tour of British India. After arriving in Port Said aboard HMY *Osborne*, the prince transferred to the *Oceana* for the final leg of the voyage to Bombay. Another high-profile passenger to sail on the *Oceana* was the American author and humourist Mark Twain, who joined the *Oceana* in Sydney in December 1895 for a voyage to Ceylon. Twain later commented about his experience on the ship in his book *Following the Equator: A Journey Around the World*:

This *Oceana* is a stately big ship, luxuriously appointed. She has spacious promenade decks. Large rooms; a surpassingly comfortable ship. The officers' library is well selected; a ship's library is not usually that ... For meals, the bugle call, man-of-war fashion; a pleasant change from the terrible gong ... Three big cats – very friendly loafers; they wander all over the ship; the white one follows the chief steward around like a dog. There is also a basket of kittens. One of these cats goes ashore, in port, in England, Australia, and India, to see how his various families are getting along, and is seen no more till the ship is ready to sail. No one knows how he finds out the sailing date, but no doubt he comes down to the dock every day and takes a look, and when he sees baggage and passengers flocking in, recognizes that it is time to get aboard. This is what the sailors believe.

In July 1902 the *Oceana* ran aground in the Suez Canal but was soon towed off by a steam tug without incurring any significant damage. A similar incident had occurred during an earlier canal transit in 1888.

In 1904 all four vessels of the Jubilee class underwent an extensive refit in preparation for a new mail service contract due to commence in February 1905. Among the improvements were completely

The *Oceana*'s valuable cargo of gold and silver was recovered from the wreck during a salvage operation that lasted ten days.

remodelled passenger accommodation, improved lighting and ventilation and renewed rigging. Down below, the engine room machinery was given a complete overhaul and all the boilers were retubed. After the new mail contract came into force the *Oceana* switched from the Australia service to the India route.

The final voyage of the *Oceana* sailed at 2 p.m. on 15 March 1912 from Tilbury for Bombay under the command of Captain Thomas Hermann Hide RNR. The captain had been in the company's service for thirty-one years and had recently rejoined the *Oceana* on 4 March, having commanded the vessel once before between November 1908 to November 1909. There were forty-one passengers on board, of which fifteen were first class and the remainder second class. The crew of 220 included 153 lascars. The ship also carried a highly valuable cargo of gold and silver ingots worth nearly £750,000.

In the early hours of the next morning the *Oceana* passed a short distance off the Royal Sovereign light vessel in the English Channel. The weather was fine and clear with a fresh north-west wind and the pilot Mr T. Penny was still on board, it being the usual practice to retain the pilot until reaching the Nab light vessel. Shortly after 3 a.m. the pilot retired to the chart room to take a rest, leaving the bridge in charge of the chief officer, Walter Naylor RNR. Shortly before 4 a.m. the forward lookout sounded the bell to indicate the presence of another vessel approaching off the port bow. This turned out to be the *Pisagua* (1892, 2,850 tons), a German-registered, four-masted steel-hulled sailing ship, homeward-bound for Hamburg with a cargo of nitrate. With the vessels little more than a mile apart the chief officer gave the order 'port 5 degrees', at which point the pilot returned to the bridge and questioned the change of course. Upon seeing the rapidly closing *Pisagua*, the pilot ordered, 'Hard-a-port'. But it was already too late to avoid a collision and the *Pisagua* struck the *Oceana* hard on the port bow, almost at a right angle.

The ship's carpenter was lying in his bunk and the force of the blow wrecked his cabin, crushing his leg against the side of the bunk. The injury was so bad that his leg was later amputated. The *Pisagua* rebounded and struck again, this time near the bridge, sweeping away all bar one of the *Oceana*'s port-side lifeboats. The most serious damage was a great gash below the waterline where the plating had been torn away for about 18ft.

Captain Hide ordered the chief officer to get all hands on deck and get the boats swung out ready for use. Unfortunately lifeboat number one was launched prematurely while the *Oceana* was still underway. This had tragic consequences when the painter fouled the forward fall, capsizing the boat and casting the occupants into the water. Two crew members managed to scramble back on board and the chief officer sent the third mate in the ship's cutter to search for the remaining

people. Despite being sent as a rescue boat, a number of passengers also managed to get themselves into the cutter before it was lowered. After getting clear, the occupants of the cutter heard a cry emanating from the upturned lifeboat and were able to rescue passenger Miss Macfarlane who had been clinging on desperately. Following a brief search for more survivors the third mate inexplicably ordered the cutter to make for Beachy Head, assuming that further boats would be sent to aid the search. None of the other occupants of lifeboat number one were found alive and in total seventeen people perished. The seven passengers in the boat included Reverend J.C. Leishman, along with his wife, baby daughter and nanny, Miss Avern. After two hours the leaking and overcrowded cutter was found by the Eastbourne lifeboat, which took all the exhausted occupants aboard.

Meanwhile, the watertight doors were closed and distress rockets were fired from the bridge. The first vessel to arrive on the scene was the cross-Channel passenger ferry *Sussex* (1896, 1,565 tons), which took all the passengers and most of the crew aboard. By 6.30 a.m. the *Sussex* had been joined by the small steamship *Queensgarth* and the tug *Alert*. A tow line from the *Alert* was secured to the *Oceana*'s stern and the tug commenced to tow the ship towards Dover, despite the protestations from the chief officer, who felt they should make straight for the shoreline and beach the ship. It wasn't long before the *Oceana* started to take on a heavy list, so the tow lines were reluctantly cut, sealing the ship's fate. At around 10 a.m. the *Oceana* sank slowly, bow first, and came to rest on the seabed with her masts and top of the funnels still showing. The *Pisagua* fared a little better and, despite having sustained considerable damage to her bow, was towed successfully to Dover for repairs, but the sailing ship never returned to her former glory. She was condemned by her owners and sold in October, rebuilt as a whaling factory and wrecked off the Shetland Islands early the following year.

A lengthy investigation into the loss of the *Oceana* commenced on 30 April 1912, but by then the collision had been vastly overshadowed by the loss of the *Titanic* earlier that month on 15 April, with the loss of more than 1,500 lives.

When the inquiry concluded at the end of June the court was left with a feeling:

> of disappointment and almost dismay, that the elaborate system built up by the Company through long years of experience in passenger traffic, should have failed at the moment of trial, in not particularly difficult circumstances.

The chief officer was ultimately found at fault for causing the collision by attempting to cross ahead of the *Pisagua* and, in doing so, failing to follow the longstanding rule of the sea that 'steam gives way to sail'. As punishment his certificate was suspended for six months. The chief officer was also found primarily to blame for the loss of life in the calamitous launching of number one lifeboat. Finally, both Captain Hide and Chief Officer Naylor were formally censured for failing to take adequate measures to rescue the people from the overturned lifeboat.

Two days after the collision a local man was walking along the beach at St Leonards when he found a photograph of a young boy mounted in an ornamental picture frame washed up among wreckage from the *Oceana*. It wasn't until seventeen years later that he removed the photograph from the frame, revealing an inscription on the back that read, 'George Seymour Hide, aged 10 years.' Not only did this turn out to be the only son of Captain Hide, but George had also attended the local school, the Hide family having been long-term residents of St Leonards up until 1910.

Salvaging the Wreck

The cargo lost with the *Oceana* included many cases of military supplies such as clothing and swords that were being sent as replacements for those previously lost in the wreck of the *Delhi* (3) a few months earlier. However, a more pressing priority was to recover the gold and silver ingots. The challenging task was given to the Liverpool Salvage Association, who arrived on site the day after the shipwreck on board the salvage vessel *Ranger* with a team of divers.

The first task was for a diver to penetrate the captain's cabin and retrieve the keys to the bullion room from his desk. Battling against vicious currents and masses of tangled wreckage, it took the diver several attempts to enter the cabin. When he finally managed to gain access, he not only recovered the keys, but also the captain's papers, sword, Naval Reserve uniform and silverware.

On his next dive, the diver located the bullion room only to discover the door had five separate locks. He managed to open three with the keys, but resorted to using a hatchet for the remaining two. Once inside, he retrieved the first few silver bars and a chest containing 5,000 sovereigns.

From then on the divers worked the wreck in two pairs: one pair forward, the other aft, with a fifth diver on constant standby in case of an emergency. The conditions were extremely hazardous and the divers often had to grope around in the dark on their hands and knees, squeezing through confusing narrow hatchways, while all the time avoiding debris. The divers took it in turn to descend into the bullion room, while one from each pair remained on the deck above, from where he dispatched the treasure to the surface

in special baskets. After ten days all the bullion was said to have been recovered, although rumours persist to this day that a few bars remain on the wreck. After the salvage work was completed the navy systematically dispersed the wreck with explosives, since it posed a serious hazard to navigation.

Diving the Wreck

Lying in a maximum depth of 30m, 6 miles south of Eastbourne, the *Oceana* is one of the most accessible P&O wreck dives on the south coast of England. A short distance to the south-east in slightly deeper water lies the wreck of the Cunard liner *Alaunia* (2). Therefore, when tidal conditions permit, it is possible to dive two classic liner wrecks in the same day.

Despite salvage activities and the use of explosives to disperse the wreck, a significant amount of the *Oceana* remains intact and recognisable. However, with strong tides and a relatively short slack water window it is challenging to explore the entire wreck in a single dive. The seabed is composed of shifting sands, which can make a

Diver Johno de Lara swims around the *Oceana*'s bow. (Catherine de Lara)

Large anchor lying on top of the *Oceana* wreck. (Catherine de Lara)

A few portholes still remain on the *Oceana*. (Catherine de Lara)

P&O silver cutlery and china from the wreck of the *Oceana*. (Tunbridge Wells Sub Aqua Club/ Newhaven Fort)

This brass coffee pot most probably belonged to a personal service.

The shifting sands often encroach upon the wreck. (Catherine de Lara)

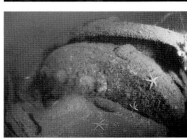

The Nottinghamshire Regiment commemorative plaque was recovered from the wreck of the *Oceana* in 2009. (Tunbridge Wells Sub Aqua Club)

difference to how much of the wreck is revealed, particularly around the more broken sections.

The bow rises vertically from the seabed, where one of the large anchors remains partially buried. One of the anchor chains is laid out across the top of the forecastle and descends into the chain locker below. This is one of the few areas where you can safely explore the interior of the wreck. Unusually a lot of the wooden decking survives on the *Oceana*. Heading aft the wreck becomes a confusing tangle of twisted metal until reaching the boilers, which typically stand several metres proud, depending on the level of surrounding sand. The remains of the triple-expansion engine is one of the most impressive features of the wreck and stands at least 5m proud. Towards the stern the outline of the wreck again becomes less defined, but it is still possible to see flattened hull plates where portholes once existed. A distinctive feature of this part of the wreck are large concrete blocks, remnants of the general cargo. The *Oceana*'s distinctive fantail stern stands upright. The end of the prop shaft

is exposed but the propeller itself has been salvaged. Lying on the seabed nearby is the steering quadrant and remains of the rudder.

Visiting divers will see a diverse range of marine life including bib, flatfish, tompot blennies, lobsters, crabs, scallops and conger eels. The wreck is covered extensively in bryozoa, a marine growth that has a dirty, turf-like appearance, described by one diver 'as if the wreck is wearing a brown fur coat'.

In 2009 Jamie Smith from Tunbridge Wells Sub Aqua Club recovered a large, unusual brass plaque from the wreck. The plaque was in commemoration of soldiers and families of the 45th Nottinghamshire Regiment who had been stationed in India from 1819 to 1838 and was to have been erected in a church at the regiment's final posting at Secunderabad. Although the regiment subsequently ordered a replacement, the original was formally returned to the plaque's commissioners, Sherwood Foresters Regiment, for display in their Regimental Museum. Many other varied and interesting artefacts from the *Oceana* wreck are on display at Newhaven Fort.

PART 3

FIRST WORLD WAR, 1914–1918

– *Harlington* (1) –

1895–1914, England

Harlington (1) (1,032 tons) was built for J.&C. Harrison of London by S.P. Austin & Sons, Greenock, and launched on 9 April 1895. The vessel was later purchased by P&O on 17 January 1896. The length was 220ft (67.0m) and beam 31.5ft (9.6m). The single screw was powered by a triple-expansion steam engine, giving a service speed of 9.5 knots. The *Harlington* (1) was a modest dedicated cargo vessel without passenger accommodation and used primarily on east coast feeder services.

On the evening of 18 September 1901 the *Harlington* (1) was on a voyage to Middlesbrough when she sighted a small boat in distress. On coming alongside, it was discovered to be a small dinghy occupied by the sole twelve survivors from the wreck of HMS *Cobra*, one of only two specially designed, turbine-powered torpedo boat destroyers. HMS *Cobra* had inexplicably foundered and broken in two the day before, with the loss of sixty-seven lives.

On 2 December 1914 the *Harlington* (1) ran aground on Middle Sunk Island in the Thames Estuary while inbound from Middlesbrough with a general cargo including iron. The ship hit the sands in a south-south-westerly gale and very heavy seas. All fifteen crew members were rescued by the Clacton-on-Sea lifeboat which was in attendance almost continually from 2 to 5 December. The coxswain, George Grigson, later received a silver medal from the Royal National Lifeboat Institution in recognition of 'exceptionally fine services'.

Although the loss was not caused by enemy action, the *Harlington* (1) was P&O's first shipwreck in the First World War.

– *Nile* –

1906–1915, Inland Sea of Japan

Nile (6,694 tons) was built for P&O by Caird & Co., Greenock, and launched on 24 May 1906. The length was 449.8ft (137.1m) and beam 52.2ft (15.9m). Twin screws were powered by quadruple-expansion steam engines, giving a service speed of 14 knots. There was accommodation for fifty-four first- and forty-two second-class passengers, with a crew of 146. The vessel was the first of the eight N-class ships, which provided moderate passenger accommodation and a large cargo capacity for the Far East services.

The maiden voyage sailed from Royal Albert Dock, London, on 18 August 1906, bound for China and Japan.

On Christmas Eve of December 1909 the *Nile* was outbound to Calcutta but forced to anchor off the Nore, in the mouth of the Thames Estuary, due to a thick fog. While lying at anchor the inbound cable-laying ship *Telconia* was proceeding cautiously but did not see the *Nile* in time to avoid a collision. The *Nile* was badly damaged and forced to return to the Royal Albert Dock for repairs.

At 10 p.m. on 10 January 1915 the *Nile* sailed from Moji, bound for Kobe, under the command of Captain H. Powell with seventeen passengers and a mixed cargo. It was raining hard with a wild sea, and although there was a pilot on board, at 2.32 a.m. the vessel struck a rock off the southern extremity of Iwaijima, a small island in the Inland Sea of Japan. With the vessel firmly fixed on the rocks and making water fast, the captain swiftly ordered the passengers to the lifeboats. The high seas posed some difficulty in getting the boats alongside but five boats were soon safely away with all the passengers and most of the native crew. Distress rockets were fired and SOS messages sent, attracting the attention of the *Fukuju Maru*, which came to render assistance. The lifeboats transferred their occupants to the *Fukuju Maru* and one returned to the *Nile* to take off the remaining ten persons still on board, the captain being the last to leave. By this time the *Nile* was settling down by the head and water was already up to the bridge, requiring the oarsmen to pull very hard to avoid the suction from the sinking ship. At 4.20 a.m. the *Nile* began to sink deeper and deeper by the head and then suddenly dived bow first, with the stern high in the air and by 4.30 a.m. the vessel had vanished from view.

No lives were lost and afterwards the passengers signed a testimonial 'expressing their appreciation of the great efficiency, courage and courtesy shown by all on board in the hour of danger'.

– *Nubia* (2) –

1895–1915, Sri Lanka

The passenger/cargo liner *Nubia* (2) (5,914 tons) was built for P&O by Caird & Co., Greenock, launched on 13 December 1894 and completed in February 1895. The length was 430ft (131m) and beam 49.3ft (15m). A single screw was powered by triple-expansion steam engines, giving a service speed of 14.5 knots. There was accommodation for ninety first- and sixty-two second-class passengers and a crew of 148. *Nubia* (2) was mainly employed on intermediate services, along with her sister ships *Simla* (2) and *Malta* (2).

On 1 March 1895 the *Nubia* (2) set sail for Calcutta under the command of Captain B.W. Hall on what proved to be quite an eventful maiden voyage. The Pacific Steam Navigation Company ship *Oroya* ran aground in Naples Bay on 4 March and some of her passengers were taken on board the *Nubia* (2). Then on 19 March the *Nubia* (2) herself ran aground near Aden. After several days spent lightening the vessel by removing cargo and ballast, the ship was eventually refloated on 25 March. Although the *Nubia* (2) only suffered minor damage, Captain Hall was later dismissed.

From 1899 to 1903 the *Nubia* (2) was taken up for transport and hospital ship duties in the Boer War. This got off to a bad start when five members of the North Lancashire Regiment died from an outbreak of cholera on board, said to be the result of fruit taken on board in Port Said.

In the early hours of 20 June 1915 the *Nubia* (2) ran aground on a sandbar in the mouth of the River Kelani, off Colombo. The ship had sailed from Bombay five days previously with thirty-five passengers and the China mails, under the command of Captain Lyndon. It was

a dark and stormy night when the *Nubia* (2) approached the harbour and the ship was seen to be getting into difficulties. The searchlights for the harbour defences were shut off in case they were hampering the vessel's progress but shortly after 4.30 a.m. the *Nubia* (2) grounded. Distress rockets were fired and a local tug, *Goliath*, soon arrived at the scene but could not help get the *Nubia* (2) off the reef. By afternoon the following day the ship had developed a heavy list to starboard and the women and children passengers became increasingly nervous. The captain wasted no time in getting all the passengers safely ashore, soon followed by all their baggage. Further tugs arrived and continued making every effort to tow the *Nubia* (2) off, but with the weather deteriorating, the ship eventually had to be abandoned.

– *India* (2) –

1896–1915, Norway

India (2) (7,911 tons) was built for P&O by Caird & Co., Greenock, and launched on 15 April 1896. The length was 499.9ft (152.3m) and beam 54.3ft (16.5m). A single screw was powered by a triple-expansion steam engine, giving a service speed of 18 knots. There was

The *India* (2) was built in 1896 and spent her first decade on the Australia service. (Allan C. Green/State Library of Victoria)

were sighted and the alarm was sounded. Within seconds the ship was struck by a torpedo fired by *U 22* (Bruno Hoppe) and quickly sank off Helligvær Island, near Bodø. This earned the *India* (2) the unfortunate distinction of becoming P&O's first ship to be lost due to enemy action. Although over 100 men were saved, there was a tragic loss of 166 lives.

Many of the survivors were taken to Narvik by the Swedish steamer *Götaland* and HMT *Saxon*, others went ashore at Helligvær in the ship's boats.

The *U 22* torpedoed the *India* (2) on 8 August 1915, making her the first P&O ship to be sunk by a German U-boat.

accommodation for 317 first- and 152 second-class passengers, or up to 2,500 troops for war service. The *India* (2) operated on services to India and Australia.

In 1892 work began to develop the mouth of the Swan river at Fremantle, Western Australia, into a port and the new harbour was eventually opened in May 1897. Recognition of Fremantle over Albany as the premier port in Western Australia followed in August 1900 when the first mail steamers called there, one of which was the *India* (2) on 20 August 1900, under the command of Captain W.D.G. Worcester RNR. To commemorate the maiden call of the *India* (2) to the port, a lavish banquet was held on board, which was attended by many local dignitaries and businessmen.

After providing over a decade of fast and efficient service to Australia the *India* (2) transferred to P&O's Far East routes.

On 13 March 1915 the *India* (2) was taken up by the Admiralty for use as an AMC. A refit took place at the Royal Albert Dock where the ship was fitted with armaments and loaded with ammunition and stores. Forty men were drafted from HMS *Pembroke*, followed by a further eighty-eight from HMS *Sutlej*. After completing gun trials, *India* (2) left to join the Northern Patrols.

At 5.40 p.m. on 8 August 1915 the *India* (2) (Commander W.G.A. Kennedy RN) was on patrol in Norway when torpedo tracks

– *Socotra* (1) –

1897–1915, France

The purpose-built general-cargo liner *Socotra* (1) (6,009 tons) was built for P&O by Palmer's Shipbuilding & Iron Co., Hebburn-on-Tyne, and launched on 3 December 1896 by Mrs A.M. Palmer, the wife of one of Palmer's directors. The length was 450ft (137.1m) and beam 52.2ft (15.9m). Twin screws were powered by two triple-expansion steam engines, giving a service speed of 14 knots. The *Socotra* (1) was the sister ship of the preceding *Candia* (2) (1896).

On the morning of 1 February 1903 the *Socotra* (1) collided with the cargo steamer *Dallington* (1900, 2,534 tons), which was at anchor in

The twin-screw cargo liner *Socotra* (1) was built in 1897 and employed on services to the Far East and Australia. (Newall Dunn Collection)

LE TOUQUET-PARIS-PLAGE — Vapeur S. S « Socotra » Newcastle, échoué à Paris Plage. le 26 Novembre 1915

Navigational error caused the *Socotra* (1) to run aground on the beach at Le Touquet, France, in November 1915. The wreck was featured on a series of French postcards.

the mouth of the River Scheldt, Belgium. The *Dallington* was very badly damaged and was taken to Antwerp for repairs. Although the *Socotra* (1) had a Belgian pilot on board, an Admiralty Division court case ruled against the P&O Company for negligent navigation.

When P&O registered the *Socotra* (1) it had always been the company's intention that the ship would eventually operate on the Australian trade, via the Cape of Good Hope. The ship's final voyage on this route sailed from London on 1 July 1915 under the command of Captain Robert Pollock Stevenson, with a full cargo of general merchandise and a crew of ninety-seven. The *Socotra* (1) called at Cape Town, Adelaide, Melbourne and Sydney before finally arriving at Brisbane. The return voyage commenced on 18 September 1915, calling again at the same ports, with a return cargo of wool and frozen meat.

On the evening of 24 November the long voyage was drawing to an end and the *Socotra* (1) rounded Ushant and set course for the final run up the English Channel. At noon the following day Captain Stevenson checked the ship's position but made an incorrect assumption, which placed the *Socotra* (1) south of Portland Bill,

A storm a few days after the wreck caused the *Socotra* (1) to part amidships.

The wreck of the *Socotra* (1) is occasionally exposed on the beach at Le Touquet, which allows people to walk out and see it.

when in actual fact the vessel had progressed much further east. The weather was fine, with passing clouds, but by 4 p.m. a haze had developed, making it impossible to see the coastline. From 7 p.m. soundings were taken at hourly intervals, but even though the results were not consistent with the master's assumed position, no significant remedial action was taken. After the 10 p.m. sounding Captain Stevenson began to seriously doubt his position and slowed the ship down to half speed, then stopping the engines completely when a green light was sighted off the starboard bow. For no rational reason the master took this to be a wreck-marker buoy, but it later proved to signify the Vergoyer Bank, off the French coast near Le Touquet. After drifting with the tide for twenty minutes the engines were set to 'slow ahead' and the *Socotra* (1) steamed on cautiously.

At 11.20 p.m. a flashing light was seen, which the master took to be Beachy Head. Although the third officer pointed out to Captain Stevenson that the light could not possibly be Beachy Head, since its flash duration and eclipses did not match, the captain persisted in his opinion. Despite yet another inconsistent sounding at 11.30 p.m., fifteen minutes later the *Socotra* (1) picked up speed and

proceeded 'full ahead' on both engines. Not long after, at 12.08 a.m. on 26 November, the ship grounded gently on the sandy seabed off Le Touquet. The crew spent the next three hours trying to get the *Socotra* (1) off, but without any success. The next day five tugs arrived and attempted to haul her off, but the vessel remained stuck fast. The crew finally abandoned the wreck on 30 November and there was no loss of life.

In a storm a few days later the vessel parted amidships at the boilers and the cargo tumbled out from the holds. Local people soon arrived to pillage whatever they could, so armed guards had to be placed at the wreck, remaining on duty until the entire contents of the *Socotra* (1) were removed. A light railway was temporarily laid out across the beach to the wreck to aid the salvage effort.

At the inquiry into the loss of the *Socotra* (1) questions were raised about Captain Stevenson's general state of health. It was revealed that since 1 July the storekeeper had provided the master with seventy-two bottles of Irish whisky, about forty-eight bottles of Scotch and about six bottles of gin, of which the Scotch was used for 'entertaining in hot-weather ports'. Despite the considerable quantity of alcohol consumed by the master during the voyage, all witnesses were unanimous in their opinion that their captain was perfectly sober. However, they also noted that he had become increasingly anxious and nervous, apparently due to the constant threat of submarines. The court subsequently ruled that 'the stranding and subsequent loss of the vessel were caused by the master neglecting to take adequate steps to ascertain and verify the position of his ship at and after noon of the 25th November, 1915, and mistaking Le Touquet light for the light at Beachy Head'. The master's certificate was suspended for six months.

Visiting the Wreck

The remains of the *Socotra* (1) lie in very shallow water just a few hundred metres out from the beach at Le Touquet on a vast expanse of flat sand. Unusually, the best way to see this wreck is actually by foot and there is no need to even get wet. During periods of very low spring tides the *Socotra* (1) is completely exposed and it is possible to spend a good couple of hours exploring the wreck before the tide starts to turn. In March 2015 Le Touquet experienced the biggest tide for eighteen years, which coincidentally marked the centenary of the ship's loss. The local community marked the occasion with a special event, a highlight of which was a folk band performing live at the wreck site amongst a crowd of many hundreds.

Le Touquet is a popular destination for sailing and other water sports so the shallow depth of water around the wreck presents a

The starboard propeller shaft dominates the stern section of the *Socotra* (1) wreck.

At low tide the *Socotra* (1)'s permanent marker buoy rests on the sand a short distance from the wreck.

The sun sets on the *Socotra* (1) a century after the shipwreck.

dangerous hazard. Therefore, the *Socotra* (1) location is permanently marked with a bright-yellow marker buoy, which, since it rests on the sand at low water, provides a useful reference point for a walk out to the wreck. To get the most from a visit and the maximum time at the wreck it is best to arrive just as the sea starts to recede, when slowly but surely the outline of the *Socotra* (1) starts to reveal itself. Although the remains of the *Socotra* (1) have stayed firmly in place for over a century, the amount that is visible depends on the constantly shifting sand. Generally it is the stern section that is the most prominent, standing a couple of metres high. The separate bow section rests about 100m away and is nearly always completely covered.

The outer hull of the stern of the *Socotra* (1) is completely intact, although rising just a metre or so above the waterline. The sternpost is the closest point to the shore and the wreck points out to sea in a north-westerly direction. It is normally possible to completely circumnavigate the wreck or 'go aboard' for a closer inspection.

The most distinctive and recognisable features are the twin propeller shafts. The port shaft is still enclosed in its tunnel, whereas the starboard one is completely exposed and hangs suspended above the rest of the wreck, terminating in a flange. Further forward there are numerous engine components, which are fused into dense wreckage. This is followed by large box sections of steel frames. If the sand has receded sufficiently then it may be possible to spot one of the boilers.

The wreck is covered with a variety of molluscs including mussels, a popular local delicacy. Small 'wreck pools' left behind by the outgoing tide contain crabs, starfish, small fish and various other marine life. The *Socotra* (1) is a very photogenic wreck and its entire mood changes depending on the weather and amount of sunlight. When the early morning sun illuminates the wreck the rusting remains are lit up in glorious shades of ochre.

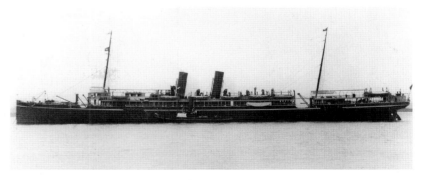

The *Persia* was completed in 1900 and was P&O's final single-screw passenger liner.

– *Persia* –

1900–1915, Mediterranean Sea

Persia (7,951 tons) was built for P&O by Caird & Co., Greenock, and launched on 13 August 1900. The length was 499.8ft (152.3m) and beam 54.3ft (16.5m). The ship was the last single-screw P&O passenger liner and was powered by triple-expansion steam engines, giving a service speed of 17 knots. There was accommodation for 320 first- and 210 second-class passengers. The *Persia* was employed on services to India and completed over seventy return voyages to Bombay.

When the Russo-Japanese War broke out in 1904 it resulted in serious disruption to P&O services transiting the Red Sea. In July both the *Malacca* and *Formosa* were seized by vessels of the Russian Volunteer Fleet. That same month *Persia* was one of many British

The *Persia*'s bullion room door was raised from a depth of nearly 3,000m. It is now on display at Buckler's Hard Maritime Museum, Beaulieu.

merchant ships to be stopped and searched for Japanese mails by the *Smolensk*.

In April 1907 the Princess Royal, Duke of Fife and their daughters, Princesses Alexandra and Maud, returned from the Mediterranean on board the *Persia*. Four years later the family were to sail from England on the *Delhi* (3) when it was shipwrecked off the coast of Morocco.

Moonstones and amethysts recovered from the wreck of the *Persia*.

Pages of music fused together in a solid mass but still legible.

Leather boot, stamped 'Peal' on the sole.

One of a pair of leather boots with spur, stamped 'Peal' on the sole.

On 11 July 1912 the *Persia* grounded in thick fog about 20 miles from Marseilles. All the passengers were safely landed and three days later the vessel was towed off, undamaged, by local tugs.

A week before Christmas, on 18 December 1915, the *Persia* sailed from London for Bombay under the command of Captain William Hall RNR. Despite the war, there were still close to 200 passengers on board from many different walks of life. Among them were the 2nd Baron Montagu of Beaulieu and his secretary (and mistress) Eleanor Thornton, who was the model for the Rolls-Royce 'Spirit of Ecstasy' mascot. That winter, Captain Hall's wife and young daughter had decided to spend the winter season in Malta, but since P&O regulations prohibited captains from taking their wives with them, his family sailed separately on the *Medina*. Mrs Hall never saw her husband again.

After calling at Gibraltar, the *Persia* proceeded to Marseilles where the ship remained berthed for Christmas Day celebrations. The vessel sailed the following morning and made one more call at Malta before heading for Port Said and the Suez Canal. At 1.10 p.m. on 30 December the passengers were dining in the saloon when the ship was struck without any warning from a torpedo fired by the German U-boat *U 38* (Max Valentiner) while some 70 miles south-east of Crete. The explosion caused one of the *Persia*'s boilers to blow up and the ship heeled over and sank within five minutes, leaving insufficient time to launch all the lifeboats.

Lord Montagu had made for the decks with Eleanor in his arms but she was swept from his grasp by a huge wall of water. Although he was dragged down by the suction from the sinking ship he survived to tell his tale, which was reported in *The Times* afterwards:

When I was blown to the surface again I saw a dreadful scene of struggling human beings. There was hardly any wreckage to grasp. Nearly all the boats were smashed, and only three remained afloat. After a desperate struggle I climbed on to the bottom of a broken boat with 28 lascars and 3 other Europeans. Our number was reduced to 19 by Thursday night, and only 11 remained on Friday, the rest having died from exposure and injuries. We saw a neutral ship pass close on Thursday evening at about eight o'clock, but she took no notice of the red flare shown by another of the *Persia*'s boats. I pulled five dead men out of the water during the first night in the water-logged boat. We saw a large steamer three miles away on the next day, but she, too, ignored our signals, probably thinking they were a ruse of an enemy submarine. Our broken boat capsized constantly, and we were all the time washed by the waves, so that we were almost exhausted when the second night began.

A memorial sundial was unveiled at Buckler's Hard on 15 June 2016 in an act of remembrance commemorating the centenary of the *Persia*'s loss.

Clicquot champagne dated 1909, cutlery bearing the P&O insignia and, on the last day of the operation, a hoard of impressive rubies. Even the bullion room door was raised, which is on display along with many other *Persia* artefacts at the Buckler's Hard Maritime Museum, Beaulieu, Hampshire, UK.

– *Geelong* (2) –

1904–1916, Mediterranean Sea

Geelong (2) (7,951 tons) was built for Wilhelm Lund's Blue Anchor Line by Barclay, Curle & Co. Ltd, Glasgow, and launched as *Australia* on 19 March 1904, but completed as *Geelong* (2). The length was 450ft (137.2m) and beam 54.5ft (16.6m), with twin screws powered by triple-expansion steam engines, giving a service speed of 14 knots. There was accommodation for ninety saloon- and 450 third-class passengers.

At 8.30 p.m. we saw the Alfred Holt steamer, *Ningchow*, near us and shouted as loudly as we could. Eventually the steamer stopped some way off, again suspecting a submarine trap, but at last she approached and rescued us on Friday night at 9 o'clock, after we had been 32 hours in the sea without water or food, except one biscuit from a tin found in the boat, since breakfast time on Thursday. Our survival and rescue were absolutely miraculous in the circumstances.

There was an appalling loss of innocent lives, with only sixty-five passengers (many of whom were women and children) and 102 crew surviving from a total complement of over 500.

The *Persia* was known to be carrying a highly prized cargo that included Egyptian coins and precious gems belonging to Maharaja Jagatjit Singh. Despite the wreck lying in a depth of over 2,816m (9,240ft) this did not deter the efforts of husband and wife salvage team Alexander and Moya Crawford, who located the wreck in 2001 and returned two years later with specialist recovery equipment. Among the items raised were several unopened bottles of Veuve

Geelong (2) of 1904 in her original Blue Anchor Line livery. The ship was sold to P&O in 1910 after her original owners went into liquidation. (Allan C. Green/State Library of Victoria)

The *Geelong* (2) was sold to P&O along with several other ships in 1910 when the Blue Anchor Line went into liquidation following the tragic disappearance of their flagship *Waratah* off the South African coast in 1909. After modification the *Geelong* (2) became the first P&O ship to carry solely third-class passengers and served on the Australia emigrant service via the Cape of Good Hope.

In August 1914 the *Geelong* (2) was leased by the Commonwealth for troop transport duties and underwent conversion at Melbourne to carry sixty-two officers and 1,539 other ranks, becoming HMAT *Geelong A2*. On the evening of 1 January 1916 the *Geelong* (2) was crossing the Mediterranean bound for London from Sydney, having recently landed her troops in Egypt, with a general cargo that included lead for the war effort. To avoid detection from submarines the ship was steaming without lights and was not seen by the approaching British cargo steamer *Bonvilston* (1893, 2,865 tons), which struck the port side of the vessel at full speed. All six of the *Geelong* (2)'s lifeboats were launched at once but were found to leak badly. Although the bow of the *Bonvilston* was severely damaged, fortunately it was not below the waterline and the vessel stood by and succeeded in taking everyone on board. There was no loss of life and all the *Geelong* (2) crew members were landed in Alexandria the following day.

– *Maloja* (1) –

1911–1916, England

Maloja (1) (12,431 tons) was built for P&O by Harland & Wolff, Belfast, and launched on 17 December 1910. The length was 550.4ft (167.7m) and beam 62.9ft (19.2m). Twin screws were powered by quadruple-expansion steam engines, giving a service speed of 19 knots. The M-class liner provided accommodation for 438 first- and 218 second-class passengers.

Although the *Maloja* (1) was ultimately destined for the mail service to Australia, the ship's maiden voyage was advertised as a 'Preliminary Yachting Trip' cruise and sailed on 23 September 1911 to Lisbon, Tenerife, Madeira and Gibraltar. The *Manchester Courier* was impressed with the latest addition to the P&O fleet: 'The vessel is a splendid example of British shipbuilding, her graceful lines, pleasing profile and arrangement of deck houses making her a very handsome vessel.'

The *Maloja* (1)'s younger sister ship *Medina* had been commissioned as the royal yacht to take King George V and Queen Mary to the Delhi Durbar in December, held in honour of their coronation earlier that year. The *Maloja* (1) sailed in company with the *Medina* carrying a large party of distinguished persons, for which the ship's black hull was dressed with a special white ribbon.

After returning from India, the *Maloja* (1) commenced her first voyage from England to Australia on 9 February 1912 under the command of Captain George Weston. The ship encountered a hurricane-force gale in the Bay of Biscay but passed her first serious test with flying colours. The *Maloja* (1) caused a great deal of excitement when she made her maiden calls at Australian ports. In Adelaide *The Register* reported on 18 March:

A noteworthy advance has been made in the class of steamship visiting Australia. The great companies which have engaged in the trade between Great Britain and the Commonwealth have invariably kept well abreast of the times, and in recent years the advent of luxuriously fitted liners has provided travellers with facilities for sea travel scarcely surpassed, except in regard to size, in any other part of the world. No company with interests in Australia has done more in this direction than the far-famed P. & O. Company, whose M class of ships now trading to Australia have been augmented by the *Maloja* and *Medina*. The first of these arrived on her maiden voyage to Australia on Saturday. The two ships are a distinct advance on their predecessors, not only in size and speed, but in point of all-round comfort and design.

The *Maloja* (1) struck a mine off the Dover coast in February 1915 resulting in the loss of 155 lives, many of whom were women and young children.

During the First World War the *Maloja* (1) was taken off the Australian mail service in order to make a return voyage to Bombay. The ship sailed from Tilbury on 26 February 1916 under the command of Captain Charles Irving RNR with 121 passengers and a general cargo, and anchored at the mouth of the Thames for the night since at that time ships were not permitted to pass through the Straits of Dover after dark. While at anchor Captain Irving took the opportunity to hold a full lifeboat drill and instructed the passengers in the use of their lifejackets, telling them to keep them about their person at all times during the voyage. At 8 a.m. the next morning the captain received permission to weigh anchor and proceeded in accordance with his issued sailing instructions. The *Maloja* (1) had just passed Dover and was steaming at full speed when at 10.30 a.m. there was a tremendous explosion in the aft end of the ship which was witnessed from the shore. The ship had struck a mine laid by *UC 6* (Matthias Graf von Schmettow).

The emergency signal was immediately sounded and everyone was at their lifeboat stations immediately. Captain Irving then ordered the vessel full astern in order that it could be brought to a halt as quickly as possible and allow the boats to be safely launched. Just as the ship slowed down the captain rang the telegraph with the order to stop the engines but there was no response. With the crew anxious to get the boats away from the listing ship he immediately dispatched the chief officer to the engine room to see that his order was carried out. The chief officer quickly returned with the bad news that the engine room was already full of water and nothing further could be done. By now the ship had picked up speed and was steaming backwards at a speed of around 8 knots. Captain Irving was acutely aware of the risk of lowering boats while underway, being familiar with the *Oceana* disaster four years earlier, but all he could do in the desperate situation was instruct his officers to make their best efforts and man the rafts. Amazingly a few boats were got away, but the majority of passengers and crew ended up jumping into the cold water. The *Maloja* (1) sank twenty-four minutes after the explosion and ultimately claimed the lives of 155 passengers and crew.

The Dover tugs *Lady Brassey* and *Lady Crundall* soon arrived on the scene and picked up as many of the survivors as they could find, the latter rescuing Captain Irving who had been in the water for forty minutes. Many of those recovered were found barely alive so were swiftly transferred to the nearby hospital ships *Dieppe*, which took in over 100, and *St David*. The small cargo ship *Empress of Fort William* (1908, 2,181 tons) had been sailing in company with the *Maloja* (1) and also stopped to render assistance, but she too was mined, fortunately without further loss of life.

Lobster on the wreck of the *Maloja* (1), which rests on a sandy seabed at a depth of 25m.

Many of those who survived did so because they had been wearing their lifejackets, which also accounted for the number of bodies later recovered from the water. The task of taking charge of all the deceased fell to Chief Constable Fox of Dover who decided to use the market hall as a makeshift mortuary. By Sunday evening forty-five bodies had been brought ashore representing a variety of passengers and crew of all ages, gender and nationality. At an inquest that was convened at the town hall the following Tuesday, efforts were made to identify the bodies, which had been given a number and description, such as this tragic example:

> No. 52 is a little baby dressed in a brown velvet jacket and about nine months old; found near the Warren the jacket was fastened with military buttons and the child was probably a soldier's.

'No. 52' was identified as the body of Henry Charles Higman, aged 14 months, son of 'No. 27', Mrs C. Higman, going out to join her husband in Gibraltar. The coroner pointed out the great difficulty in identification and suggested that every person on a vessel should be supplied with an identification disc. The inquest was also surprised to learn that merchant navy ships did not posses the capability of stopping the engines from the bridge, which would have made a significant difference to the outcome of the *Maloja* (1) disaster. Ultimately the jury returned a verdict that 'the fifty-eight persons on whom the inquiry was held met their deaths from immersion as the result of the liner *Maloja* (1) being struck by a mine and sunk'.

Morse telegraph key recovered from the *Maloja* (1).

Many of the deceased were buried locally in Dover at St Mary's Cemetery. A funeral procession left the market hall, headed by a firing party of the Royal Fusiliers and the band of the same regiment. The remains of Lieutenant Henry Harris on a gun carriage came first, followed by four transport wagons driven by soldiers conveying the remainder of the coffins, which were covered with Union Jacks. Captain Irving was amongst those at the graveside, accompanied by one of the directors of the P&O Company.

A separate funeral service took place for the lascar crew a few days later in the nonconformist section of St Mary's Cemetery. One large grave held eighteen of the Indians who were of the Mohammedans religion, and two lascars and a nurse who were Catholics were buried close by in separate graves. Men of the Royal Garrison Artillery had dug the graves, due to there not being sufficient civilian labour.

Diving the Wreck

The wreck of the *Maloja* (1) was dispersed in 1917 because it presented a serious hazard to shipping. In the mid 1960s Risdon Beazley Ltd undertook extensive salvage operations on the wreck, which was further dispersed. Consequently, what remains of this grand ocean liner is a shadow of its former glory. The *Maloja* (1) lies a short boat ride from the busy port of Dover, less than 2 miles out from the Samphire Hoe country park on the Kent Downs. A short

distance away the modern-day P&O ferries ply their trade back and forth across the English Channel.

Unfortunately for the visiting diver this is an area of notoriously poor underwater visibility which is compounded by a seabed dominated by shifting sand dunes. The amount of sand encroaching on the wreck varies all the time so the profile of the wreck is changing constantly. Despite this, the *Maloja* (1) on a good day (or evening!) can still make an excellent dive.

The author first dived the wreck in April 2015, entering the water as the sun was setting at 8 p.m. Night dives are not regularly undertaken in the UK coastal waters, least of all in the cold spring (7°C) waters of one of the busiest shipping lanes in the world. The time of the dive had been dictated by local knowledge for the cleanest tides with the best slack-water window. Although dark, the water was clear and the wreck was easy to navigate with the aid of good lights – the diving conditions around Dover can certainly be a lot worse during daylight hours! Part of the attraction of night dives can be the nocturnal marine life. On this occasion the usual lobsters and crabs were out in force, but the sight of a lone squid swimming across the wreck was most unexpected.

In 2005 volunteers from the Kent Seasearch underwater survey team dived the wreck and observed:

A large liner, partially buried in the side of a large and mobile sand and gravel bank, with occasional common starfish and dragonets and a number of other fish like bib and pollack. Exposed wreck structures were covered in a dense animal turf, dominated by oaten pipe hydroids, small orange anemones and small patches of mussels.

Occasionally in the summer months it can be possible for the visibility to reach in excess of 5m and divers will be rewarded with a large area of interesting wreckage to explore. The maximum depth on the dive is typically around 25m but it can become up to 7m shallower in places. One notable feature is the intact foremast, which stretches out from the wreck across the seabed at a right angle. Sections of collapsed hull plating are marked by rows of rivets the size of golf balls.

Over the years the *Maloja* (1) has revealed some interesting items. One good example was a Morse telegraph key, now on display in a local dive facility. The brass key was found complete with its wooden base and only required a replacement spring to make it functional again.

The wreck of the Canadian cargo ship *Empress of Fort William* lies a short distance to the north-west in a similar depth.

– *Simla* (2) –

1894–1916, Mediterranean Sea

Simla (2) (5,884 tons) was built for P&O by Caird & Co., Greenock, and launched on 13 October 1894. The length was 430ft (131m) and beam 49.3ft (15m). A single screw was powered by a triple-expansion engine, giving a service speed of 15 knots. The passenger/cargo liner provided accommodation for ninety first- and sixty-six second-class passengers, and was also suited to trooping duties.

The maiden voyage of the *Simla* (2) sailed for Calcutta under the command of Captain Field, with mails and passengers, calling at Gibraltar, Naples, Port Said, Ismalla, Aden, Colombo and Madras.

The *Simla* (2) took on an active role throughout the Boer War, during which the vessel was converted into a hospital ship with accommodation for 250 patients, on one occasion carrying as many as 264 invalids. The ship made numerous round-trip voyages from England to the Cape and her master, Captain Sidney de Bohun Lockyer RNR, was later decorated with a Transport Medal (1899–1902).

During the First World War the *Simla* (2) acted as an Admiralty transport for which she was armed with a gun. The weapon proved of little use when the vessel was attacked without warning at 1 p.m. on 2 April 1916 by a torpedo fired from *U 39* (Walther Forstmann). The *Simla* (2) was about 45 miles north-west of Gozo and making around 11 knots when the torpedo exploded into the port side, killing ten lascar firemen instantly. One of the lifeboats was destroyed but

the remainder were successfully lowered and all the remaining 150 crew were able to get away safely. After the *Simla* (2) had been abandoned the submarine surfaced and fired seven shells into the ship, sending her to the bottom at 2.30 p.m. The survivors were picked up later that afternoon by a French patrol vessel and landed at Malta.

– *Arabia* –

1898–1916, Mediterranean Sea

Arabia (7,903 tons) was built for P&O by Caird & Co., Greenock, and launched on 10 November 1897. The length was 499.9ft (152.3m) and beam 54ft (16.5m). A single screw was powered by a triple-expansion steam engine, giving a service speed of 18 knots. There was accommodation for 317 first- and 152 second-class passengers, or 2,500 troops if required. The *Arabia* was primarily employed on the UK–India service.

In December 1898 Lord Curzon sailed on the *Arabia* from Marseilles to Bombay so that he could relieve Lord Elgin as the new Viceroy of India.

In February 1910 the *Arabia* was involved in an unofficial 1,000-mile race from Gibraltar to Plymouth with the rival Orient Line's *Omrah*

Above: The *Arabia* entered service in 1898 and had a top speed of 18 knots. The ship was designed for the accelerated Indian and Australian mail contracts.

Left: The *Arabia* making one of her many Suez Canal transits.

Right: Paula Scotland and her 9-month-old daughter Norah boarded the *Arabia* in Fremantle in October 1916 for the ship's fateful voyage. (Scotland family)

Left: Paula and Norah on board the *Arabia*. (Scotland family, © National Archives of Australia, 2016)

within range of the *Arabia*'s defensive gun. The smoke from the *Arabia*'s twin stacks also laid an effective smoke screen, enabling the liner to steam away at full speed. The *Arabia* experienced two further encounters within a period of five hours on 3 July 1915 when the vessel reached the English Channel on the return voyage. Once again, through the diligence of the lookouts and effective use of the ship's superior speed, the *Arabia* was able to evade the danger.

On 24 July 1915 the *Arabia* sailed for Sydney on the first of three voyages to Australia, but when returning from the third voyage sixteen months later the ship's luck was to finally run out when she was sunk in the Mediterranean by *UB 43* (Hans von Mellenthin).

The *Arabia* sailed from Sydney for the last time on 30 September 1916, calling at Melbourne, Adelaide and Fremantle before proceeding via Colombo and Bombay. The cargo consisted of wool and wheat from Australia, silk from Colombo and pearls from Bombay. Among the passengers to board the ship in Fremantle were Paula Scotland and her baby daughter, Norah.

Paula Scotland's Story

Paula's mother, Pauline Oceana Weidenbach, had been born at sea during her family's migration from Germany to South Australia in 1848. After settling in Adelaide, Pauline met and married Ernst Wilhelm Pustkuchen, another of the increasing number of German migrants attracted to the growing colony, and Paula was born in 1881.

(1899, 8,291 tons). The *Arabia*, from India, left Gibraltar two hours ahead of the *Omrah*, which was inbound from Australia. At Cape Finisterre the *Omrah* passed the *Arabia* and an exciting race ensued. Both liners steamed full speed and kept almost abreast throughout the day, just a couple of miles apart. The contest created much excitement amongst the passengers, who placed bets on the outcome. The *Omrah* ultimately took the lead and anchored in Plymouth twenty minutes ahead of the *Arabia*. A representative from P&O later attributed the defeat to bad coal!

On 12 October 1912 the *Arabia* was involved in a collision with the steamer *Powerful* of Liverpool, off the Nore lightship at the mouth of the Thames estuary. The *Arabia* was holed in the starboard quarter above the waterline, killing a lascar crewman. The *Powerful* proceeded on her voyage, but the *Arabia* had to put back and anchored off Southend Pier.

Following the outbreak of the First World War the *Arabia* continued making regular passenger sailings to India under the command of Captain Walter Benjamin Palmer, the ship's master since June 1910. The *Arabia* experienced her first encounter with an enemy submarine on the evening of 9 May 1915 while outbound for Bombay in the English Channel. After sighting the submarine Captain Palmer repositioned the ship to place the threat astern and

A woman being lowered into a lifeboat after the *Arabia* had been torpedoed in the Mediterranean without warning by *UB 43* in November 1916.

A boatload of survivors pulls away from the sinking *Arabia*.

During a visit to her homeland at the age of 12, Paula met one of her German cousins, Herbert 'Harry' Pustkuchen, who was to become a decorated First World War U-boat commander, with commands of *UC 5*, *UB 29* and *UC 66*. When hostilities commenced in 1914 life became increasingly difficult for the German migrants in Australia, many of whom were subjected to suspicion and sometimes hostility due to their heritage. As a consequence many Germans changed the spelling of their names or adopted new surnames. Despite the differences, many of the men to enlist in the newly formed Australian Imperial Forces (AIF) were sons and grandsons of German migrants and fought and died for Australia in the First World War.

In February 1915 Paula married the English migrant Lieutenant Thomas Scotland, who served in the AIF 10th Light Horse regiment in the First World War. A year later their first child, Norah, was born in Western Australia. Upon learning that her husband had been injured in Egypt and invalided to England for medical attention, Paula and 9-month-old Norah (Babs) booked passage on the *Arabia* and Paula commenced a diary of the voyage:

> The 10th October, 1916 was a hot and muggy day, particularly on the Fremantle wharf where we boarded the P. & O. Liner *Arabia*, a huge dark grey and dismal looking vessel. I remember not feeling too happy when we went aboard and said as much to my friends. I was glad when the parting was over and I settled down as best as I could in a crowded cabin, trying to make things comfortable for Babs and myself.

The voyage started badly for Paula with the discovery that her trunk lid had been smashed and the lock broken. This was followed by an uncomfortable passage to Colombo during which a rough and heavy sea caused her and Norah to be sick:

> I had my hands full with Babs, for we were both very sick at first, but she was the best and pluckiest little one.

All 437 of *Arabia*'s passengers including 169 women and children were saved.

Once the *Arabia* reached Colombo and started to unload the cargo Paula was able to spend two very enjoyable days ashore before sailing for Bombay where more passengers embarked. There she received an important message:

> I received my first shock of Bombay, in the form of a cable from Australia readdressed from England 'Do not come. Tom leaving for Egypt'. I would not turn back, so I cabled Tom's brother who was paymaster at Cairo to try and get me landed at Port Said.

It was a huge disappointment to Paula when the *Arabia* reached Suez, only to find that the necessary permission had been refused:

> No permission granted to land, but I was advised to proceed to England on the chance of meeting my husband there. Tom hearing I had left Australia, also tried to get me landed, but all in vain. So I was not to see Tom after all!

It was during the next part of the journey that the passengers began to fully comprehend the possible danger they could confront from attacks by German submarines:

> Boat practice had begun. Not till then did we really realise the amount of danger we might encounter. It sent a cold shiver through me to read the various instructions on discipline, etc. It was particularly exciting when the siren blew and belts had to be hurriedly adjusted and a rush made to our different boat stations. How well I remember ours was No. 12.

Paula found that a separate belt for Norah was not helpful and was advised by the *Arabia*'s master, Captain Palmer, to strap the baby in her belt:

> This was quite a success as we proved later. Little did we think of falling prey to one of those deadly submarines.

On arrival at Port Said, Paula was able to meet her husband's brother William, who came aboard and had breakfast with her, but was rather concerned when the preparation was being completed for the next part of the voyage:

> The port-holes had been tightly closed and the deadlights applied; also the boats swung out. A 4.7-inch gun had been taken aboard, together with three gunners. Some of the passengers thought this added to our security. I dreaded the sight of it, to say nothing of the sound when they shot off for practice, although it acted as a sort of a bait for submarines.

At Port Said the *Arabia* embarked a large number of troops and officers, but Paula was dismayed at the thought that they had permission to parade on deck in full uniform:

> Any submarine stalking ships and seeing troops on board would have no hesitation but to attack, regardless of whether or not it was carrying passengers.

The *Arabia* departed Port Said at 10 a.m. on Saturday 4 November, but life aboard had changed and passengers concerned about their safety would start to gather together in groups:

> The nights were dark and dreary, as no lights were permitted anywhere. At night, quite a number of us slept in the music-saloon. The boat was fearfully crowded – mostly men of course. We carried our life-belts with us by strict instructions.

Paula and her fellow passengers felt some security in having other ships acting as escorts:

> These escorts or patrol boats proved a wonderful comfort to the passengers. The boat was zigzagging to a very great degree. It was impossible to follow the route by the maps, as these had been carefully removed when we entered the danger zone. All we knew was that we were going well out of the way of the general route. What an enormous responsibility fell on the poor captain's shoulders. I am sure he had a terribly anxious time, for there were nearly 140 women and about 60 children on board.
>
> There was such a feeling of uncertainty among us all. We were kept very much in ignorance of how things were going, though worry and anxiety could be detected on the faces of the ship's staff.

Paula described the Sunday that followed as a 'rough, cold and bleak day'. Church services were held in the morning by the Church of England and in the afternoon there was a Presbyterian service. Monday turned out much calmer with plenty of sun, but Paula noted the changing feelings on board as the *Arabia* steamed onwards:

> It is surprising how unsuspecting we became, even with the knowledge of danger ahead. We had been carefully escorted

up till the previous evening, but we never saw another escort after 9 p.m. Strange why we had been left now entirely on our own.

In the early morning some passengers thought they had seen the trail of a submarine following the *Arabia*, but because the liner was steaming at 16 knots on a zigzag course they probably assumed the ship could safely outrun any submarine. But any confidence was misplaced because at 11 a.m. Paula and two other passengers were having refreshments while Norah was playing at their feet when they heard the shout, 'Here she comes!' *UB 43* had attacked without warning:

We were all thrown to the floor with the force of a terrific bump. The *Arabia* rocked to and fro, swung half round and for a second everything stopped. Some had been hurt by the concussions, which threw them to the floor several times. Then, with an almost unearthly silence, everyone rushed hither and thither. A low murmur broke out as lifebelts were adjusted.

The *Arabia*'s 4.7in gun started firing but only managed to shoot off the submarine's periscope. Meanwhile Paula grabbed Norah and a lifebelt and another passenger assisted by tying the lifebelt round them both:

There was not a sound from the little darling, she just clung onto two tiny playthings. Water and coal had showered us from head to foot, for the torpedo had lodged in the freezing chambers, having first struck the coal bunkers. We did not sink immediately, as expected at first. The boat took a big list and begin to settle down stern first. Well knowing our appointed boat stations, we rushed to our places. No panic ensued. The calmness and order were marvellous. Crossing the well-deck to get to the boat was a difficulty. The tarpaulin covering had been partly smashed and torn down.

Paula was very concerned about the panic that had set in amongst some of the lascar crew, who were pushing passengers aside while rushing to commandeer a number of lifeboats, which they sailed off in. Paula managed to reach her lifeboat, although it proved quite a daunting task getting into it:

We found our No. 12 lowered to the sea. Orders were to scramble on to the railing, grab a rope and let ourselves down into the boat as speedily as possible. It seemed to take ages

and was a most peculiar sensation. Norah was tightly strapped in my lifebelt, but I found her no trouble; in fact remarkably easy considering. The boat was packed with 65 instead of 35 to 40, and was leaking at first. Some had cut and bleeding faces and skinned hands, with other injuries.

The *Arabia* was evacuated within fifteen minutes and all 437 passengers, including 169 women and children, were saved, the only confirmed fatalities being two engineer officers and a small number of firemen who had been killed by the explosion. There appeared to be more submarines in the vicinity and three were seen cruising around, but they quickly disappeared when patrol boats surrounded the area. It was fortunate that the attack had been witnessed by other ships, since the *Arabia*'s radio apparatus had been destroyed when the torpedo struck and the Marconi operator was unable to send an SOS message:

What a relief it was to see the trails of smoke on the horizon. Within an hour and a half our rescuers, four minesweepers and the *City of Marseilles* [Ellerman Line], had us aboard. The minesweepers were manned by 8 or 10 men and a good gun or two. They do splendid work, these brave, fearless fellows, and I am afraid they do not get nearly enough recognition for their splendid services. How they regretted being unable to avenge us, but there was no sign of the submarines now.

Life aboard the rescue ships was challenging, but the survivors were relieved to be safe:

The first trawler was overcrowded, having about 280 people aboard. The others were slower and carried much less. The *City of Marseilles* could offer some comfort, but carried the passengers back to Port Said, for each vessel carried the passengers to the port for which she was bound. I pressed my little one to me and wept silently, thanking God for His goodness in saving us. How near death we had been one and all of us. We had lost our temporary home and all our personal possessions, but what was that compared to the saving of hundreds of lives.

The next few days for the survivors were especially difficult due to rough weather causing sickness, and, despite the crew providing them with some basic food, it was not always possible to eat it. The cold was intense and Norah became unwell and unable to eat or drink, but Paula had been given a table cover, which was thick and warm, to cover Norah and they remained huddled up on deck until the trawler reached Malta. However, there was one complication due to it being nightfall when they arrived at the harbour entrance, as ships were forbidden to enter after sundown, causing further grief among the survivors:

A cry of distress went up. The children could not stand much more and the women were nearly as bad. A wireless message was sent out to that effect and only under these particular circumstances would they permit the bar to be opened. A dim light showed, then some more sprang to view. At last! There seemed to be signs of a little vitality among some of the people, but most of them did not care. It seemed that ages passed before we entered the harbour. I imagine we must have looked an extremely pathetic crowd to the many who were looking for us from the pier entrance to the harbour.

We glided in silently and up to the welcoming lights of the Hospital Ship, *Glenart Castle* [Union-Castle Line], at 2 a.m. I remember hearing voices, 'Women and children first!', and we were carefully handed up by the sailors; such a sad, starving crowd. Then we were put to bed. Oh, the joy and comfort of rest and food, when such was given a quarter of a cup of steaming chicken broth; even Babs enjoyed it. It was strange how such a small quantity hurt to swallow. Later a little soda water followed by a quarter of a cup of arrowroot. The doctors, sisters and orderlies flitted about, like angels, they seemed, administering warmth and ease. I had little sleep, suffering violently from headaches and sickness. Some of them had a very bad time.

The Red Cross visited the ship later and supplied the survivors with clothing to enable them to go ashore as soon as they felt fit enough. Paula welcomed the support and help given to them:

We were treated well and the P&O were kind, giving us assistance to get necessary clothing. Then we just had to wait, until we received orders to proceed to England. Shopping in Malta was not easy. Most things had to be made and were poor at that, but cheap. A few days after my arrival a cable came from Egypt with the information that Tom had left England and I was granted permission to land in Egypt for one month.

I cabled back to say I was proceeding to England with the rest of the passengers, having no funds left. A few days later, there came a cable from Tom at Marseilles saying to await his coming, by the first opportunity. Then I made arrangements to stay behind, despite objections from the P&O. All except the

sick passengers left on the following Wednesday. For several days I waited on my own and then Tom arrived on a troopship.

Tom and Paula were finally together again and spent eleven days in Malta while Norah recovered from her illness and Tom got to meet his daughter for the first time.

The sinking of the *Arabia* without prior warning by *UB 43* caused international outrage, since it was seen to be in breach of the Sussex Pledge – a promise made by the Germans to the United States following the attack by *UB 29* (coincidentally commanded by Paula's cousin, Herbert Pustkuchen, on the French cross-Channel ferry *Sussex* off Dieppe on 24 March 1916, resulting in the loss of fifty-five lives). By further coincidence, the *Sussex* had been the first vessel to attend the wreck of the P&O liner *Oceana* in March 1912. The pledge stipulated that passenger ships would not be targeted, merchant ships would not be sunk unless the presence of weapons had been established and merchant ships would not be sunk without provision for safety of all passengers and crew. However, the *UB 43* commander had justified his attack on the *Arabia* by claiming that he was convinced that the ship was being employed as a troop transport and that he had observed 'large batches of Chinese and other coloured persons in their national costumes on board', whom he considered to be 'workmen soldiers'.

Captain Palmer was praised for the low number of lives lost in the *Arabia*, which was largely attributed to his insistence on conducting regular lifeboat drills for passengers and crew. He remained with P&O until his retirement as commodore in 1923.

– *Harlington* (2) –

1913–1916, England

The small cargo ship *Harlington* (2) (1,089 tons) was built as *Figulina* for French owners by Osbourne, Graham & Co., Sunderland, and launched on 17 September 1913. The length was 210ft (64m) and beam 32ft (9.8m). The single screw was powered by a triple-expansion steam engine, giving a service speed of 9.5 knots. P&O purchased the ship in January 1915 and renamed it *Harlington* (2), after the ship of the same name wrecked the month previously. Like her predecessor, the *Harlington* (2) was employed on the east coast feeder service.

On the cold winter night of 9 December 1916 the *Harlington* (2), under the command of Captain W.B. Potts, struck a mine laid by *UC 11* (Benno von Ditfurth) when 4 miles (6.5km) south-west of the Shipwash Lightship off Harwich while on a voyage from Newcastle to London with a cargo of coal. The mine blew the bottom of the *Harlington* (2) away and the ship sank within three minutes. Despite rough weather, all the crew escaped by lifeboat and were soon picked up by the collier *Harlyn* (1911, 1,794 tons). Many of the *Harlington* (2)'s crew were soaking wet and very cold, so the crew of the *Harlyn* provided them with fresh clothes while they recovered in the warmth of the boiler room. But then tragically the *Harlyn* also struck a mine and quickly sank, claiming the lives of two of her own crew and seven of those just rescued. Another coasting vessel arrived at the scene and later landed Captain Potts and the other survivors at Sheerness.

A wreck found in the area that could well be the *Harlington* (2) lies partially buried in shallow water at a depth of just 11m and appears to be upside down. A second wreck lying upright about 800m to the north-west is a strong candidate for the *Harlyn*.

– *Ballarat* (1) –

1911–1917, England

Ballarat (1) (11,120 tons) was built for P&O by Caird & Co., Greenock, and launched by Mrs F.C. Allen, wife of the manager of the P&O Branch Line, on 23 September 1911. The length was 500.1ft (152.4m) and beam 62.8ft (19.1m). Twin screws were powered by two quadruple-expansion steam engines, giving a service speed of 14 knots. There was accommodation for 302 passengers in a permanent 'one class' and a further 750 in temporary quarters.

When P&O took over the Blue Anchor Line's emigrant service in 1910 they placed orders for five new ships to serve on the route around the Cape of Good Hope, all of which were named after Australian towns beginning with the letter 'B'. The *Ballarat* (1) was named after a town in the state of Victoria, which is derived from an Aboriginal word meaning 'resting place'. A previous vessel in the P&O fleet, *Ballaarat* (1882, 4,764 tons), used an alternative earlier spelling of the town's name. The new service, known as the Branch Line, was run separately from the rest of the P&O operation because Australian regulations mandated that the ships sailed with all-white crews. For

her first few years on the route the *Ballarat* (1)'s single funnel retained the Blue Anchor emblem, but in 1914 the funnel was dressed solely in black, in keeping with all other vessels in the P&O fleet.

The *Ballarat* (1) sailed on her maiden voyage from London to Sydney on 18 November 1911 under the command of Captain Windeger Lingham, formerly of the *Wakool* (ex-Blue Anchor Line), making his fifty-fourth passage to Australia. The ship arrived in Sydney in record time on 10 January 1912 and docked at Brown's Wharf, Woolloomooloo Bay, where 400 immigrants disembarked to start their new lives in Australia.

For the first few months after the outbreak of the First World War, the P&O immigrant service continued to operate as normal. Regular newspaper advertisements advised the cost of the passage commenced at £10 for the Cape and £18 for Australia.

It wasn't long before the *Ballarat* (1) was taken up for transport service. Upon returning to London from a routine voyage to Sydney the ship was dispatched to India under the command of Captain F.W.A. Hanson to repatriate a large number of Civil servants who had been stranded in England at the outbreak of the war. The *Ballarat* (1) sailed for Bombay where a large convoy of sixty-four merchant vessels was being assembled to transport Indian troops to the war zone. The ships sailed from Bombay under naval escort in formation of eight abreast, with the *Ballarat* (1) designated as the flagship. The ships remained in formation as far as Perim, where they

The *Ballarat* (1) was built in 1911 for the P&O Branch Line service to Australia. All 1,752 lives were saved when the ship was torpedoed by *UB 32* on Anzac Day 1917.

were reduced to four abreast for the passage through the Red Sea. In addition to carrying a full complement of troops, there were also a large number of horses on board which required daily exercise on the open decks. After passing through the Suez Canal in single file, ten ships dropped out of the convoy for East Africa and the Persian Gulf and the remainder proceeded safely to Marseilles.

On 6 August 1915 the *Ballarat* (1) arrived in Melbourne to a rapturous reception, with thousands of people lining the streets to welcome home over 600 wounded Australian soldiers, many of whom had taken part in the historic landing at Gallipoli on 25 April 1915. An array of motor cars lent by members of the Australian Patriots' League was lined up near the dock, ready to help transport the invalids directly to the base hospital. Similar scenes greeted the ship in Sydney a few days later and every disembarking soldier was met with loud cheers. Despite receiving some horrific injuries, all the men had remained in high spirits during the voyage and never complained once.

For the next couple of years the *Ballarat* (1) served as a hospital transport under the designation HMAT A70 *Ballarat*, embarking medical staff and troops in Australian ports and returning with war wounded.

On 19 February 1917 the *Ballarat* (1) sailed from Melbourne on her fourth transport voyage from Australia with troops, Unit 15 of the Australian Railway Operating Division and members of the Australian Army Medical Corps (AAMC). The cargo included copper, bullion and antimony ore. The master was Captain George Wallace Cockman RD RNR (retired) who had been awarded with the Distinguished Service Cross in December 1916 for his conduct on the P&O *Benalla* earlier in the war. The troops' commanding officer was Lieutenant Colonel Robert Morrison McVea, who had been invalided home on the *Kyarra* (of the Australian United Steam Navigation Company) prior to joining the transport service.

A huge crowd gathered to give the *Ballarat* (1) a rousing send off and friends and relatives waved farewell to their loved ones. The ship was festooned with colourful streamers that stretched between the decks and the pier, creating an atmosphere more like a carnival than a departure to war. After calls at Albany and Fremantle, the *Ballarat* (1) made for Cape Town where the troops were able to enjoy a few days of shore leave. The last port visited on the voyage was Freetown, Sierra Leone, where the ship spent four nights at anchor over the long Easter weekend. After a passage of nine weeks and steaming a distance of 13,000 miles the *Ballarat* (1) finally arrived in the approach to the English Channel where she was joined by the Royal Navy destroyer HMS *Phoenix*, sent to escort her the rest of the way to Plymouth.

A strong sense of camaraderie had developed among the Australians during the long voyage on the *Ballarat* (1), epitomised by the satirical content of the unofficial on-board newspaper *The Ballarat Beacon*. Towards the end of the journey the highlights from the newspaper were compiled into a censored souvenir booklet entitled *The Book of the Ballarat*, which required some hasty last-minute changes due to the dramatic events that took place just a short distance from Plymouth, as written in the article titled 'Exit H.M.A.T. Ballarat':

On every deck the troops are preparing for disembarkation and bringing out their web equipment.

Most important on this day – 25th April – are the 'Anzacs' on board. In a few minutes they are to take part in a memorial service. Already the padres are preparing for it. This tribute paid, they are to sit down to a simple repast, intended to remind them of their first soldier's meal, eaten on Gallipoli's grim heights. Bread and bully beef, washed down with water. (This was to be the frugal fare, and no Anzac would have exchanged it for the sumptuous banquet the ship had offered to provide.)

Meanwhile, in ship's orderly room, papers of all descriptions are being catalogued and packed; at the same time, the C.O. is trying the last offender; while outside, guesses are being hazarded as to the time we shall see the shores of England.

At the ship's side the submarine guard is on duty. The sentries still gaze over the sea, searching for the first sign of the dreaded periscope, yet hoping that danger from such a source is now over. The very fact of being within a few hours of port gives a sense of security to all on board.

The scene is animated. Never since our first day on board has there been such bustle. Excitement is in the air. Anticipation is on tip-toe. That which for nine weary weeks has been to us a land of dreams is about to become a reality. The descendant of Irish stock conjures up visions of a trip to the little green isle of the West; the son of Scotia dreams of the hills and heather; while the man who boasts English parentage thinks of green lanes, hedgerows, and – London! Thus were we musing at 2 p.m. on Wednesday, 25th April, 1917.

Five minutes later –

Boomp! The ship shivers from stem to stern.

No need for any bugle to call. Though few have heard the dread sound before, there is no one ignorant of its meaning. 'She's got it!'

All we dreaded and planned to avert has happened.

The ship has been torpedoed!

For a moment a strained silence prevails. Even the engines have ceased to throb.

The awed silence is cut by the sharp notes of the bugle: 'To the lifeboats!'

Despite over fifty extra lookouts being stationed on either side of the ship, no one detected the lurking submarine *UB 32* (Max Viebeg) before it was too late. The force of the explosion blew away the starboard propeller, bent the port propeller shaft and breached the watertight bulkheads that separated the tunnel from the engine room. The *Ballarat* (1) started to take on water rapidly and within minutes the engines were completely submerged. With the vessel sinking fast the troops prepared for the worst and shook hands with their mates, but there was no panic and every man kept his head. Lifeboat drill had been rehearsed countless times during the course of the voyage and it wasn't long before twenty boats were away, quickly followed by additional life rafts. There was a brief period when the possibility of saving the ship was entertained and some men were surprised to be called back on board. But it soon became clear that the badly damaged port screw and pumps could not compete with the incoming water and the plan was quickly abandoned. HMS *Lookout* approached and came alongside so that many of the troops could be transferred directly to the small destroyer.

As soon as Captain Cockman had seen all the troops and the majority of the crew safely away his thoughts turned to making an attempt to save his ship. The *Ballarat* (1) was taken in tow by several naval vessels and other additional drifters stood by to assist. With HMS *Phoenix* remaining on station to ward off any potential further attacks, the *Ballarat* (1) was towed slowly towards The Lizard where it was hoped the ship could be beached in shallow water. However, at 4.30 the following morning the *Ballarat* (1) finally sank while still 7 miles from shore.

Amazingly not a single life was lost and the entire ship's company of 1,752 souls were landed safely. Lieutenant Colonel McVea was 'thundering proud' of the conduct of his troops and Captain Cockman and his crew were praised in an official announcement made by the Secretary of the Admiralty published in the press:

With reference to the official announcement, dated the 2nd inst., reporting that the troopship *Ballarat* had been sunk by a German submarine, it is desired to add that Commander G.W. Cockman, D.S.C., Royal Naval Reserve (retired), was in command of that vessel, and the fact that all hands were safely transferred from the transport to the patrol craft reflects the highest credit on the captain, officers, and crew.

Diving the Wreck

The wreck of the *Ballarat* (1) lies in a maximum depth of 88m, 7 miles south of Lizard Point, Cornwall. It was first located in 1954 by salvage company Risdon Beazley Ltd. Another much later salvage operation took place in 1985 when lead and copper ingots were raised from the wreck, with munitions being reported in the midships area. It was also at this time that the *Ballarat* (1)'s bell was recovered, leaving no doubt over the wreck's identity.

Being the deepest P&O wreck in the English Channel the *Ballarat* (1) is seldom visited by recreational divers. When Leigh Bishop dived the wreck in 2004 he found that despite the destructive salvage operations the 'troopship' still makes an interesting dive. The wreck lies with a strong list to port and is relatively simple to navigate, with significant sections still easily recognisable. The bow is intact but broken away at the forecastle where the wreck flattens to the seabed, yielding visible evidence of the earlier salvage activities in the forward hold. There are reports of a few copper ingots remaining in this area, most probably having spilled from salvage grabs in the past. P&O crockery and other interesting artefacts are often found in the midst of scattered wreckage surrounding this location. Heading aft, the wreck starts to rise again, reaching as high as 7m from the seabed. A significant amount of teak decking remains, which leads to an area of collapsed upper decks and exposed engine cylinder heads.

– Medina –

1911–1917, England

Medina (12,350 tons) was built for P&O by Caird & Co., Greenock, and launched on 14 March 1911. The length was 550ft (167.6m) and beam 62.8ft (19.1m). Twin screws were powered by quadruple-expansion steam engines, giving a service speed of 16.5 knots. There was accommodation for 460 first- and 216 second-class passengers. The ship was the last in the series of ten M-class ships that commenced with *Moldavia* (1) in 1903.

Within days of the launch it was reported in the press that the *Medina* was to be chartered by the Admiralty and commissioned as the royal yacht to carry King George V and Queen Mary to the Delhi Durbar. It was believed that the beautifully furnished

The *Medina* sailed on her maiden voyage in 1911 commissioned as the royal yacht to carry King George V and Queen Mary to the Delhi Durbar. (Allan C. Green/State Library of Victoria)

Brass vases were amongst the extensive Lord Carmichael collection recovered from the wreck in 1986. (Salcombe Museum)

fly the necessary flags, a third mast was fitted immediately in front of the forward funnel. The ship was painted in the customary royal yacht livery: the hull and superstructure in white, buff funnels and a ribbon of blue and gold.

The *Medina* sailed from Portsmouth on her maiden voyage as HMS *Medina* on 11 November 1911 and was joined at Spithead by her four naval escorts: HMS *Argyll*, HMS *Natal*, HMS *Cochrane* and HMS *Defence*. Despite an exceptionally rough passage through the Bay of Biscay, in which heavy seas forced water into the Queen's cabin, the rest of the voyage passed smoothly and the *Medina* arrived safely in Bombay on 2 December. After spending six weeks in India the *Medina* sailed for home and arrived back in Portsmouth on 5 February 1912. The ship was then returned to her original builders on the Clyde for a refit prior to commencing commercial P&O service.

The *Medina*'s first P&O sailing departed from England on 28 June 1912 under the command of Captain Franke Notley who, upon arrival in Sydney, praised the *Medina* as 'the finest ship I have ever had'. Great interest was also shown in the ship's Marconi wireless operator, who was none other than Harold Bride, of recent *Titanic* fame. Bride had been the deputy of Jack Phillips, who died in the disaster, but he refused to discuss the tragedy with the Australian press.

After completing a successful inaugural voyage the *Medina* became firmly established alongside the other vessels on P&O's fortnightly UK–Australia mail service.

Unlike many other merchant vessels, the *Medina* was not commandeered by the Admiralty during the First World War and the ship remained on the mail run to Australia. Early in 1917 the *Medina* sailed from Australia with a cargo of meat, butter, tin and silver bullion, bound for England via India. When the *Medina* called at Bombay she embarked Lord and Lady Thomas Gibson Carmichael, who were returning to England after six years in India, where Lord Carmichael had served as governor of Madras and later governor of Bengal. Lady Carmichael was very concerned about travelling to England at a time when merchant ships were so susceptible to attacks by enemy submarines, so the Carmichaels were relieved to transfer to HMS *Sheffield* at Port Said for the remainder of the voyage. Lord Carmichael was an avid art collector and entomologist and his expansive collection and personal effects remained on board the *Medina*. After reaching Plymouth and offloading the bullion, the *Medina* commenced her way up the English Channel for her final destination of Tilbury, London.

The *Medina* had only steamed as far as Start Point, Devon, when late in the afternoon of 28 April 1917, just three days after the loss of the *Ballarat* (1), the ship was hit by a torpedo fired by *UB 31* (Thomas Bieber). The torpedo struck in the vicinity of the starboard engine

midships staterooms on the luxury liner would afford a much more comfortable voyage for the royal party than the accommodation on any existing navy ship. The internal design was further modified to provide two expansive royal suites, one for the king on the port side, another for the queen on the starboard side. In keeping with other contemporary P&O vessels, the *Medina* had been designed with two masts, but in order to meet the requirements of a royal yacht and room, instantly killing Fourth Engineer William Palmer and five lascar crew. All the remaining passengers and crew managed to get away in the lifeboats, which were soon taken in tow by local boats and destroyers to Dartmouth and Brixham. The *Medina* sank shortly after 7 p.m., along with Lord Carmichael's unique and valuable collection.

Salvaging the Wreck

In 1936 the Italian salvage firm Sorima based themselves in Dartmouth for an extensive salvage operation, which targeted over thirty war wrecks, one being the *Medina*, from which much of the cargo of tin was recovered. Much later, in the early 1970s, the wreck attracted the attention of the leading British salvage company Risdon Beazley Ltd, who worked the wreck for 25 tons of tin in 1973 and 1975. They were also acting on information that 100 tons of copper was stowed in an unknown location, but none was found. However, the salvage grab would frequently come to the surface with passenger trunks that had been stowed in the holds. Amazingly, the contents were often still dry and included such items as elaborate dressing-table sets, which comprised cut-glass jars and bottles, brushes, combs and mirrors. The ship was also found to carry several tons of golf balls, which were frequently found rolling around the deck of the salvage vessel.

In 1984 the salvage company Consortium Recovery decided to attempt to locate Lord Carmichael's possessions, having recently learned that they were still on board when the *Medina* had sunk. At first the project was delayed by severe weather and difficulty determining the exact location of the baggage, which was due to the damage caused by the earlier use of explosives on the wreck. However, in 1986 the salvage operation commenced in earnest, with saturation divers working from the *Holger Dane* in eight-hour shifts, twenty-four hours a day. The divers were hampered by unstable decks and working in dark compartments thick with mud, but eventually their efforts were rewarded when finally a box marked 'GCIE' (Knight Grand Commander of the Indian Empire) was found. It wasn't long before eighty-eight cases of Lord Carmichael's belongings were raised, with much of the contents found to be in an excellent state of preservation. The collection was auctioned off by Sotheby's in May 1988 but the revenues were disappointing, due to many of the items being modest historical curiosities and with limited commercial value.

The illustrated Sotheby's catalogue listed 194 lots categorised as: 'Oriental Brass and Other Metal Work' (e.g. an Indian articulated brass fish); 'Porcelain and Pottery' (e.g. a pair of Satsuma vases); 'Oriental Works of Art' (e.g. a Chinese rock crystal figure of a cat); 'Personal Effects, P&O Tableware and Various European Artefacts' (e.g. a brass-mounted shooting stick); 'Letters Documents and Personal Papers' (e.g. a nickel Automobile Association badge); and 'Jewellery and Objects of Vertu' (e.g. a pair of sapphire and diamond sleeve links). The latter proved to be one of the most highly prized items and it sold for £1,800.

Diving the Wreck

The substantial remains of the *Medina* rest at a depth of 63m on the Western side of Lyme Bay, 4 miles east of Star Point. It is not quite the largest P&O shipwreck on the south coast of England – that honour goes to the *Maloja* (1), which at 12,432 tons is just fractionally bigger. However in terms of how much there is to see and explore then there is no contest. Despite the numerous salvage operations that have taken place over the years and the ravages of time, the *Medina* remains in very good condition. The most impressive and intact part of the wreck is the forward section which stands upright with a slight list to port, whereas the stern area is detached and very broken. The top of the wreck was once reported to be as shallow as 39m and although it is now showing signs of collapse, the *Medina* still stands 15m proud of the silted seabed.

In 1994 a team of technical divers known as Starfish Enterprise undertook a pioneering dive expedition to the 93m-deep wreck of the Cunard Liner *Lusitania* off the south coast of Ireland. The *Medina* made an ideal choice for one of several build-up dives that took place during their final preparations. Gary Gentile was one of three American divers to join the expedition and recalled the *Medina* dive in his book *The Lusitania Controversies*:

> There were lots of openings and rust holes in the hull, so I wasted no time in shooting inside. Visibility was around twenty feet [6m]. Standing bulkheads sectioned off the interior into good-sized compartments. I picked my way from room to room, careful not to disturb the ultra fine white silt that lay many inches thick. During my wandering I took note of alternative exits, so I was not much concerned about finding my way back.

Gentile's solo penetration to the interior of the wreck came as something of a surprise to the other divers, but he was rewarded for his efforts when he returned clutching a china plate bearing the distinctive P&O emblem. The divers that day were fortunate to experience such good visibility as it is notoriously bad in the area, seldom extending much beyond a few metres.

Andris Nestors recalled his memories from diving the *Medina* two decades later:

> The superstructure was quite intact and it was very easy to swim into the upper decks, along the walkways that run both sides of the ship and into the rooms and cabins on the upper deck level. A lot of the walls had fallen away and there were plenty of holes in the ceiling so lots of comforting green glows showing the exits.
>
> The bow was particularly impressive, with a post standing up a couple of metres at the bow which you could hold onto and look straight down at the flanks of the wreck, anchors intact. However the last time I went, the bow area was really beginning to collapse into the middle of the ship, the plates were at right angles, the large deck winches were hanging precariously.

Divers report that the upright hull is still lined with rows of portholes and a lot of handrailings remain in place. The stern section is less interesting but a highlight is one of the massive boilers.

The depth of the *Medina* places the wreck beyond normal recreational diving limits. As such most divers visiting the wreck in the modern era will breath trimix instead of regular compressed air. Trimix is a gas mixture where the narcotic effect of breathing nitrogen at depth is reduced by replacing a percentage of it with helium. The *Medina* is a unique and special wreck and, despite the murky conditions and technical challenges, many divers who have visited it feel compelled to return.

In 1905 the *Mongolia* (2) made a record passage from Marseilles to Fremantle of just twenty-three days and sixteen hours. (Allan C. Green/ State Library of Victoria)

– *Mongolia* (2) –

1903–1917, Indian Ocean

Mongolia (2) (9,505 tons) was built for P&O by Caird & Co., Greenock, and launched on 13 August 1903. The length was 520.9ft (158.7m) and beam 58.3ft (17.8m). Twin screws were powered by triple-expansion steam engines, giving a service speed of 16.5 knots. There was accommodation for 348 first- and 166 second-class passengers.

The maiden voyage of *Mongolia* (2) sailed from London to Bombay and Kurrachee on 20 November 1903, but the vessel was ultimately destined for the fortnightly mail service to Australia. In January 1905

the ship made a record passage from Marseilles to Fremantle of just twenty-three days, sixteen hours.

The *Mongolia* (2) had a lucky escape in March 1908 when a fire broke out in the baggage hold while the ship was en route from Gibraltar to Marseilles. The fire was eventually brought under control and none of the 400 passengers were harmed, but much of the cargo and baggage was destroyed.

A second incident at the end of the same year had much more serious consequences. Shortly before 1 p.m. on 28 December 1909 the *Mongolia* (2) was approaching her berth in Fremantle Harbour when she was met by the harbour tug *Susan* carrying the customary officials from the Health and Customs Department. As the *Susan* was manoeuvring to come alongside the *Mongolia* (2) on the port side, the tug managed to cut underneath the bows of the incoming liner and was struck heavily. All the occupants managed to leap overboard, with the exception of fireman John Wright who was down in the stokehole and went to the bottom with the tug. The

Mongolia (2) immediately launched two lifeboats to recover the officials and crew from the water and there was no further loss of life.

The *Mongolia* (2) was one of many P&O ships represented at the Coronation Naval Review at Spithead on 24 June 1911.

On 17 May 1915 the *Mongolia* (2) was outward-bound from England to Australia under the command of Captain Herbert Lewellin when the ship narrowly escaped an encounter with the enemy off the coast of Spain. The chief officer caught site of a submarine about a mile off the port quarter so the *Mongolia* (2) increased speed and put on a zigzag course. A suspicious, unidentified vessel then approached and commenced to speed south on a parallel course but could not keep up with the *Mongolia* (2), which was making 17.5 knots.

Captain Lewellin and the *Mongolia* (2) got through the next two years of the war unscathed, but the ship's luck ran out in the Indian Ocean on 23 June 1917 during a voyage to Bombay when the ship struck a mine laid by the German armed merchant raider SMS *Wolf* (Karl August Nerger). The explosion claimed the lives of three passengers, three engineering officers, three European crew and fourteen native crew. Fortunately a full lifeboat drill had been held the day before and this helped account for over 400 survivors making it into the boats, despite the fact that the *Mongolia* (2) went to the bottom after just thirteen minutes. Captain Lewellin was the last to leave and just before the final plunge he was seen to dive from the promenade deck, cheered on by two nearby boats. The captain was soon picked up and gave orders for the boats to make for shore and try to land before nightfall. Battling against monsoon weather, it wasn't long before the boats became separated, so Captain Lewellin and one of the other boats decided to make directly for Bombay. Most of the others landed in a cove at Janjira, about 60 miles south of Bombay, where they were taken good care of by the local Nawab. One other boat was picked up by the passing coastal steamer *Sabarmati*.

The elderly Australian wool broker and politician Frederick Winchcombe was returning from England on the *Mongolia* (2) after paying a visit to two sons on active service with the Australian Imperial Force. Although he survived the wreck he contracted pneumonia as a direct result and died in hospital in Bombay just six days later.

One of the surviving passengers was the world champion tennis player Norman Brookes, winner of the men's singles at Wimbledon in 1907 and 1914. During the war Brookes served in the Australian branch of the British Red Cross in Egypt.

– *Salsette* (2) –

1908–1917, England

Salsette (2) (5,842 tons) was built for P&O by Caird & Co., Greenock, and launched on 2 April 1908. It had a length of 440ft (134.1m) and a beam of 53.2ft (16.2m). Twin bronze screws were powered by 10,000hp quadruple-expansion steam engines, giving a service speed of 20 knots. Capacity was for 140 first- and 121 second-class passengers.

The *Salsette* (2) was a modest-sized vessel in comparison to two larger 10,000-ton passenger liners that were also built on the Clyde for P&O in 1908 – the *Morea* and *Malwa* (2). But anything the *Salsette* (2) lacked in size was amply compensated for by both the ship's impressive speed, which made her the fastest ship in the fleet, and her striking appearance. Because the *Salsette* (2) was destined to sail exclusively in the tropics, P&O made the decision to paint the hull white, rather than the traditional black of the other vessels in the fleet. The perfectly proportioned funnels were painted buff yellow. The new livery, used just once before on the *Caledonia* in 1894,

The express passenger liner *Salsette* (2) entered service in 1908 and was the fastest ship in the fleet with a service speed of 20 knots. (Allan C. Green/State Library of Victoria)

served to further enhance the sweeping lines of the hull, graceful counter stern and straight stem. One of the *Salsette* (2)'s future masters, Captain Albert Armitage, later described the vessel as 'the most beautifully modelled ship that I have ever seen'.

P&O took delivery of the *Salsette* (2) in July 1908 and during the same month the ship undertook a short round-trip trial voyage from Tilbury, with calls at Southampton and Plymouth. This was followed by two cruises, which were extensively advertised in the press:

P. & O. Pleasure Cruises,
By the New Express Steamer 'SALSETTE'
6,000 tons, 10,000 h.p.
AUGUST 8th, 24 Days. — The BALTIC and RUSSIA
SEPTEMBER 9th. 30 Days. — ALGIERS, VENICE, DALMATIA, and SICILY.

Captain Albert Armitage (left) became master of the *Salsette* (2) in 1915. Seen here on board *Karmala* in 1921 reunited with fellow Antarctic explorer Captain Evans RN.

In October the *Salsette* (2) sailed for India, completing the passage from Marseilles to Bombay in a record time of eleven days, twenty-one hours, breaking the previous record held by the *Caledonia* since 1895 by twelve hours. From November onwards the *Salsette* (2) was employed on the fortnightly express mail service, running between Bombay and Aden, where the ship provided the connection with the outward- and homeward-bound Australian mail steamers. The *Salsette* (2) remained almost exclusively on this route for the next six years, consistently making fast and efficient passages and setting new records. The only significant downside to a voyage on the *Salsette* (2) was that the ship had a tendency to pitch and roll heavily, which could cause discomfort for the passengers, especially during the monsoon season.

One of the worst monsoons encountered by the *Salsette* (2) occurred in the Arabian Sea in July 1914 while on a voyage from Aden to Bombay under the command of Captain Vines. Not long after leaving Aden the ship ran into exceptionally heavy weather and waves crashed relentlessly over the decks, causing considerable damage. Somehow water managed to penetrate the stokeholds, most probably through the coaling chutes, and several of the boilers were extinguished. To make matters worse the pumps became clogged and the crew had to resort to bailing out the water with buckets. The *Salsette* (2) was hove to for thirty-six hours while the problems were dealt with, by which time the vessel had crawled about 50 miles back towards Aden. Despite doing everything they could, the engine room crew were unable to fully overcome the trouble and Captain Vines had to make for Bombay at reduced speed, eventually arriving two and a half days late.

The outbreak of the First World War did not cause any immediate disruption to the *Salsette* (2), which continued to operate the express service as normal. At the start of 1915 Captain Albert Borlase Armitage sailed as a passenger in the *Medina* to Bombay in order to relieve the *Salsette* (2)'s current master. Armitage, who eventually rose to commodore of the P&O line, had an unusual background to his career.

Captain Albert Borlase Armitage RD, RNR

In 1878, at the age of 14, Albert Armitage joined the Royal Navy training ship HMS *Worcester*, moored on the River Thames, where he spent the next two years. He then commenced his apprenticeship at sea on the sailing ship *Plassey*, which was wrecked off the Kent coast at the end of his second voyage in January 1883. Armitage completed his apprenticeship in the sailing vessel *Lucknow*, after which he applied to join P&O, despite strong objections from his

Salsette (2) was torpedoed off the Dorset coast by *UB 40* in July 1917. The wreck rests in Lyme Bay at a depth of 50m and is very popular with divers. (Painting by Stuart Williamson)

father, who felt the Royal Navy offered a better career. Armitage joined *Bokhara* in 1873 as fifth officer and spent the next ten years on a variety of P&O ships, by which time he had risen to the rank of second officer on the *Bombay* (3).

In 1894 the secretary to the Royal Geographical Society, Sir Clements Markham, approached Armitage with an invitation to be navigator and second-in-command of the Jackson–Harmsworth Expedition. He was given leave of absence from P&O and spent the next three years in the Arctic, where his excellent work as an ice-navigator and Polar explorer resulted in him being awarded the Murchison Award.

Armitage resumed his career with P&O as chief officer of the *Osiris* in 1898 but three years later, at the age of 37, he was asked to join the Discovery Antarctic Expedition (1901–04), led by Robert Falcon Scott, once again as second-in-command and navigator.

When Armitage returned to P&O for the second time he was frustrated to learn that, despite an earlier agreement from the company, he had fallen behind on the seniority list and six other chief officers had been promoted over his head. Finally in 1906 Armitage gained his first command, the *Isis*, sailing on the Brindisi–Port Said shuttle service, where he remained until he joined the *Salsette* (2) in 1915.

In the autumn of 1915 Captain Armitage was ordered to take the *Salsette* (2) to England on a voyage that proved to be very eventful. When the ship sailed from Bombay on 3 October it had not been supplied with a gun, the captain being advised that *Salsette* (2)'s speed would provide its greatest protection. Armitage felt that even a dummy gun would be better than nothing and at Port Said he managed to acquire a 4.7in gun handbook from a navy commander, from which the *Salsette* (2)'s carpenter was able to construct a life-size wooden replica. The fake gun soon proved to be convincing

enough to successfully ward off an enemy submarine that was encountered lurking off the Spanish coast. Upon arrival in London at the end of the month the *Salsette* (2) was finally armed with a real gun.

On the return voyage the ship called at Marseilles where the arrest of two spies revealed that the *Salsette* (2) was to be a target for enemy submarines in the Mediterranean. Despite receiving wireless messages daily that submarines were following the ship, no harm was done, but apparently a French ship of the same name was attacked.

By the time the *Salsette* (2) had cleared the Suez Canal, Captain Armitage had been on his feet for sixty hours and was mentally and physically exhausted, so he retired to his cabin for some much-needed rest. On 21 November, ten minutes after sighting the Zafarana light, the captain came up to the bridge where he was shocked to discover

the *Salsette* (2) aground on a sandbank, with the officer of the watch oblivious to the fact. Both engines were put full astern but sand had choked the condensers and the ship remained stuck fast. HMS *Fox* and HMS *Porcupine* arrived at the scene the following morning, followed by the French armoured cruiser *Montcalm*. *Salsette* (2) soon came off with minimal assistance without sustaining any damage and safely completed her voyage to Bombay.

At the end of 1916 the *Salsette* (2) made the first of two voyages on the Australia run, where she was required as a replacement for the *Arabia*, which had been torpedoed on 6 November. In between voyages to Australia the *Salsette* (2) remained on the Bombay–Aden express service until she was recalled to England once more, arriving in July 1917.

On 19 July 1917 *Salsette* (2) sailed from London, bound for Bombay, with passengers, general cargo and pay for the troops in Egypt. At 10.30 p.m., after spending several hours at anchor in the Downs off the east coast of Kent, orders were eventually received to get underway, with instructions to hug the coast around Portland Bill. However, as the *Salsette* (2) approached the Shambles Lightship a minelayer dashed out and demanded that the ship keep further out into the English Channel. The *Salsette* (2) proceeded at 19 knots, steering a zigzag course, with multiple lookouts all around the ship. Captain Armitage was in the chartroom plotting the course when he heard the chief officer, who was up on the flying bridge, suddenly shout down the order, 'Hard a starboard!' Just as the captain rushed onto the bridge an explosion of volcanic proportions erupted. It was

a moment that he never forgot, later describing the vivid memory in his autobiography *Cadet to Commodore*:

> The ship seemed to be uplifted and drop and sag; the air was filled with blackness. I couldn't see my hand a foot from my face, and a blast hurled me against the chart-room, the Q.M. being blown out of the open door.
>
> Gathering my dazed senses together, I dimly noted that the sounding-boom was sticking through the chart-room, it having gone up like a rocket and come down like a stick, penetrating flying bridge and lower bridge into the Third Officer's cabin, nearly imprisoning him and another officer. I rushed to the engine-room telegraph and gave a prearranged order to abandon ship. I knew that she was doomed.

The captain's next priority was to dash down to his cabin and retrieve about thirty bags containing secret and confidential government despatches, which had come aboard in London. The weighted bags were hastily thrown overboard and Captain Armitage bore witness to further scenes of devastation:

> Five boats out of twelve were wrecked by the blast; the foremast rigging came down by the run just as the crow's nest look-out slid down to the deck; water was being ejected from the swan-neck ventilators as though by a powerful steam-pump: gush – gush – gush! A fireman – Indian – crawled from out the cowl-head of one of the great engine-room ventilators with the flesh hanging down his legs – never a murmur – quietly into a boat. Four and a half minutes; seven boats filled with humanity; the *Salsette*, *my Salsette*, wounded to death, rolling over in her death-agony.

Captain Armitage was the last to leave the *Salsette* (2) and witnessed the ship's final moments from his departing lifeboat, seeing the ship turn and nosedive fifty minutes after the torpedo had struck. All the passengers had got off safely but fifteen lascar engine room crew lost their lives: ten firemen, four trimmers and one tindal. The captain also lost his beloved cat, Otto, although another cat was found alive on a raft and later became a torpedo boat's mascot. All the survivors were picked up after twenty minutes and landed in Weymouth.

A diver is dwarfed by one of the *Salsette* (2)'s large anchors. (Catherine de Lara)

The *Salsette* (2) attracts a lot of fish life, which makes the wreck popular with both anglers and divers. (Catherine de Lara)

Engine room telegraph from the *Salsette* (2) on display at the Shipwreck Project in Portland.

An Alfred Grahams Patent Navy Phone that was found on the wreck of the *Salsette* (2). (Julian Hale)

This pewter ram's head is one of the more unusual items to have been found on the wreck of the *Salsette* (2). (Callum Beveridge)

After a couple of months off to recuperate from injuries incurred in the blast, Captain Armitage took command of the *Karmala* (1), which had been requisitioned for transport duties in the North Atlantic, where he remained until the end of the war. With the compulsory P&O retirement age rapidly approaching, Armitage asked for a larger ship and was transferred to the passenger liner *Mantua* (1), where he enjoyed one year as commodore before retiring in 1924.

The *Salsette* (2) had been struck by a torpedo fired from *UB 40* (Hans Howaldt), which during the course of the war was responsible for sinking 100 ships, totalling 134,537 tons, and inflicting damage on a further fifteen. Hans Howaldt was one of four *UB 40* commanders, serving on the U-boat from 3 December 1916 to 14 December 1917. He also commanded *UC 4* and *UB 107* and was personally responsible for sinking sixty-five ships during the First World War. He received numerous awards, including the Pour le Mérite, and was later active in the Second World War. Before the end of July 1917 German submarines would claim a further two P&O vessels – *Mooltan* (2) and *Candia* (2).

Diving the Wreck

The impressive wreck of the *Salsette* (2) lies in Lyme Bay 9 miles due west of Portland Bill, within easy reach from Weymouth and many other Dorset ports and launch sites. The wreck of the sleek ocean liner is instantly recognisable and rests on the port side at 45 degrees on a flat, sandy seabed. Although much of the upper-deck superstructure has collapsed, the hull is still largely intact for the entire 134m length of the vessel. The maximum depth is 45m and the highest point of the wreck is the starboard railings at 32m.

With a typical thirty-minute bottom time it is just possible to swim the entire length of the wreck, but this won't leave much time for stops along the way or any forays into the interiors. The *Salsette* (2) attracts a lot of fish life, which includes shoals of pout and some massive pollock. Unfortunately this has the downside of making the wreck just as popular with fishermen as with divers. Consequently, there is monofilament line trailing all over the wreck, requiring extra diligence, particularly in poor visibility.

When the wreck was first positively identified as that of the *Salsette* (2) in the 1970s it was said that it was still possible to read the imprint of the ship's name left behind by the removal of the brass nameplate letters above the stern. The *Salsette* (2) carried a solitary, defensive 4.7in gun and this is still mounted on the deck above. Below the stern, the starboard prop shaft is exposed but the bronze propeller has been salvaged. A lot of wooden decking remains in place and is observed throughout the length of the wreck.

Moving forward, there is a brief break in the starboard side of the hull. Beyond this are the remains of a cargo crane and the aft mast, which reaches out across the seabed. This is followed by an open space in the deck that permits access to engine room areas. From here it is possible to penetrate deeper into the wreck and then out through the torpedo hole on the starboard side.

There are two large cylindrical tanks side by side on the open deck, beyond which is a large winch. From here the central third of the wreck follows a similar pattern of holes and deck until reaching the forecastle section where there are two further cranes. Conger eels are common on the *Salsette* (2) and have been known to swim brazenly out in the open rather than hiding in the deeper recesses of the wreck. Just past the forward hold and down inside a hole is a bathtub. A large anchor winch indicates arrival at the bow where the anchor chains file down through the hawse pipes, ending with the anchors, which both still sit snugly in place. The bow terminates with the classic straight stem commonly preferred by early twentieth-century liners.

Before starting the slow ascent to the surface some divers may elect to spend the last few minutes swimming along the starboard edge at the shallowest depth. This provides a good opportunity to view some of the many hundreds of portholes that once lined the *Salsette* (2)'s hull.

The underwater visibility is definitely a significant influencing factor in how divers rate their experience diving on the *Salsette* (2). During the summer months of a single season it has been known to vary from an undivable 1m to an astounding 20m.

Without doubt, one of the biggest attractions to the *Salsette* (2), especially for the divers in the late twentieth century, has been the abundance and diverse range of 'souvenirs' waiting to be found. As a well-appointed luxury liner carrying affluent passengers, the wreck has been a treasure trove of interesting and valuable artefacts. Some of the items recovered over the years have included the bell and all manner of brass fixtures and fittings such as portholes, bridge equipment, engine room gauges, fans and ornamental bench ends. More delicate items have included P&O crockery and etched water decanters. P&O china chamber pots have been a particularly prized find. The medical officer's cabin has yielded a variety of specialist equipment, including some very large and intimidating syringes. Among more personal effects there have been gold chains and fob watches. One particularly unusual discovery has been a large quantity of small, ornamental gilded pewter ram heads, deep inside the forward part of the ship.

– *Mooltan* (2) –

1905–1917, Mediterranean Sea

Mooltan (2) (9,621 tons) was built for P&O by Caird & Co., Greenock, and launched on 3 August 1905. The length was 520.4ft (158.6m) and beam 58.3ft (17.8m). Twin screws were powered by quadruple-expansion steam engines, giving a service speed of 18 knots. There was accommodation for 348 first- and 166 second-class passengers.

Before embarking on her maiden voyage to Bombay on 3 November 1905, the *Mooltan* (2) spent two days open for public inspection at Tilbury Dock. Visitors were charged a nominal fee, the proceeds of which went to the Seamen's Hospital Society, Greenwich.

In January 1908 Empress Eugénie, widow of Napoleon III, joined the *Mooltan* (2) in Marseilles for the passage to Colombo. Travelling under the name of Comtesse Pierrefonds, the 81-year-old caused much excitement among her fellow passengers, who were charmed by her bright personality and cheerful conversation. The empress showed particular interest in the transit of the Suez Canal, having been the most valued guest present at the grand opening in 1869.

The *Mooltan* (2) carried P&O's guests to the Coronation Naval Review at Spithead on 24 June 1911, where the ship was joined by several other vessels of the P&O fleet.

Second-class dining saloon on *Mooltan* (2). (Mick Lindsay)

Second-class music room on *Mooltan* (2). (Mick Lindsay)

Mooltan (2) was built in 1905 and made over thirty trips to Australia before being sunk by *UC 27* in 1917. (Mick Lindsay)

On 9 June 1917 the *Mooltan* (2) sailed from Sydney under the command of Captain A.L. Valentine, carrying a large compliment of passengers, many of whom were Australian nurses. The nurses were disembarked in Egypt and, after a largely uneventful voyage, the *Mooltan* (2) reached Malta, from where she sailed in the company of the French steamer *Lotus*, under escort of the Japanese destroyers

Ume and *Kusunoki*. The presence of the destroyers was not sufficient to deter the German submarine *UC 27* (Gerhard Schulz), which in the evening of 26 July surfaced a short distance away and unleashed two torpedoes. The first passed just astern but the second exploded violently into the forepeak on the starboard side. Most of the passengers were just finishing dinner when the alarm was sounded, but they immediately rushed to their lifeboat stations and within ten minutes everyone was safely away – apart from two lascar crew who were killed in the explosion. One of the destroyers promptly gave chase, unleashing a barrage of depth charges in an unsuccessful attempt to sink the submarine, while the other circled the *Mooltan* (2). After an hour they returned to the lifeboats and quickly and efficiently took all the 552 survivors on board. The *Mooltan* (2) was abandoned and eventually sank some 100 miles south of Sardinia. The conditions on the Japanese ships were crowded and basic, but everyone was well cared for by the Japanese crew, who landed them at Marseilles after an uncomfortable journey lasting thirty-eight hours.

For some of the passengers and several engineers the experience was all too familiar, having been on board the *Mongolia* (2) when it was mined the previous month.

Completed in 1896, the *Candia* (2) was P&O's first purpose-built cargo liner and also the company's first twin-screw ocean-going vessel. (Newall Dunn Collection)

– *Candia* (2) –

1896–1917, England

Candia (2) (6,482 tons) was built for P&O by Caird & Co., Greenock, and launched on 7 November 1896. The length was 450.6ft (137.3m) and beam 52.3ft (15.9m). Twin screws were powered by triple-expansion steam engines, giving a service speed of 14 knots. The dedicated cargo liner had a capacity of 432,921 cubic feet (12,257 cubic metres).

Towards the end of the nineteenth century the cargo-carrying capacity of new vessels entering the P&O fleet had steadily increased, but the *Candia* (2) was the first P&O ship to be commissioned for the sole purpose of carrying cargo. A unique feature of the design was the provision of a number of steam cranes, fore and aft, for cargo handling. The *Candia* (2) was also the company's first ocean-going twin-screw vessel. The *Candia* (2) was followed by the sister ship *Socotra* (1) the next year. Unlike the ships servicing the mail contracts, the cargo fleet were not restricted to specific routes or timetables, and therefore free to seek the most profitable trading voyages.

The maiden voyage of the *Candia* (2) sailed from London on 9 January 1897 for Hong Kong and Yokohama. After returning from Japan, the *Candia* (2) sailed once more for the Far East, but this time returned via Australian ports, from where a large cargo of wool was loaded. When the *Candia* (2) called at Adelaide at the end of November she became the largest ship so far to sail up the Port river and dock alongside the wharf.

The *Candia* (2) narrowly averted a major disaster in November 1902 on a return voyage to London from Yokohama. The ship was near Ismailia in the Suez Canal when a major fire broke out in the aft hold. The local authorities rendered every possible assistance and eventually the fire was brought under control and extinguished. A similar incident occurred in May 1916 after the ship had sailed from Adelaide, homeward-bound for London. The *Candia* (2) put in at Albany where the fire was extinguished and the cargo reloaded.

One of the more unusual items to be listed on the *Candia* (2)'s manifest was in December 1909 when a Blériot XI monoplane, the same model of aircraft that Louis Blériot had himself flown in the first flight across the English Channel on 25 July 1909, was transported to Melbourne.

During the First World War the *Candia* (2) was fitted with a single 4.7in gun and continued to make regular commercial voyages to Australia. In May 1917 the ship sailed from Melbourne under the command of Captain Charles Smith, with a cargo that included

9,000 tons of grain, 3,400 cases of boiled rabbits, lead, zinc and general cargo. After a long but uneventful voyage the *Candia* (2) called at Falmouth, where the master received his route orders for the final leg of the voyage to London, which was to pass close to south of the Owers light vessel off Selsey Bill. Captain Smith also received further written instructions advising him that a particularly dangerous area existed 4 miles to the south and east of the light vessel.

By nightfall on 26 July the *Candia* (2) had reached Portland Bill, where the marine traffic became particularly busy, requiring extra caution because all ships were steaming without lights. At 3.38 a.m. the next morning, the ship reached the edge of the danger zone and Captain Smith commenced a zigzag course, maintaining a speed of 12 knots. Twenty minutes later the *Candia* (2) was altering to a north-easterly course, in the direction of Brighton, when an explosion erupted on the starboard-side aft. Falling debris killed a lascar lookout named Karim Qasim instantly and the ship quickly started to go down by the stern. Captain Smith wasted no time giving the order to abandon ship. Fortunately the weather was fine and clear with smooth seas and the lifeboats got away without too much difficulty. At 4.20 a.m. HMT *Willonyx* arrived on the scene and with the assistance of two drifters picked up all ninety-nine surviving crew members. The *Candia* (2) sank ten minutes later.

The loss of the *Candia* (2) was caused by a torpedo fired by *UC 65* (Otto Steinbrinck), just one day after *UC 27* sank the *Mooltan* (2) in the Mediterranean.

Diving the Wreck

The twin screws of the *Candia* (2) possessed unique overlapping arcs, which helped lead to a positive identification of the wreck in 1952. Risdon Beazley Ltd went on to salvage 1,025 tons of lead and 1,000 tons of zinc from the forward holds. The wreck was salvaged again in 1987 by divers operating from the *Holger Dane*, the same vessel that had worked on the *Medina* the previous year.

The wreck of the *Candia* (2) lies amongst sandy dunes in a general depth of around 50m, a distance of 14 miles south of Littlehampton. The shallowest section is the top of the midships superstructure in 40m, with the deeper bow and stern sections in excess of 50m. Deep scours around the wreck can result in depths closer to 60m.

The midships area is the most intact part of the wreck and sits completely upright, with lots of open interior areas that can be explored safely. The engines and boilers are embedded deeper inside the wreck, towards the aft. On either side of the central superstructure the wreck drops off steeply to sandy holds and collapsed hull plating. There is a large anchor winch at the bow.

The skeletal remains of the upper midships superstructure on the *Candia* (2) wreck.

Typical marine life on the wreck of the *Candia* (2).

A significant quantity of P&O crockery and cutlery has been found on the wreck over the years. The china plates were made by Ashworth Brothers in Hanley, England, and bare the distinctive starburst P&O crest. A diver reported a stern hold to be full of green bottles laid out like a 'carpet of glass'. The usual crustaceans such as lobsters and edible crabs are in residence. There is also abundant fish life, making the wreck a popular location for fishing. The *Candia* (2) makes an excellent dive and is a welcome alternative to the more popular deep passenger liner wrecks such as the *Salsette* (2) and *Moldavia* (1).

– *Peshawur* (2) –

1905–1917, Irish Sea

Peshawur (2) (7,634 tons) was a passenger/cargo liner built for P&O by Barclay, Curle & Co., Glasgow, and launched on 8 March 1905. The length was 479.5ft (146.1m) and beam 57.3ft (17.46m). Twin screws were powered by two triple-expansion steam engines, giving a service speed of 14 knots. The ship's primary purpose was to carry cargo, and a large amount of insulated space was provided for refrigerated goods. There was limited accommodation for just twelve first-class passengers.

The *Peshawur* (2) experienced a minor mishap a few months after entering service. On 4 December 1905 the ship was leaving Antwerp Dock with heavy cargo for China when two hawsers broke, causing the vessel to run into the quay, breaking her rudderpost and sustaining other damage.

For the next ten years the *Peshawur* (2) sailed on the Far East and Australian services, and in 1910 became the first P&O ship to sail on the former Blue Anchor Line route via the Cape to Australia.

Immediately after the outbreak of the First World War the *Peshawur* (2) was requisitioned by the Admiralty for service as a stores carrier. The ship was placed under the command of Captain Francis Andrews RD RNR, who, despite having been placed on the Royal Naval Reserve retired list since 1910, was recalled for war service. Captain Andrews had previously served as chief officer on the *Nubia* (2) during the Boer War, for which he was awarded the Transport Medal. In May 1915 the *Peshawur* (2) became an Expeditionary Force Transport vessel, importing stores from Canada to Great Britain, an unusual route for a vessel of the P&O fleet.

On the afternoon of 9 October 1917 the *Peshawur* (2) arrived off Tor Head, Ireland, having crossed the Atlantic from Sydney, Nova Scotia, in an escorted convoy. The convoy was given the signal to disperse and Captain Andrews proceeded south, in company with several other vessels, hugging the Irish coast. The *Peshawur* (2) had just passed the South Rock Lighthouse when she was struck without warning on the port side by a torpedo fired from *UC 96* (Heinrich Jeß), flooding the engine room and destroying one of the lifeboats. The captain ordered all hands on deck and the lifeboats swung out. At first he hoped that the ship might remain afloat, but after a thorough search to ensure that no one remained on board he finally gave the order to abandon ship. This proved to be a prudent decision as within minutes of leaving the ship a second torpedo ripped into the starboard side of the *Peshawur* (2), just forward of

This unusual brass badge (diameter 6cm) bearing the initials 'P&O' was found on the wreck of the *Candia* (2).

A pair of P&O teaspoons. The top one was recovered from the *Candia* (2) nearly a century after the ship was sunk by *UC 65* in 1917.

the bridge. The ship settled deeper in the water but still did not show any immediate signs of sinking, but with the wind picking up Captain Andrews ordered the boats to make sail and head for land.

After about an hour and a half the survivors were picked up by the patrol yacht *Albion III* and taken to Belfast. From the crew of 125, at least eleven men lost their lives, most of whom were lascar firemen and trimmers. The third engineer, George Caws, was also among the deceased.

Diving the Wreck

The wreck of the *Peshawur* (2) lies in a maximum depth of 58m, 7 miles south-east of Ballyquintin Point, County Down, and was first dived by the Northern Ireland Advanced Diving Group in the 1980s. Divers visiting the wreck have reported low visibility, poor light and snagged fishing nets, and because the wreck also lies on the prawn ground it is seldom visited.

– *Pera* (3) –

1903–1917, Mediterranean Sea

Pera (3) (7,635 tons) was a cargo liner built for P&O by Workman, Clark & Co., Belfast, and launched on 10 June 1903. The length was 480ft (146.3m) and beam 57.2ft (17.4m). Twin screws were powered by two triple-expansion steam engines, giving a service speed of 14 knots. There was limited passenger accommodation for twelve people.

The *Pera* (3) was the sister ship of the *Palermo*, which had been launched on the Clyde two weeks previously. Both ships belonged to the new series of five P-class cargo liners, which was completed by the *Palma* later the same year and followed by *Poona* and *Peshawur* (2) in 1905. The *Pera* (3) operated on services to Calcutta and the Far East.

The *Pera* (3) was immediately taken up at the start of the First World War for transport duties from Australia and given the designation HMAT *A4 Pera*. In October 1914 the *Pera* (3) was one of the many ships in the first convoy assembled in King George's Sound, Albany, for transporting the First Detachment of the Australian and New Zealand Imperial Expeditionary Forces overseas.

During the period from October 1915 to September 1916 the *Pera* (3) transported four Light Horse regiments, two Mobile Veterinary sections and medical officers. The vessels' lease to the Commonwealth ended in January 1917.

The end came for the *Pera* (3) on 19 October 1917, just ten days after the loss of the *Peshawur* (2), while on a voyage from Liverpool to Calcutta under the command of Captain Sidney Finch. The ship was steaming through the Mediterranean in convoy with ten other vessels, all of which were abreast, with the *Pera* (3) on the far right, when an incoming torpedo was sighted. The helm was immediately turned hard to port and the engines put full ahead but it was too late to avoid impact. The torpedo fired by *UB 48* (Wolfgang Steinbauer) struck the *Pera* (3) on the starboard side in No. 5 hold and water rushed into the engine room. When the order was given to stop the engines it was discovered that the telegraph was jammed and no response could be received from the engine room by telephone. Someone was sent down to investigate and found that a pani-wallah had been killed by the explosion, and also that the engineer on watch had been badly injured. At considerable risk to himself, Third Engineer Wilkinson worked his way in through the stokehold and managed to shut off the steam.

Meanwhile the *Pera* (3) had developed a heavy list to port and was in danger of capsizing so Captain Finch had to risk lowering the boats, even though the ship still had some way on. As a result, two of the boats capsized but fortunately all the occupants were wearing lifebelts and were picked up quickly by the remaining boats. The *Pera* (3) went down by the stern forty minutes after the impact and sank about 100 miles east by north of Marsa Susa. The survivors were picked up by the escort sloop HMS *Clematis* and landed at Alexandria two days later.

– *Namur* –

1906–1917, Gibraltar

Namur (6,694 tons) was built for P&O by Caird & Co., Greenock, and launched on 26 July 1906. The length was 449.8ft (137.1m) and beam 52.2ft (15.9m). Twin screws were powered by quadruple-expansion steam engines, giving a service speed of 14 knots. There was accommodation for fifty-four first- and forty-two second-class passengers. The *Namur* was an intermediate passenger/cargo liner and employed on the London–Far East intermediate service.

The *Namur* typically made two to three annual round-trip voyages to India and Japan, and had a largely uneventful career. After the commencement of hostilities in 1914, the ship continued operating commercial services as normal. The *Namur* narrowly escaped an encounter with an enemy submarine in the early hours of 14 June 1916 while inbound for London from Kobe, Japan. The ship was halfway between Malta and the island of Pantelleria on a bright, moonlit night when a torpedo passed within 50yd of her stern.

On 29 May 1917 the *Namur* sailed from London to the Far East for the last time, with just twenty passengers on board. On the homeward voyage the ship was approaching Gibraltar in convoy, steering a zigzag course, when she was struck at 9 a.m. on 29 October 1917 by a torpedo fired by *U 35* (Lothar von Arnauld de la Perière). Although the weather was fine and very clear and multiple lookouts were stationed around the vessel, no one saw the torpedo until the last instant, when it exploded into the port side between hatches four and five. The engines were stopped immediately, an SOS was sent out and all passengers and crew were mustered at their lifeboat stations. The *Namur* started to settle slowly by the stern, so, as soon as the way was off the ship, all seven boats were got away. Although no one was injured by the blast, two native firemen fell out of a lifeboat as it was being lowered, rendering one of them unconscious. He subsequently died from his injury. The captain and senior officers were the last to leave the ship at 9.20 a.m. and twenty-five minutes later the *Namur* slipped slowly beneath the waves.

The escort destroyer HMS *Larne* went in search of the submarine and returned after about an hour to pick up the survivors from the lifeboats, who were then taken to Gibraltar. The escort arrived in Gibraltar shortly after 1 p.m., where everyone was taken on board the P&O passenger/cargo liner *Kashgar* (2) and served lunch.

The *U 35* was the most successful German submarine to participate in the First World War and was responsible for sinking over 200 ships, with a combined tonnage in excess of half a million. Commander Lothar von Arnauld de la Perière was personally responsible for 194 of the losses, making him the most successful submarine ace of all time. Many of the targets were sunk with his 88mm deck gun, which he frequently used in preference to torpedoes.

At the time of her loss the *Namur* was believed to be carrying gold, diamonds and rubies from Penang, Malaysia. In 2013 the Spanish Navy arrested the research and survey vessel *Endeavour*, which was believed to be undertaking a clandestine search for the treasure.

– *Moldavia* (1) –

1903–1918, English Channel

Moldavia (1) (9,500 tons) was built for P&O by Caird & Co., Greenock, and launched on 28 March 1903 by Helen Sutherland, daughter of Sir Thomas Sutherland, chairman of P&O. The length was 520.6ft (158.6m) and beam 58.3ft (17.8m). Twin screws were powered by triple-expansion steam engines, giving a service speed of 16.5 knots. There was accommodation for 348 first- and 166 second-class passengers, with a crew of 370.

The *Moldavia* (1) was the first of four new M-class passenger liners, and at the time of her launch was the largest P&O vessel to be built. The other three ships were also launched in 1903: *Mongolia* (2), *Marmora* and *Macedonia*. Only the *Macedonia* survived past the First World War and lived on to provide her owners with many more years of service until finally being scrapped in 1931.

The M-class passenger liner *Moldavia* (1) of 1903 was torpedoed in the English Channel in 1917 while serving as an AMC. The wreck lies in 50m and ranks alongside the *Salsette* (2) as one of the classic UK wreck dives. (State Library of Western Australia)

William Sandell, naval rating of 'boy first class', was commended by the Admiralty for his service to the captain when the *Moldavia* (1) was lost. (Sandell family)

The passenger accommodation on the *Moldavia* (1) was very well appointed and set a new benchmark for P&O with regard to comfort, space, lighting and ventilation. The impressive public rooms designed by architect Thomas Collcutt featured solid-oak woodwork and took on a quintessentially English character. A unique feature of the internal arrangement was the magnificent drawing room, which was raised several feet from the deck in order to increase the height of the dining saloon on the deck below. It had large rectangular windows all round, and doors at one end gave a clear view along the forepart of the ship. The dome above the picturesque music room was decorated with two large lunettes by the English painter Gerald Moira, illustrating scenes from Shakespeare's *Tempest* and *King Henry V*.

The privilege of being given command of the new vessel went to Captain Ernest 'Fighting' Gordon, an experienced and popular master who had been with P&O for twenty-eight years. On Saturday

15 August 1903 the *Moldavia* (1) sailed from Gravesend on a short trial voyage with a party of distinguished guests hosted by the company chairman, Sir Thomas Sutherland. The ship spent the night anchored off Margate and resumed her voyage the following morning, reaching the Needles on Sunday afternoon. The *Moldavia* (1) spent the night off Netley, Southampton, and arrived back in London on Tuesday morning. The trip proved to be very satisfactory and the *Moldavia* (1) managed to record a speed of 18 knots on a test run up the Channel. A few weeks later the ship was opened to the public for inspection and hundreds of visitors flocked to Tilbury Docks for an opportunity to explore the new liner.

Although the *Moldavia* (1) was intended for the Australian mail service, the ship's inaugural commercial voyage was to Bombay and sailed from England on 25 September 1903. The *Moldavia* (1)'s first sailing on the Australia run left London on 11 December 1903. The ship reached Gibraltar on the 14th, after encountering heavy gales in a typically rough passage through the Bay of Biscay. The *Moldavia* (1) next called at Marseilles on the 18th, where Lord and Lady Northcote were among the many passengers to embark at the port. Lord Northcote was travelling to Australia where he was to succeed Lord Tennyson as the new governor general. The *Moldavia* (1) sailed again the following day and the passengers soon settled into the typical routine of on-board activities which included dining, deck sports and fancy-dress dances. The ship arrived at Port Said on the 22nd, where she took on mail and passengers from the *Isis*. The Suez Canal was cleared on the morning of the 24th and the passengers celebrated Christmas Day in the Red Sea. The *Moldavia* (1) arrived at Aden on the 27th, where the passengers and mails for India were transferred to the *Peninsular*. The liner sailed for Colombo the next day and arrived on 3 January 1904, where she connected with the *Malta* for transfer of passengers and mail to China. The *Moldavia* (1) sailed again the next day, crossed the equator on the 5th and passed the Cocos Islands on the 8th.

At 9.30 a.m. on 13 January 1904 the *Moldavia* (1) reached Fremantle, Australia, and was thrown open to the public, leaving again at 6 p.m. the same day. After rounding Cape Leeuwin and crossing the Great Australian Bight, the vessel made for Largs Bay, Adelaide, where she anchored on the 17th. After an overnight stay the *Moldavia* (1) continued east to Melbourne. On the afternoon of the 19th the ship berthed in Melbourne, alongside the smaller *India* (2). The *Moldavia* (1) finally arrived in Sydney on the 22nd, where she remained until 6 February when she set sail for the return voyage to London. Over the course of the next three years the *Moldavia* (1) firmly established herself on the Australia run and was always welcomed enthusiastically in the Australian ports.

The *Moldavia* (1)'s career could have easily come to a premature end on 19 January 1907 when the vessel ran aground in thick fog, opposite Deal Pier on the Goodwin Sands. The ship was homeward-bound from Sydney and had already landed most of her passengers at Plymouth. The Dover tug *Lady Crundall* was first on the scene, followed by the Walmer lifeboat and another tug. Since the *Moldavia* (1) had grounded at low water, Captain Gordon declined any assistance and managed to float the vessel off unaided six hours later. On reaching Tilbury a survey revealed that the hull had not been damaged and the mail service was able to continue as normal.

In March 1911 the *Moldavia* (1) made the first of several extended voyages to Auckland, New Zealand. Instead of remaining in Sydney for the customary two weeks, the stay was cut short to just a few days and the vessel continued eastward across the Tasman Sea.

Captain Ernest Henry Gordon retired in 1914, by which time he had become commodore of the P&O line after nearly forty years of service with the company. The command of the *Moldavia* (1) passed to Captain George William Gordon (no relation), previously of the *India* (2).

Following the outbreak of the First World War the *Moldavia* (1) continued to make regular voyages to Australia, up until November 1915 when the vessel was requisitioned for use as an AMC. After undergoing conversion at the Royal Albert Dock, the ship was commissioned into the Royal Navy as HMS *Moldavia* on 1 February 1916 and placed under the command of Acting Captain Adrian Holt Smyth RN. A month later the *Moldavia* (1) joined the 10th Cruiser Squadron and commenced regular patrols in the waters between the north of Scotland and Iceland. The ship was tasked with intercepting merchant ships and placing an armed guard aboard to ensure each ship sailed to an Allied port for its cargo to be inspected.

In early November 1916 the *Moldavia* (1) encountered several days of particularly bad weather in the North Atlantic, after which she picked up survivors from the Norwegian cargo vessel *Patria* (465 tons), which had been abandoned on 9 November. The *Patria* was sunk for target practice the following day. The same month the *Moldavia* (1) was compulsorily purchased by the Admiralty, together with *Macedonia* and *Marmora*. However, this was strongly contested by P&O and ownership was returned to them in February 1917.

On 9 February 1917 the *Moldavia* (1) intercepted the Italian cargo ship *Famiglia* and found it to be in possession of a German prize crew from *U 43*. The Germans set off explosive charges to scuttle the ship and abandoned the vessel, but were soon captured by a boat dispatched from the *Moldavia* (1). At the end of July 1917 the *Moldavia* (1) completed her last Northern Patrol and soon sailed

to Dakar to take up a new role as a convoy escort between West Africa and Plymouth. The ship remained on this route until March 1918, during which time she completed three voyages transporting gold bullion.

The next duty assigned to the *Moldavia* (1) was to assist in the transportation of troops across the Atlantic from North America. On 11 May 1918 the *Moldavia* (1) sailed from Halifax, Nova Scotia, as escort to the five merchant vessels in convoy HC.1. There were close to 500 American troops on board, many of whom belonged to the 58th Infantry Regiment of the Fourth Division. The ship also carried a similar number of naval officers and ratings. The cargo mainly consisted of frozen meat, butter and general stores. On 20 May the *Moldavia* (1) arrived off the Western Approaches, where the ship was joined by five escort destroyers for the remainder of the voyage up through the English Channel. In the early hours of 23 May most of the troops were sleeping soundly in their bunks and looking forward to disembarking in London the following morning when they were awakened by a violent explosion, followed by the alarm signal for everyone to muster on deck. The *Moldavia* (1) had been struck on the port side, just below the bridge, by a torpedo fired by *UB 57* (Johannes Lohs) of the Flanders Flotilla. Over fifty men from B Company who were sleeping in the compartment where the explosion took place were killed instantly.

William George Frederick Sandell was just 12 years old when the First World War began, but four years later he found himself serving as a naval rating of 'boy first class' on *Moldavia* (1). When the torpedo struck, William was up on the bridge where he was on duty as a messenger. He was later commended by the Admiralty for his 'gallant manner' and 'invaluable services' in assisting the captain, services which William later described for an American newspaper:

> The explosion flung me high in the air, and then I was hit with a grating from the deck. When I came around, our Captain ordered me to the engine room for the signal apparatus was broken and I found everything was alright, so he ordered full steam ahead.
>
> We tried to throw a tow line to a destroyer, but it was no use. The Captain ordered the first lieutenant to get the men away on the port side, and then I carried his further orders to the second lieutenant. As we went through the Captain's cabin, I asked if he had thrown the confidential books overboard. 'I forgot, you saved my life,' he told me. I saw his revolver there, and I asked him if he thought he would need it. 'No, we have discipline aboard this ship,' he said. Then I ran aft to see that the propectiles [sic] and cartridges were thrown overboard,

and when I reported to the Captain again, he ordered me to the engine room to see if any stokers were left there. There were some, so I transmitted the Captain's orders to abandon ship, and followed them out. The engine room deck was covered with water. The Chief Engineer was last out after me. When the ship was cleared, the Captain, the Chief Engineer, a yeoman of signals and I dived from the stern. We swam about for an hour, and then a destroyer picked us up.

Everyone was evacuated within fifteen minutes of the explosion and many of the survivors were transferred directly on to two of the escort destroyers, which came alongside the stricken vessel.

Some of the other destroyers circled the ship and unleashed a barrage of depth charges in retaliation to the submarine attack. However, *UB 57* managed to escape and sunk the *Kyarra* (Australian United Steam Navigation Company) a few days later off Swanage. The troops kept perfect discipline throughout their ordeal and began to laugh and sing after they had been rescued. When the *Moldavia* (1) finally heeled over to port and sank at 3.55 a.m. they even gave three cheers.

Fixty-six lives were lost in the wreck of the *Moldavia* (1), all of whom were American soldiers. A further serviceman lost his life during a leg amputation on board one of the rescue ships. All the survivors were landed at Dover.

After a century on the seabed the bow of the *Moldavia* (1) is showing signs of collapse. (Steve Jones)

Diving the Wreck

The *Moldavia* (1), or 'The Mol' as she is affectionately known, is without doubt one of the classic UK wreck dives. Many divers throughout the diving fraternity who have dived the wreck would even rate it as superior to the enduring *Salsette* (2). Although the *Moldavia* (1) was five years older than the *Salsette* (2) the ship was larger by 3,658 tons and was 25m longer. The wreck lies at a depth of 50m in the middle of the English Channel, 24 miles south of the Sussex port of Littlehampton. For divers undeterred by the long boat journey of two to three hours it is well worth the reward. The visibility is seldom less than 10m and 15–20m is common, further enhanced by a seabed of light sand and shingle.

The *Moldavia* (1) lies on its port side, with the shallowest point near the stern at around 37m. The wreck is largely intact, but with a notable break around the midships section where the torpedo struck and also where later salvage operations took place. To fully appreciate everything that the wreck has to offer definitely requires multiple visits.

Exposed tubes in one of the *Moldavia* (1)'s boilers. (Steve Jones)

The *Moldavia* (1) was armed with eight guns, one of which points
menacingly to the surface. (Steve Jones)

The stern of the *Moldavia* (1) presents an imposing sight. (Catherine de Lara)

The bathtub is an easily recognised feature on the *Moldavia* (1). (Catherine de Lara)

Heading forward from the stern and swimming about 5m above the seabed the wreck presents an imposing presence on the diver's right, giving a true sense of just how big the *Moldavia* (1) was. A popular photographic opportunity along the way is a large bathtub wedged on its side among the wreckage and surrounded by shoals of fish. This is soon followed by the more exposed midships area and two of the boilers, one of which has opened up to reveal dozens of the tubes. The starboard hull then regains its shape and provides an easy point of reference to proceed towards the bow. Items of interest along the way include remains of cabins, winches, lifeboat derricks, water tanks and bollards. There are several more guns and, in contrast to the rear starboard gun, the forward-port gun points downward with the muzzle embedded in the sand.

Left: Porthole from the *Moldavia* (1), complete with drip tray. (Nick Ellerington)

Below: A Royal Navy china bowl recovered from the wreck of the *Moldavia* (1) is evidence of the ship's final years spent as HMS *Moldavia*.

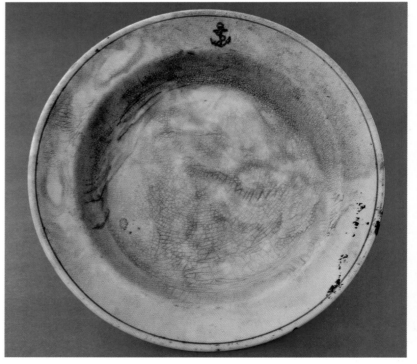

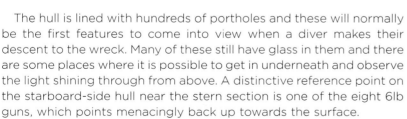

The hull is lined with hundreds of portholes and these will normally be the first features to come into view when a diver makes their descent to the wreck. Many of these still have glass in them and there are some places where it is possible to get in underneath and observe the light shining through from above. A distinctive reference point on the starboard-side hull near the stern section is one of the eight 6lb guns, which points menacingly back up towards the surface.

The stern has a distinctive appearance where the outer hull plating has fallen away, leaving the exposed ribs arrayed in a crescent shape. A considerable amount of the wooden decking has survived a century of immersion and is evident over much of the wreck. Both of the large bronze propellers have been salvaged, leaving just the exposed shafts and rudder. Up until as recently as 2009 the stern telegraph was still in place. Another of the guns has fallen down into the wreckage nearby.

The bow section is without doubt one of the visual highlights of the *Moldavia* (1), but sadly it is starting to collapse, like all wrecks of this era. At the beginning of the twenty-first century it was still largely intact, but in more recent years the top deck has separated from the hull and dropped down by several metres. Occasionally large trawl nets get caught on the wreckage, no doubt a contributing factor to the degradation of the wreck. Nevertheless, it is still possible to see the anchors, chains, hawse pipes and winch gear.

– *Marmora* –

1903–1918, Celtic Sea

Marmora (10,509 tons) was built for P&O by Harland & Wolff, Belfast, and launched on 9 April 1903. The length was 530.4ft (161.6m) and beam 60.3ft (18.4m). Twin screws were powered by quadruple-expansion steam engines, giving a service speed of 17 knots. There was accommodation for 367 first- and 187 second-class passengers.

The *Marmora* was the third ship completed in the M-class series of liners and the first P&O ship to be fitted with quadruple-expansion steam engines. She was also the first vessel in the fleet to exceed 10,000 tons. The maiden voyage of the *Marmora* sailed from London for Bombay on New Year's Day 1904, under the command of Captain George Langborne. After returning from India the ship commenced the first of her regular sailings on the Australia service on 18 March.

On 11 December 1909 the *Marmora* sailed from Tilbury carrying HRH The Princess Royal Louise Victoria, her husband the Duke of Fife

and Princesses Alexandra and Maud on the first of the family's regular winter trips to Egypt. A later voyage on the *Delhi* (3) in 1911 ended in a shipwreck off the coast of Morocco.

Immediately upon the outbreak of the First World War the *Marmora* was requisitioned by the government for use as an AMC and commissioned as HMS *Marmora*. The ship's first assignment was to form part of the Cape Verde Islands division of 10th Cruiser Squadron, intercepting shipping on the trade routes between Madeira and St Vincent. In one of her first engagements on 4 September the *Marmora* boarded and sank the small German cargo ship *Rheinland*.

Early in 1915 the *Marmora* took part in an unsuccessful search for the German auxiliary cruiser *Kronprinz Wilhelm*, which had been responsible for sinking fifteen Allied merchant vessels. Afterwards the *Marmora* continued to make regular patrols in the Atlantic and did not return to England until June 1916, when the ship underwent an extensive three-month refit in Liverpool before returning to the Cape Verde Islands once more. At the end of the year the *Marmora* docked in Devonport for another refit, after which she took up a new role as an Atlantic convoy escort.

On 22 July 1918 the *Marmora* sailed from Cardiff with instructions to escort HMAT *A36 Boonah* to Dakar, Senegal, where she was

Torpedoed by *UB 64* in July 1918, the *Marmora* was the last P&O ship to be lost in the First World War.

also joined by the destroyers *P66* and *P77*. At 3.45 p.m. on 23 July the four ships were halfway between the Old Head of Kinsale and the Scilly Isles, steering a zigzag course, when the *Marmora* lookout saw the wake of two torpedoes appear perilously close to the ship. Before any evasive action could be taken, one struck amidships on the port side, right between the two funnels. The *Marmora* settled a few metres by the head and developed a slight list to starboard, but did not show any immediate signs of sinking, so for a while the ship proceeded slowly on both engines. However, both stokeholds were soon reported to be flooded and at 4.15 p.m. the master, Commander Walter Woodward RN, made the decision to abandon ship.

The *Boonah* was signalled to keep her distance, while the two destroyers circled the *Marmora* to ward off any further threats from the submarine *UB 64* (Otto von Schrader). After all the survivors had been picked up ten men were found to be missing, one of whom was leading fireman Edward Gallagher. The surviving crew later paid glowing tributes to Gallagher, who had made several trips down through the smoke and dust to the lower decks in order to help lead his colleagues up to safety. When he descended for the fourth time the ladders collapsed and he fell to his death. The other nine men who lost their lives comprised three Royal Navy able seamen, along with four fireman and two trimmers from the Mercantile Marine Reserve. The *Marmora* was the last P&O loss during the First World War.

Top: Stowing passenger baggage in the *Marmora*'s hold. (Andy Usher)

Far left: Deck life on board the *Marmora* in 1912. (Andy Usher)

Left: The Duke of Westminster relaxing with a cigar on board *Marmora*. (Andy Usher)

PART 4

BETWEEN THE WARS, 1919–1938

– *Egypt* –

1897–1922, France

Egypt (7,912 tons) was built for P&O by Caird & Co., Greenock, and launched on 15 May 1897. The length was 499.8ft (152.3m) and beam 54.3ft (16.5m). A single screw was powered by triple-expansion steam engines, giving a service speed of 16 knots. There was accommodation for 312 first- and 212 second-class passengers, with a crew of 283.

The maiden voyage of the *Egypt* sailed from London to Bombay on 15 October 1897 under the command of Captain Robert Briscoe RNR. The *Egypt* remained primarily on the India route for many years, during which time the ship sailed under a number of different captains. In June 1914 the *Egypt* made the first of three voyages to Sydney, Australia, until the First World War caused her regular passenger service to be disrupted.

In August 1915, shortly after returning from Australia, the *Egypt* was hired by the Admiralty for use as hospital ship HMHS *Egypt* No. 52. The *Egypt*'s sister ship, *China* (2), had already been taken up for the same purpose the previous year, and of the five vessels in the India class, these were the only two to survive the First World War. The hospital ships were fitted out with all the equipment and amenities required to care for wounded soldiers on their voyages home. The hull was painted white and a large red Geneva cross was painted on each side. Powerful electric lamps were rigged to vividly illuminate the red cross during hours of darkness.

In February 1916 the *Egypt* got caught up in a Zeppelin bombing raid at Salonika Bay. The airship appeared to be targeting the warships in the port but did not manage to score any direct hits. However, the *Egypt* suffered some blast damage to portholes, boats and the forward funnel.

After peace was declared, the *Egypt* remained in government service and was refitted for use as an ambulance transport. The ship was later employed for repatriating military officials, civil servants

The single screw passenger liner *Egypt* (1897, 7,912 tons) sailed on P&O services to India and Australia.

During the First World War the *Egypt* was hired by the Admiralty for use as hospital ship HMHS *Egypt* No. 52. (Mick Lindsay)

and their families to India. The ageing *Egypt* was finally returned to regular commercial service in October 1921 and made her first post-war sailing for P&O to Bombay the following month.

On 10 March 1922, the *Egypt* sailed for Bombay under Captain Andrew Collyer, who was taking command of the ship for the first time. The ship returned safely to London two months later where a big change oversaw ninety-five new crew join the ship, many of whom had transferred from the P&O cargo liner *Palermo*. On 18 May a full inspection of the *Egypt* was carried out by the P&O managing director, Frank Ritchie, along with the marine superintendent, Franke Notley. On the same day, Chief Officer Charles Cartwright mustered the crew for a brief boat drill, but many were absent on account of the inspection and other duties. The next day the *Egypt* sailed from Tilbury, bound for Bombay, with a crew of 294 and small complement of just forty-four passengers; more were scheduled

to embark in Marseilles en route. In addition to the usual mails and general cargo, the *Egypt* also carried a consignment of gold, silver and sovereigns, worth in excess of £1 million.

On 20 May the *Egypt* encountered the first of many fog banks so the ship's whistle was sounded regularly at two-minute intervals and the speed was moderated to 12½ knots. By 5.30 p.m. the ship was off Ushant and an hour later the fog had lifted a little, improving the visibility to about 1 mile. The weather was fair, with a slight swell and light westerly wind. Then, just before 7 p.m., the fog descended once more, so the officer on watch rang 'stand by' on the telegraph. Just as Captain Collyer came onto the bridge, a faint whistle was heard off the port bow. The whistle was heard again two minutes later, but before its source could be determined the French cargo steamer *Seine* (1,383 tons) suddenly loomed out of the fog and struck the *Egypt* hard on the port side between the two funnels. The bows of

Scenes of 'horror and heroism' were witnessed when the
Egypt collided with the _Seine_ off Ushant in 1922.

the _Seine_ were reinforced for ice breaking in northern
waters and easily tore open the _Egypt_'s hull plating.
The two ships then broke away from each other and
the _Seine_ disappeared once more into the fog.

Captain Collyer issued orders to man the lifeboat
stations, but when the emergency signal was sounded
the whistle failed after the first two blasts, which was
before the minimum four blasts could be given. He also
gave orders for the watertight doors to be closed, but
several were found to be inoperable due to damage
caused by the collision. The carpenter was sent to take
soundings and reported that there was already 18ft of
water in the forward stokehold. An SOS was sent but
the closest vessel to receive the message was about
9 miles distant. The desperate situation was further
compounded by the _Egypt_ taking on a heavy list to
port, which made it very difficult for the crew to ready
the lifeboats.

Many of the passengers were dining in the saloon
when they felt the shock of the collision. Scenes of
mass confusion arose and heartrending cries were
heard from all over the ship. The impact was so violent
that many people were dashed against the bulkheads
and fatally injured before they could even reach their
lifeboat stations. Panic ensued among elements of
the non-European crew, many of whom were still
unfamiliar with the _Egypt_. Stricken by fear, they rushed
into the boats before the passengers, from where they
had to be forcibly removed by the officers. It became so bad at one
stage that passenger Captain Carr of the Indian Army produced his
revolver and fired warning shots, which accidently caused injuries to
a couple of crew members. Unfortunately the first boat to get away
took the Serang (lascar boatswain), making it even harder for the
chief officer to maintain discipline among the Asiatic crew.

Boat No. 18 got away under the command of Second Officer
Cameron but, finding it impossible to get alongside the _Egypt_
to embark passengers, he decided to go in search of the _Seine_.
Fortunately he soon found the ship and was able to guide her
master, Captain Le Barzic, back to the scene of the wreck, where
every possible assistance was rendered. Only five of the eighteen
available lifeboats were launched successfully, but not without
further incident. A steward called Eagles got caught in the falls of
Boat No. 8 and was dashed against the davit and killed.

The _Egypt_ sank just twenty minutes after the collision and went
down stern first, leaving many people in the cold water, desperately
clinging onto anything that would float. Captain Collyer stayed with
his ship to the last and was rescued from the water by Boat No. 17.
The _Seine_ remained at the scene for several hours and picked up all
the survivors and a number of dead bodies.

A total of eighty-six people lost their lives in the disaster, of whom
fifteen were passengers. One surviving passenger lost his wife,
3-year-old daughter and 4-month-old baby daughter, the only two

The unique observation shell used by the Sorima divers to salvage the *Egypt* in the 1930s.

Nearly all the *Egypt*'s gold was raised from a depth of 130m using a mechanical grab.

children on board the *Egypt*. But, as with so many shipwrecks, scenes of individual bravery and compassion were witnessed. The *Egypt* carried three Marconi wireless operators and distress messages continued to be sent right until the final moments; only one operator survived. The ship's painter had put on a lifebelt and was about to jump overboard when he saw a lady rushing up and down the deck, frantically calling for help. He called out to her and strapped his own lifebelt round her body, saying, 'I can't swim, but take this and good luck to you.' He was never seen again. Another passenger took off his lifebelt in the water and gave it to a lady whom he had been supporting, after which he threw up his arms and sank. A nun named Sister Rhoda refused to enter a boat, asking that somebody else should take her place if there was not room for all, and that she would wait for the last. She then knelt on the deck in prayer and was an inspiration to the other passengers in the *Egypt*'s final moments.

A comprehensive Board of Trade inquiry into the loss of the *Egypt* commenced on 24 July 1922 and over the course of the next few weeks the court heard detailed evidence from officers, crew and passengers. No witnesses were called from the *Seine*, since the vessel was not under British ownership and therefore under no obligation to participate. The court did not find the captain or officers at fault for the collision and subsequent loss of the ship, which was an unfortunate accident in a notoriously hazardous stretch of water. The *Seine* had been steaming northbound from La Pallice to Le Havre and would normally have taken a coastal route, but on this occasion had steered further out to sea in order to give Ushant a wide berth in the fog. As a consequence, the *Seine* unexpectedly crossed into the path of the *Egypt*, which had been following the regular southbound trade route. However, when addressing the efforts taken to save life, and even taking into the account the difficulties faced by the master, officers and crew following the collision, the court came down hard on Captain Collyer, the chief officer, and P&O, concluding:

> that the loss of life was mainly due to default on the part of the Master and Chief Officer in failing to take proper measures to save life; default on their part in failing to exercise their authority to ensure good order and discipline at the time of the casualty; default on their part in failing to make the crew efficient in collision and boat drill; and failure on the part of the owners through their officials and servants to take proper and effective measures to ensure compliance with their regulations and to exact good discipline on the ship.

The court suspended Captain Collyer's certificate for six months and Chief Officer Cartwright was severely censured. Captain Collyer, who had not yet recovered from injuries received in the wreck of the *Egypt*, was shocked by the damning verdict. In a long career at sea that spanned nearly forty years he had never once met with an accident. In a statement to the press the captain claimed that given the 'absolutely abnormal conditions' no amount of additional lifeboat drill could have averted the panic, which in his opinion had been brought on by the belief that the ship was going to turn turtle on top of the passengers and crew. He concluded:

> The panic occurred not through people not knowing where to go, such as the lascars, but through them going towards their boats and finding that they could not be used. They then

rushed for the other side. In the confusion they lost their heads, and that started the whole trouble.

Captain Collyer received more than 200 letters of condolence from fellow seamen and several powerful mercantile marine associations took up the cause for his reinstatement. However, the captain had since been retired by P&O on full pension and was reluctant to take the matter further. Chief Officer Cartwright remained with P&O and eventually received his first command, which was the *Comorin* (1) in 1930.

Salvaging the Wreck

The insurance on the lost treasure was paid out by Lloyd's within ten days of the wreck, but the underwriters entertained little hope of recovering their loss. Although they now had legal entitlement to the *Egypt*, the exact position of the wreck was not known with any degree of certainty, especially since the vessel had sunk far from any visible landmarks. But a bigger obstacle faced was the depth of the seabed in the region, which, at over 100m (328ft), was far too deep for a diver wearing contemporary dress. Neither did any technical apparatus exist to recover the gold by any other means. However, the treasure-hunting business seldom lacks optimism and it wasn't long before Lloyd's were approached by various enterprises keen to try their hand at recovering the treasure.

The first expedition was undertaken by a Swedish company in 1923 under the command of Captain Hedbäck and consisted of the salvage ship *Fritjof* and two trawlers. After two months searching by means of dragging a cable over the seabed an obstruction was located which was believed to be the *Egypt*. The team then returned to Sweden with the intention of coming back the next year with a new design of diving apparatus. However, nothing further materialised and two years later a French company took up the challenge, employing a new design of diving shell designed by Neufedt & Kuhnke of Germany. Although the new apparatus was proven to work well, the expedition failed to locate the wreck.

In 1928 the Italian salvage company Sorima, led by Commendatore Giovanni Quaglia, made a technical breakthrough by salvaging the wreck of the Belgian steamer *Elisabethville* (7,017 tons) off the French coast in a depth of 73m (240ft). This gave the company the confidence to go in search of the *Egypt*'s riches and in August that year they were awarded the contract to do so. In June 1929 Sorima established a base of operations at Brest and commenced the search for the *Egypt* using their salvage vessels *Artiglio* and *Rostro*. The season was plagued by bad weather and with morale low the *Rostro* was sent to resume work on the *Elisabethville*. Meanwhile the *Artiglio* went to the nearby wreck of the Union-Castle liner *Drummond Castle* to test some new electric search equipment.

The search resumed once more in June the following year and additional input was received from Captain Hedbäck and Captain Le Barzic, who had conflicting theories on the *Egypt*'s exact position. On 30 August 1930 the wreck of the *Egypt* was finally found and positively identified by the Sorima divers. A few days later the captain's safe was recovered from the wreck, but all it contained were the sodden remains of Foreign Office documents. The next task was to get to the bullion room, which was three decks down. By the end of September the divers had blown away the deck houses and boat deck and had made their first cut in the main deck. Sadly, the year ended tragically in December when the *Artiglio* was engaged in the demolition of the wreck of the *Florence H.* at Saint-Nazaire. One of the salvage charges detonated live munitions in the wreck and the resulting explosion blew up the *Artiglio*, killing two divers and ten crew.

Diving operations on the *Egypt* recommenced in May 1931 from the newly commissioned *Artiglio II*. The system employed by the Sorima divers was for a diver to descend in a sealed, upright cylindrical steel shell, which had viewing ports at eye level. The diver remained in constant radio contact with the surface crew, to whom he issued instructions for lowering and raising the salvage grab. By the end of July the divers were tantalizingly close to reaching the bullion room but bad weather intervened once more. Work resumed again in May 1932 and on 22 June the salvage grab finally brought the first two gold bars to the surface. By the end of the year a significant quantity of gold and silver had been recovered and landed at Plymouth. Sorima continued to work the wreck for the next three years and when the salvage operations finally concluded in 1935, 98 per cent of the gold bars, 97 per cent of the silver ingots and 91 per cent of the sovereigns had been recovered. It was an unprecedented achievement that had defied all the experts and pioneered a new era of deep-sea salvage diving.

In 1987 the *Egypt* caught the attention of Consortium Recovery, who thought they would try their hand at recovering some of the remaining treasure using modern methods. Operating from the salvage vessel *Holga Dane*, they recovered one gold bar and silver bars with a market value of around £100,000. With operating expenses in the region of £10,000 per day it was deemed unprofitable to continue.

Rectangular skylights surround the edges of the cargo hatch combings on the forward holds of the *Egypt*. (Leigh Bishop)

Diving the Wreck

Of the many diveable P&O shipwrecks, the *Egypt* is by far the deepest. A depth to the seabed of 130m makes it a highly specialised and technical dive which can only be undertaken by the most experienced and dedicated of divers. This is further complicated by the wreck lying 30 miles due west from the closest point of land and close to busy shipping lanes. For experiencing just twenty minutes on the wreck divers are required to spend in the region of three to four hours decompressing. This introduces another important consideration for planning dives in an area that is prone to changeable weather, fog and unpredictable Atlantic currents.

The first scuba-diving expedition to the *Egypt* took place in 2001 and was led by Chris Hutchison of the Starfish Enterprise deep-wreck-exploration dive team. The first divers to descend to the wreck were Richard Stevenson and David Wilkins, who were soon followed by five others (a few months later Stevenson became one of the first divers to dive the wreck of the Cunard Line *Carpathia* at an incredible depth of 158m). During these initial dives the wreck's identity as the *Egypt* was positively confirmed by the discovery of china bearing the

A porthole on the *Egypt* encrusted with thick marine growth. (Leigh Bishop)

Remains of spare lamps lying in the *Egypt*'s portside lamp locker. (Leigh Bishop)

P&O emblem. The divers also observed portholes of the distinctive design used on P&O vessels of the era, featuring drip trays and square fastening dogs. The team were further rewarded with excellent water clarity, and deep-wreck photographer Leigh Bishop was able to capture the first underwater images of the *Egypt*.

The 2001 expedition paved the way for other divers in the years that followed but the currents have been a constant challenge, just as they were for the Sorima divers of the 1930s. Even when the tide is slack on the surface it can be very strong at depth, sometimes making it too exhausting to safely reach the wreck or to return to the shotline for the ascent. Although dark at such depths, the visibility on the *Egypt* is often in excess of 10m with a good degree of ambient light, aided by a seabed of light sand and pebble. Most dives take place on the forward half of the ship, ahead of the gaping hole left by the salvage operations. The bow is upright and largely intact, with a depth to the mooring bollards of around 115m. The anchor cables run out across the foredeck and pass an open hatch adjacent to one of the capstains. There is a large winch and the starboard anchor lies flat on the deck. Many of the deck railings are in place, adorned with a light covering of white and orange anemones. Apart from a few sea urchins there is little other marine growth, giving the wreck a relatively clean appearance.

An unusual site on the forecastle deck is the presence of a large spare propeller blade, fastened to the deck and standing bolt upright. Adjacent to this is the unmistakable sight of a toilet bowl, the lavatory walls having collapsed. On the portside the lamp locker is likewise exposed and many navigation lamps lie scattered amongst other debris. From this deck an entrance leads into the interior, where it is possible to follow a passageway and peer into the remains of crew cabins and washrooms.

The hatch combings on the forward cargo hold are completely intact and surrounded by rows of rectangular skylights. These hinged skylights are a distinctive feature on the open decks and have two large porthole dogs on the lower edge to fasten them down. Many are wide open, making it easy to look down into the interior.

Conger eels are common on wrecks in this part of the world but they tend to lurk in the recesses and seldom bother divers. However, those on the *Egypt* have been reported to be quite brazen, coming out of their lairs and approaching divers in a threatening manner. Large ling are also common but rather more docile. Everywhere you look on the wreck there are interesting features, fixtures and scattered items, including china, portholes and brass bench ends. But to recover any of the remaining gold, first you need to get past the guardian congers!

Spare propeller blade carried on the well deck. (Leigh Bishop)

Large ling fish and conger eels guard the wreck of the *Egypt*.
(Leigh Bishop)

PART 5

SECOND WORLD WAR, 1939–1945

– *Rawalpindi* –

1925–1939, Iceland

Rawalpindi (16,619 tons) was built for P&O by Harland & Wolff and launched at Greenock by Lady Birkenhead, wife of the Secretary of State for India, on 26 March 1925. The vessel was towed to the builder's Belfast yard to be engined and fitted out. The length was 547.7ft (166.9m) and beam 71.3ft (21.7m). The twin screws were powered by quadruple-expansion four-cylinder engines, giving a service speed of 17 knots. There was accommodation for 307 first- and 288 second-class passengers. The crew numbered 372.

The *Rawalpindi* was the second of four sisters in the new R class, the last class of vessel in the post-war rebuilding programme. The other ships were *Ranpura*, *Ranchi* and *Rajputana*, all of which were delivered to P&O in 1925. All four ships were to be requisitioned as AMCs during the Second World War, but only *Ranpura* and *Ranchi* survived the war. Like her sisters, the *Rawalpindi* initially operated on services to India and the Far East. Later, in the early 1930s the ship joined the *Viceroy of India* in a new cruising programme, offering month-long voyages to destinations such as the Holy Land, Greece and Egypt.

In August 1927 the *Rawalpindi* was anchored in Hong Kong Harbour when a monstrous typhoon swept over the area, causing the anchor to drag. The ship drifted to within a cable length of another ship and a collision was only narrowly averted when the *Rawalpindi* dropped her second anchor, coming to a stop just a short distance from the sea wall. On the return voyage to England the *Rawalpindi* was fogbound for thirty hours between Gibraltar and Plymouth. Whilst fog hindered the liner's progress, hundreds of migratory birds, which had evidently lost their bearings in the mist, flew aboard; they invaded all parts of the ship and many were captured by passengers. After the ship docked at Plymouth several of the birds were still flying about the music room and the smoke room.

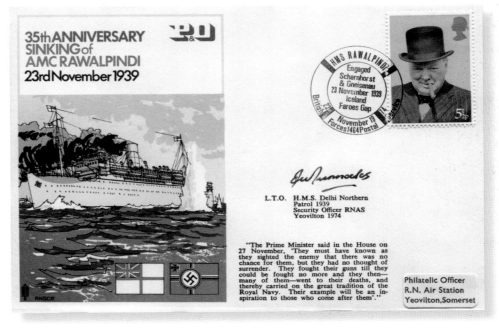

The AMC *Rawalpindi* lost her brave battle with the German battlecruisers *Scharnhorst* and *Gneisenau* on 23 November 1939 and became the first P&O casualty of the Second World War.

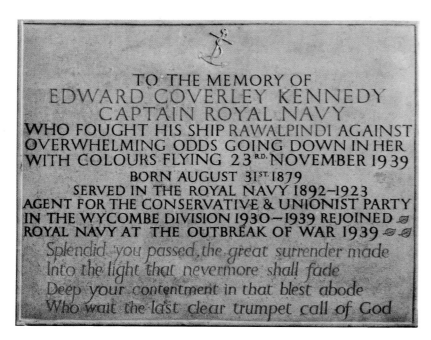

Captain Edward Coverley Kennedy RN was one of over 250 men who lost their lives in the sinking of the *Rawalpindi*. (All Saints Church, High Wycombe)

In September 1937 *Rawalpindi* was in Hong Kong when the colony was hit by a typhoon much worse than the one a decade previously. This time the ship rode out the storm without any difficulties, but thirty vessels were driven ashore. Later that month the *Rawalpindi* came to a stop 100 miles out from Hong Kong after the captain became concerned over the menacing presence of a Japanese destroyer. After communicating her peaceful intentions the *Rawalpindi* proceeded safely on her way again.

In late August 1939 the *Rawalpindi* became the first P&O vessel to be requisitioned by the Admiralty for service in the Second World War. The ship immediately underwent conversion to an AMC, which necessitated the removal of her dummy aft funnel. The ship was armed with eight 6in guns and two 3in anti-aircraft guns. In October the ship joined the Northern Patrol as HMS *Rawalpindi*, under the command of Captain E.C. Kennedy RN (father of broadcaster and journalist Sir Ludovic Kennedy), but her navy service proved to be short-lived.

On the afternoon of 23 November 1939 the *Rawalpindi* was on her third patrol in the waters between the Faroes and Iceland when she sighted the German battlecruisers *Scharnhorst* and *Gneisenau*. The Germans demanded that the *Rawalpindi* surrender, but, despite being hopelessly outgunned, Captain Kennedy chose to hold his ground. An attempt was made to lay a smoke screen, but although thick, black smoke belched from the funnel, the smoke floats failed to operate properly due to the extreme cold. It wasn't long before the German ships opened fire with deadly accuracy on either side of the vessel. The first hit struck the wireless cabin and then two more demolished the bridge. The *Rawalpindi* immediately opened fire in retaliation and managed to score several hits against one of the battlecruisers, but after forty minutes fighting a losing battle the order was given to abandon ship. The Germans continued to bombard the ship long after the *Rawalpindi*'s guns had ceased firing and fires broke out all over the vessel, resulting in the destruction of many of the lifeboats. The *Rawalpindi* continued to burn and finally foundered at around 8 p.m.

More than 250 men died on the *Rawalpindi*, including Captain Kennedy, who was later mentioned in dispatches. Thirty-seven survivors were rescued by the German ships and taken prisoner, and a further eleven were picked up from a drifting lifeboat the next day by HMS *Chitral*, another AMC taken up from the P&O fleet. The *Rawalpindi* was the first P&O vessel to be lost in the Second World War and also had the unfortunate distinction of accounting for the highest number of fatalities on a P&O ship for the duration of the war.

In 1969 the Hull trawler *Kingston Sapphire* snagged her nets on a submerged obstacle, which due to its size and position was believed to be the wreck of the *Rawalpindi*. The depth to the seabed was charted at 307m, with the wreck standing nearly 30m proud.

– *Eston* –

1919–1940, England

Eston (1,487 tons) was laid down for the Shipping Controller by Goole Shipbuilding & Repairing Co., Goole, purchased by P&O and launched on 13 September 1919. The length was 240.2ft (73.2m) and beam 36.1ft (11m). A single screw was powered by a triple-expansion three-cylinder engine, giving a service speed of 10 knots. The *Eston* was a dedicated cargo vessel with a capacity of 102,940 cubic feet (2,914 cubic metres). There was a small crew of twenty-one and the ship was employed on the east coast feeder service.

The *Eston* was a small general-cargo vessel of 1,487 tons that was employed on the east coast feeder service. (Newall Dunn Collection)

Diving the Wreck

The wreck of the *Eston* lies at a depth of 27m in Whitley Bay just a short distance from shore on a rocky seabed. A few miles to the south is the entrance to the Tyne and consequently the visibility can often be quite poor. The wreck was positively identified as the *Eston* by the recovery of the bell in 1978.

The two boilers form the highest point of the wreck and are populated by a rich growth of dead man's fingers. The remains of the triple-expansion steam engine lies on its side, with various interesting features to explore. Heading north towards the bow the wreck flattens out over the steel double hull. There are still some recognisable features such as a section of the forward mast, mooring bollards and a cargo winch. Colourful sea urchins look strangely out of place amongst the silty tangle of dispersed wreckage. The bow has collapsed to just a few metres from the seabed but one of the anchors remains in place, along with a significant length of chain. The stern section is a short distance to the south-west of the engines and one of the props rests on the seabed close by.

Being close to shore and not too deep, the *Eston* is popular with local clubs and dive centres.

At the time of her launch the *Eston* was the largest vessel to have been built at Goole and left the ways at such a speed that the ship was carried across the River Ouse, onto the opposite bank. When the tide receded it was possible to walk under a large portion of the keel. Fortunately the *Eston* was pulled off on the next high tide.

On 27 January 1940 the *Eston* sailed up the coast from Southend under the command of Captain Herbert Roser Harris, in company with six other vessels as part of convoy FN.81. After calling at Hull the *Eston* fell behind the other vessels and made for Blyth, but soon disappeared. A few days later the body of the ship's bosun was found washed up on Blyth beach, along with an empty lifeboat. A second lifeboat was also found a short distance further down the coast. It was believed that the *Eston* had struck a mine on 28 January that had previously been laid by *U-22* (Karl-Heinrich Jenish). All seventeen crew were lost, including the master. Also among the deceased was 14-year-old mess room boy Robert Robinson, who was making his first voyage.

Anchor chain on the wreck of the *Eston*. (Richard Booth)

One of the *Eston*'s two boilers. (Richard Booth)

– Lahore –

1920–1941, North Atlantic

The general-purpose cargo liner *Lahore* (5,252 tons) was laid down for the Shipping Controller by Robert Thompson & Sons, Sunderland, purchased by P&O and launched on 5 February 1920. The length was 400.6ft (122.1m) and beam 52.3ft (15.9m). A single screw was powered by a triple-expansion three-cylinder engine, giving a service speed of 11.5 knots. There was a crew of 102 and a limited amount of accommodation for four first-class passengers.

The *Lahore* was one of many B-class standard design cargo ships bought by P&O after the First World War, all of which were given a name ending in 'ore'. The ship operated on services to India, China and Japan.

On 1 March 1941 the *Lahore* sailed from Freetown, Sierra Leone, under the command of Captain Geoffrey Stable in convoy SL.67, which contained fifty-four vessels bound for Liverpool. The ship was carrying a cargo from Calcutta which included timber, pig iron, tea and 50 tons of matches. At dawn on 8 March the convoy came under attack from *U-124* (Georg-Wilhelm Schulz) while north-east of the Cape Verde Islands. The *Lahore* was hit in the port side of No. 1 hold,

which caught fire and soon afterward the ship had to be abandoned. Fortunately there was no loss of life and all the crew were rescued by one of the escort vessels, destroyer HMS *Forester* (H74), and landed at Gibraltar one week later. Three other merchant navy vessels were also sunk in the attack.

– Somali (2) –

1930–1941, England

Somali (2) (6,809 tons) was ordered for the P&O subsidiary Hain Steamship Company, built by Harland & Wolff, Glasgow, and launched on 9 October 1930. The ship was transferred to P&O ownership before it's completion at the end of the year. The length was 459ft (139.9m) and beam 60.7ft (18.5m). A single screw was powered by a quadruple-expansion four-cylinder engine, giving a service speed of 15 knots. The *Somali* (2) was a general-purpose cargo vessel and did not provide any formal passenger accommodation. There was a crew of seventy-two. A sister ship, *Soudan* (2), was completed soon afterwards and both ships were employed on the London service to the Far East.

In June 1939, in anticipation of an outbreak of hostilities with Germany, the Admiralty initiated the Defensively Equipped Merchant Ships (DEMS) programme, which aimed to arm 5,500 British merchant ships with an adequate defence against enemy submarines and aircraft. As part of the programme the *Somali* (2) was fitted with a stern-mounted 12lb anti-aircraft gun, which was manned by two dedicated DEMS gunners. Despite the protection, the *Somali* (2) had a lucky escape in 1940 while loading cargo in London for a voyage to Singapore. The ship was

The *Lahore* was one of many B-class standard design cargo ships purchased by P&O after the First World War. (Bert Moody)

Left: The general-purpose cargo vessel *Somali* (2) was originally ordered for the P&O subsidiary Hain Steamship Company but completed for P&O in 1930. (Bert Moody)

Above: The effects of the *Somali* (2) explosion were seen and felt for several miles along the Northumberland coast. (Seahouses Lifeboat Station)

struck by five incendiary bombs, which fell into a hold containing army vehicles, but fortunately no fires were started.

During the war the *Somali* (2) typically sailed in large convoys with other merchant navy cargo vessels and on 25 March 1941 convoy FN.442 assembled in Southend, bound for Methil, Scotland. The *Somali* (2)'s final intended destination for the voyage was Hong Kong and the ship was heavily laden with a 9,000 tons of cargo that included a diverse range of items such as medical supplies, cosmetics, clothing, bicycles, paint, fire extinguishers, gas masks, lorry tyres, mercury, copper cable and 100 tons of toy lead soldiers. The ship was also carrying horses, along with a large quantity of hay. The *Somali* (2) made an unscheduled call en route at Middlesbrough where several hundred tons of radioactive white metal ingots destined for India were loaded.

On 26 March the *Somali* (2) was off Blyth, Northumberland, when the ship came under an airborne attack from a squadron of German Heinkel III bombers. Although the DEMS gunners put up a valiant fight, the *Somali* (2) received three direct hits, one of which exploded in the No. 3 hold and set alight the highly flammable cargo of hay. The crew struggled for hours to contain the raging flames but by late evening the situation had begun to worsen so everyone was taken off by the armed trawler *Pelican*. The smoke and flames from the stricken vessel were visible from the shore, and not realising that no lives were in immediate danger, lifeboats were launched from several different stations along the coast. When the lifeboats arrived in the

early hours of the morning their crews were asked to assist with the attachment of tow cables from the former US Navy tug *Sea Giant* to the *Somali* (2). By 9.30 a.m. the tow was underway and the vessels proceeded slowly north, towards the shelter of the Farne Islands.

The salvage vessel *Iron Axe* was next on the scene and, with the assistance of the Boulmer lifeboat *Clarissa Langdon*, put a few men aboard the burning steamer, who then decided the best course of action was to tow the *Somali* (2) south and attempt to beach the vessel. The *Sea Giant* struggled to make headway against the strong tide so the salvage officer decided to try and get a line aboard from the *Iron Axe* to assist with the tow. The fire was now burning fiercely from the bridge forward, but the *Clarissa Langdon* made for the *Somali* (2) once more and was barely 65m away when the forepart blew up with a terrific explosion. The force of the blast blew off the *Somali* (2)'s bow, lifted the lifeboat right out of the water and knocked the crew flat on their backs. Large pieces of metal debris rained down on *Clarissa Langdon* and one man had his head badly wounded. The North Sunderland lifeboat, *W.R.A*, was still in attendance and two of its crew also sustained injuries. The effects of the explosion were seen and felt for several miles along the Northumberland coast, where windows were broken in properties as far as 5 miles away. Despite the considerable risk, the *Clarissa Langdon* coxswain James Campbell did not hesitate to approach the *Somali* (2) to rescue the two salvage crew remaining on board. No sooner had the lifeboat pulled away than the propeller became

fouled on the wreckage and the coxswain had to resort to sail. Fortunately the *W.R.A* came to his aid and everyone got clear.

James Campbell was later awarded the bronze medal by the Royal National Lifeboat Institution in recognition of his courage. The wreck of the *Somali* (2) claimed one life – an Indian merchant seaman, who died when the vessel was bombed.

Diving the Wreck

On the north-east coast of England a short distance from shore lie the Farne Islands. This is a very popular location for scuba divers and has a multitude of dive sites which are suitable for divers of all certification levels. There are many wrecks in the area but the biggest attraction is the large grey seal colony, which numbers in excess of 5,000. Seals are not shy of divers and are very playful underwater, often likened to boisterous puppies. The wreck of the *Somali* (2) is just 3 miles south of the Farne Islands and 1 mile out from Beadnell Point. Of all the P&O wreck dives in English waters, the *Somali* (2) is both the newest ship and the most recent loss. It also happens to be one of the most popular wreck dives in the north-east.

When the wreck was first discovered in the 1960s a considerable amount of the hull was still intact and parts stood as high as 9m from the seabed at 30m. However, a combination of valuable non-ferrous metals and the varied cargo have made the *Somali* (2) a target for salvage work ever since. Consequently, much of the wreck

The wreck of the *Somali* (2) near the Farne Islands is one of the most popular dive sites on the north-east coast of England. (Richard Booth)

One of the *Somali* (2)'s five imposing boilers. (Richard Booth)

Although the wreck of the *Somali* (2) has been heavily salvaged over the years, a substantial amount of the ship's structure remains. (Richard Booth)

Lorry tyres were part of the *Somali* (2)'s mixed cargo. (Richard Booth)

The *Somali* (2) cargo included a diverse range of domestic items, such as this razor. (Ben Burville)

Small lead soldiers are a common find on the wreck of the *Somali* (2). (Alan Leatham)

has been flattened and dispersed, but sections still stand at least 5m proud and it remains an excellent dive. Despite all the attention and the amount of diving that takes place in the area, one mystery remains – the bow section was detached from the wreck when it blew up and has never been found.

The highest and most central point of the wreck is the enormous quadruple-expansion steam engine, which stands completely upright with the four cylinder heads at a depth of just 23m. Descending deeper it is easy to identify the conrods and crankshaft, where it is possible to swim through the middle of the engine block amongst the powerful pistons.

Forward of the engine is the imposing sight of all five boilers, arranged in rows of two and three. From here the diver can navigate through the gaps in between them then out through the broken bulkhead to the flattened remains of the forward holds. Scattered all over the seabed here are the solidified remains of numerous bags of cement. This is also an area where many of the smaller domestic items have been discovered, such as ceramic jars, bottles, shaving kits and toy soldiers. Brass fire extinguishers are also a prized find.

On the aft end of the engine block are further cargo holds. These contain more cement and a large quantity of truck tyres, which give the appearance of an underwater scrapyard. The final hold was refrigerated and is notable for an abundance of metal piping. Off

to the starboard side are numerous large gas cylinders and a spare propeller. A short distance further aft, the 12-pound anti-aircraft gun rests on the seabed. This points to the stern where the remnant of the rudder lies amongst the debris with the outline of the propeller shaft close by.

There are further scattered remains off to the side of the wreck, which lies on a rocky seabed surrounded by scenic reefs. Visibility is generally very good and there is plenty of varied marine life, including pollock, sea urchins, starfish, dead man's fingers and lobsters. The area is very tidal and the *Somali* (2) can only be dived during slack water.

– *Comorin* (1) –

1925–1941, North Atlantic

Comorin (1) (15,116 tons) was built for P&O by Barclay, Curle & Co., Glasgow, and launched on 31 October 1924 by the Hon. Mrs Alexander Shaw, wife of the P&O deputy managing director

Comorin (1) was completed in 1925 and commissioned as an AMC in 1939. The ship sank in April 1941 after catching fire in the North Atlantic. (Bert Moody)

and eldest daughter of Lord Inchcape. The length was 523.5ft (159.5m) and beam 70.2ft (21.4m). Twin screws were powered by quadruple-expansion four-cylinder engines, giving a service speed of 16 knots. There was accommodation for 203 first- and 103 second-class passengers, with a crew of 278.

The *Comorin* (1) was the second of three new medium-sized C-class passenger liners built primarily for the London–Sydney service, but also well-suited to the Far East route. The other two ships were *Cathay* (2), launched on the same day at the same shipyard, and *Chitral* (1). The maiden voyage of the *Comorin* (1) sailed from London on 24 April 1925, bound for Sydney, Australia.

On 12 March 1930 *Comorin* (1) was at Colombo on a return voyage from Sydney when fire broke out in two of the three cargo holds. All the passengers were put ashore while the crew and local fire services fought the blaze, which wasn't fully extinguished until the following day. P&O were very fortunate not to lose the ship, which at one stage listed by as much as 30 degrees. The fire badly damaged the first-class dining saloon and much of the first-class accommodation. All the cargo in No. 2 and No. 3 holds was lost, along with most of the Australian mails. The ship was able to sail a few days later after undergoing temporary repairs but all the first-class passengers had to embark on a later ship.

Towards the end of 1930 *Comorin* (1) and *Chitral* (1) both underwent improvements to their machinery, which included the installation of new low-pressure exhaust turbines, resulting in a slight increase in service speed to 17 knots.

In November 1938 the famous science-fiction writer H.G. Wells sailed for Australia on the *Comorin* (1) in order to present two papers at the Science Congress in Canberra. He later published an essay based on his voyage entitled 'SS *Pukka Sahib*' but was rather derogatory about his experiences on the ship.

Comorin (1) was in Australian waters at the start of the Second World War and immediately upon return to England was taken up by the Admiralty for service as an AMC and commissioned as HMS *Comorin (F 49)*. During the conversion the dummy rear funnel was removed and the ship was armed with eight 6in guns and two 3in anti-aircraft guns.

For the first few months of 1940 the *Comorin* (1) was stationed in the South Atlantic, based out of Simonstown. In April the ship transferred to escort duties sailing from Bermuda and Halifax and, apart from taking a break to undergo a refit on the Tyne in the autumn, remained on that service until January 1941. From then on the *Comorin* (1) joined the Freetown escort forces. On 4 April 1941 the *Comorin* (1) sailed from the Clyde under the command of Captain Hallett RN carrying naval personnel out to Freetown as

part of a convoy that included three merchant vessels and the destroyer HMS *Lincoln*. At 2 p.m. on 6 April the ships were well out into the Atlantic when a fire broke out in the *Comorin* (1)'s engine room and quickly took hold. The situation was compounded by gale-force winds and heavy seas, with some waves estimated to be as high as 20m. Despite the atrocious weather conditions, two lifeboats and seven rafts were launched, the occupants of which were picked up by HMS *Lincoln* and the *Glenartney*. However, hundreds of men still remained gathered on the deck at the aft end of the burning ship.

At 8.10 p.m. HMS *Broke* arrived in the darkness in response to receiving distress signals and her master, Captain Scurfield, commenced a daring rescue operation. First his ship's foredeck was covered with padding and the port side was lined with fenders. Then HMS *Broke* made repeated runs alongside the *Comorin* (1) from where the stranded crew had to make a leap of faith onto the ship. With both vessels pitching and rolling violently in the heavy seas it was an extremely challenging manoeuvre and it was inevitable that HMS *Broke* would sustain some damage in the process. Only a small handful of men could make the jump with each approach, and many were injured in the process, with at least one fatality, but soon after midnight all the men had been transferred. Although twenty men from a complement of well over 400 died in the loss of the *Comorin* (1), it was fortunate that the death toll was not much higher. When dawn broke on 7 April the *Comorin* (1) was still afloat, fully ablaze from stem to stern, but the vessel was sent to the bottom by gunfire from HMS *Lincoln*.

– *Rajputana* –

1925–1941, North Atlantic

Rajputana (16,568 tons), the last of the four post-war R-class vessels, was built for P&O by Harland & Wolff, Greenock, and launched on 6 August 1925. The length was 547.7ft (166.9m) and beam 71.3ft (21.7m). Twin screws were powered by quadruple-expansion four-cylinder engines, giving a service speed of 17 knots. There was accommodation for 307 first- and 288 second-class passengers, with a crew of 370.

The *Rajputana* was delivered to P&O on 30 December 1925 and sailed on her maiden voyage from London to Bombay a few weeks

P. & O. S.S. RAJPUTANA, 16,600 TONS GROSS.

India Mail and Passenger Service.

Completed in 1925, the *Rajputana* was the last of the four post-war R-class liners and was employed on the India mail service.

The AMC *Rajputana* sank by the stern after being torpedoed by *U-108* in the North Atlantic in April 1941.

later on 22 January 1926. This was the first of many regular voyages on the India mail service.

One of the most famous passengers to be carried on the *Rajputana* was RAF airman T.E. Shaw, commonly known as Lawrence of Arabia. Shaw sailed from Bombay for England on 12 January 1929 and travelled discreetly as a second-class passenger in civilian clothing. The original intention had been for him to disembark at Tilbury, but midway through the voyage he was advised that special arrangements had been made for him to leave the ship in secret at Plymouth, due to the significant amount of public interest that surrounded him at the time.

In April 1931 the ageing Chinese steamer *Hwah Yang* foundered in fog near Wenchow, 300 miles west of Shanghai, and the passengers and crew managed to make it to a small nearby island where they spent a difficult night. The following morning their distress signals were noticed by the *Rajputana*, which wasted no time in coming to their aid. The *Rajputana*'s lifeboats were launched in treacherous seas and in a remarkable feat of seamanship all 114 passengers and crew were safely rescued.

In the summer of 1937 several thousand British nationals were evacuated from Shanghai as a result of hostilities between China and Japan and the *Rajputana* was one of six liners employed to help. Two years later, the *Rajputana* was docked in Yokohama when the Second World War broke out and was ordered to Vancouver Island, Canada, for conversion to an AMC, becoming HMS *Rajputana* (F35). The ship then took up a role as a North Atlantic convoy escort, based out of Halifax, under the command of Captain Frederick Taylor RN.

On 11 April 1941 the *Rajputana* arrived in the waters off Iceland, having recently received orders to take up patrol duties in the Denmark Strait. The ship was following a high-speed zigzag course when she was spotted and chased by *U-108* (Klaus Scholtz). The submarine's efforts were hampered by pack ice, snow and difficulties with the periscope, but shortly after 6 p.m. *U-108* managed to unleash two torpedoes. Fortunately both missed their target, as did two more that were fired later the following evening. By the morning of 13 April the U-boat commander was homing in on his target and a fifth torpedo fired at 7.40 a.m. narrowly missed. Then three minutes later a further torpedo struck the *Rajputana*'s stern, stopping the engine and starting a fire on board. Captain Taylor gave the order to abandon ship but Commander Scholtz still wasn't content with his efforts so he fired a seventh torpedo, which just missed. At 9.30 a.m. the *Rajputana* was hit once more and started to go down by the stern, taking a heavy list to port.

Forty-one lives were lost, which included the convoy commodore, Commander Cyril Richardson RNR, the last P&O civilian master of the *Rajputana*. The survivors were sighted by a Sunderland flying boat and most of them were soon rescued by HMS *Legion* and landed at Reykjavík. The remainder were later found drifting and taken to Canada by naval destroyers. The loss of the *Rajputana* came just six days after the *Comorin* (1) had also sank in the Atlantic, following a fire on board.

– *Surat* (2) –

1938–1941, Sierra Leone

Surat (2) (5,529 tons) was built for P&O by Alexander Stephen & Sons, Glasgow, and launched on 15 June 1938. The length was 442.2ft (134.7m) and beam 57.9ft (17.6m). A single screw was powered by a four-cylinder diesel engine, giving a service speed of 12 knots. The ship was a dedicated cargo liner with a capacity of 524,030 cubic feet (14,837 cubic metres).

The *Surat* (2) was ordered together with a sister ship, *Shillong* (1), which in March 1939 became the last new P&O vessel to enter service before the Second World War. Both ships operated on services to India but neither of them managed to survive the war.

The *Surat* (2)'s short career came to an end on 6 May 1941 during a return voyage from Karachi to the UK under the command of Captain Thomas Daniel. After calling at Table Bay the ship proceeded unescorted up the west coast of Africa, fully laden with a cargo of pig iron, peas and rapeseed. On the afternoon of 5 May the *Surat* (2) was sighted west of Freetown by *U-103* (Viktor Schütze) and shortly before midnight the submarine fired and missed with its first torpedo. The lookouts on *Surat* (2) realised that they were under attack, so the ship continued on its zigzag course in an effort to evade the enemy. At 5.10 a.m. the following morning the *U-103* fired two more torpedoes, both of which the *Surat* (2) successfully evaded. Five minutes later another two torpedoes were fired and this time the second one caused a direct hit on the stern and disabled the *Surat* (2)'s engine. The *U-103* showed no mercy and unleashed three more torpedoes, of which the last two struck amidships, causing the *Surat* (2) to sink soon after. Captain Daniel and most of the crew were picked up by the British hopper barge *Foremost 102*, but two engineer officers and an Indian oiler were lost.

– *Soudan* (2) –

1931–1942, South Africa

Soudan (2) (6,677 tons) was originally ordered for the P&O subsidiary Hain Steamship Company but transferred to P&O before construction commenced. The cargo liner was built by Barclay, Curle & Co., Glasgow, and launched on 24 November 1930. The length was 459ft (139.9m) and beam 60.7ft (18.5m). A single screw was powered by a quadruple-expansion four-cylinder engine, giving a service speed of 15 knots. The cargo capacity was 514,857 cubic feet (14,577 cubic metres) and she was manned by a crew of seventy-seven. The *Soudan* (2) was the younger sister ship of the *Somali* (2) and was employed on the London–Far East service.

On 15 April 1942 the *Soudan* (2) sailed from the Clyde in convoy WS.18 bound for Durban, and onwards to India via Burma. The ship

The cargo liner *Soudan* (2) was ordered for the P&O subsidiary Hain Steamship Company but completed for P&O in 1931.

carried a cargo of 8,000 tons of military stores, including 400 tons of explosives. After calling at Freetown, where various vessels joined and left the convoy, the ships proceeded south to Cape Town where a portion of the convoy detached itself in the early hours of 15 May. The remaining vessels sailed on towards Durban but later the same day, just before 4 p.m., the destroyer depot ship HMS *Hecla* struck a mine off Cape Agulhas and diverted to Simonstown. Then two hours later at 6.10 p.m. *Soudan* (2) also struck a mine and the crew took to three lifeboats. The occupants of the first two boats were picked up forty hours later, but it was six days before the third boat was rescued by *Clan Murray*. Fortunately there was no loss of life. The minefield had been laid the previous month by the German mercantile minelayer *Doggerbank*.

– Alipore –

1920–1942, British Guiana

The general-cargo liner *Alipore* (5,273 tons) was laid down for the Shipping Controller by Palmer's Shipbuilding & Iron Co., Jarrow, purchased by P&O and launched on 6 May 1920. The length was 400.1ft (121.9m) and beam 52.3ft (15.9m). The single screw was powered by a triple-expansion three-cylinder engine, giving a service speed of 11.5 knots. The cargo capacity was 393,690 cubic feet (410,00 cubic metres) and there was a crew of 104, with some limited accommodation for four passengers.

The *Alipore* was one of the standard design B-class cargo ships bought by P&O after the First World War and was primarily employed on the India–Japan service, with occasional voyages back to the UK.

In June 1940 the *Alipore* was discharging a cargo of cotton at Shanghai when fire broke out on board. The blaze was eventually brought under control but most of the cargo was lost and the ship was badly damaged. Sabotage was suspected to be the cause, since the fire had started in several parts of the ship simultaneously.

On 6 September 1942 the *Alipore* sailed unescorted from Cape Town under the command of Captain Ernest Lee, bound for Trinidad and New York. The ship was carrying a cargo that included 1,500 tons of chrome ore and 400 tons of olive oil, on a long voyage that had commenced from Alexandria. After crossing the Atlantic the *Alipore* arrived off the coast of British Guiana, where the ship was struck on the starboard side at 11 p.m. on 29 September by a torpedo fired from *U-516* (Gerhad Wiebe). One of the boilers instantly exploded and the engine room quickly flooded, killing all the occupants. The rest of the crew took to rafts and lifeboats and were sighted the next day by the fishing schooner *United Eagle* which towed them to Georgetown. The *Alipore* was finished off by gunfire from *U-516* and sank in the early hours of 30 September. Twelve lives were lost, which included the chief engineer, fourth engineer and cook.

– Nagpore –

1920–1942, North Atlantic

Nagpore (5,283 tons) was ordered for the Shipping Controller, purchased by P&O, built by Earle's Shipbuilding & Engineering Co., Hull, and launched on 6 June 1920. The length was 400.4ft (122m) and beam 52.2ft (15.9m). A single screw was powered by a triple-expansion steam engine, giving a service speed of 10.5 knots. The *Nagpore* was a standard design B-class cargo ship and operated on India and Far East services.

In September 1926 the *Nagpore* was steaming down the Yangtze river towards Shanghai when she became caught up in the siege of Hankow and was struck by indiscriminate gunfire from Cantonese troops. Fortunately none of the crew were injured during the brief encounter, but the *Nagpore*'s decks were badly splintered.

On 1 October 1942 the *Nagpore* rescued all thirty-nine officers and crew from the *Siam II* who had taken to their lifeboats the day before when their vessel was sunk off Freetown by *U-506* (Erich Würdemann). Two weeks later the *Nagpore* sailed from Freetown for Liverpool under the command of Captain Percy Tonkin, as commodore ship for convoy SL.125, carrying Rear Admiral Cecil Ryne. On the evening of 28 October the convoy was north-west of the Canary Islands when it came under attack from *U-509* (Werner Witte) and *Nagpore* was one of the unfortunate vessels to be sunk. Captain Tonkin, the first and second radio officers, and eighteen other crew members were lost. Rear Admiral Ryne and many of the survivors were picked up by the convoy escort HMS *Crocus*. However, one lifeboat remained at sea for two weeks until it eventually landed at Tenerife in the Canary Islands on 10 November.

– *Jeypore* –

1920–1942, North Atlantic

The cargo liner *Jeypore* (5,318 tons) was laid down for the Shipping Controller and built by William Gray & Co., Sunderland. The ship was launched as *War Moth*, but purchased by P&O before completion and renamed *Jeypore*. The length was 400ft (121.9m) and beam 52.3ft (15.9m). A single screw was powered by a triple-expansion three-cylinder engine, giving a service speed of 11.25 knots.

The *Jeypore* was the third of the standard design B-class cargo ships bought by P&O after the First World War. She was also the third such vessel to be lost in the Second World War within the space of just five weeks, following the *Alipore* at the end of September 1942 and *Nagpore* in October. A fourth B-class ship, *Lahore*, had been lost a year earlier. Prior to the war the *Jeypore* was employed on the India–Japan service.

On 24 October 1942 the *Jeypore* sailed from New York under the command of Captain Thomas Stevens. The ship formed part of convoy SC.107 bound for Liverpool and carried the convoy commodore, Vice Admiral Bertram Watson. On 2 October the convoy was south of Greenland when it was ambushed by the thirteen-strong U-boat wolfpack 'Veilchen' and nine vessels were sunk. The attacks continued the following day when two further ships were sunk, the second of which was *Jeypore*, claimed by a torpedo fired from *U-89* (Dietrich Lohmann). The vessel was abandoned after twenty minutes, but two Indian firemen died. The survivors were picked up by the US Navy tugs *Uncas* and *Pessacus* and transferred to the convoy rescue ship *Stockport*, which landed them in Reykjavík five days later. A further four ships from the convoy were sunk on 4 November, the last of which was a second victim of *U-89*.

– *Viceroy of India* –

1929–1942, Algeria

Viceroy of India (19,648 tons) was built for P&O by Alexander Stephen & Sons Yard, Glasgow, and launched by Lady Irwin, wife of the Viceroy of India, on 15 September 1928. The length was

On 24 October 1942 the *Jeypore* became the third P&O standard design B-class cargo ship to be lost within five weeks when she was targeted by wolfpack '*Veilchen*' in the North Atlantic. (Bert Moody)

Built in 1929, the *Viceroy of India* was the first European-owned turbo-electric passenger liner. (Bert Moody)

The Scots baronial-style first-class smoking room on the *Viceroy of India.*

586.1ft (178.6m) and beam 76.2ft (23.2m). Twin screws were powered by two steam turbines driving electric generators, which fed electric motors, giving a service speed of 19 knots. There was a crew of 414, with accommodation for 415 first- and 258 second-class passengers.

Following the launch ceremony on the Clyde, the *Viceroy of India* was nicknamed the 'Ship of the Year' by the press, and for good reason. Unlike many other contemporary vessels of the P&O fleet, the *Viceroy of India* was intentionally designed as a unique ship, and showcased many advancements for P&O and for shipbuilding in general. The ship was the first European passenger liner to adopt oil-fired turbo-electric propulsion machinery, which made the vessel much more economical in both manpower and fuel costs. The stylish interior decorations and furnishings were designed by Miss Elsie Mackay, daughter of Lord Inchcape, and included a variety of classic British and French eighteenth-century designs. The first-class passenger accommodation consisted entirely of single-berth cabins, which could easily be converted into larger two- or three-berth suites through an innovative system of interconnecting doors. Another first for P&O was the incorporation of a Pompeiian-themed indoor swimming pool.

The maiden voyage of the *Viceroy of India* sailed from Tilbury for Bombay under the command of Captain Basil Ohlson on 28 March 1929. The voyage coincided with a new P&O programme offering reduced fares for passengers making holiday voyages to Marseilles and Egypt. After returning from

The *Viceroy of India*'s indoor swimming pool featured Pompeiian themes.

The *Viceroy of India* was the first vessel to come to the aid of the White Star liner *Doric* after it collided with the French coaster *Formigny* off Cape Finisterre on 5 September 1935. Between the combined efforts of the *Viceroy of India* and the Orient Line's *Orion* all 735 passengers were rescued. The *Doric* managed to make it to port but was later declared a constructive total loss.

The *Viceroy of India* was returning unescorted from Operation Torch when she was sunk off the coast of Algeria by *U-407*.

The dramatic final moments of the grand passenger liner *Viceroy of India*.

India, the *Viceroy of India* spent a couple of months making short cruising voyages, something that would become a popular feature in the ship's itinerary over the next decade. A few years later the ship broke the London–Bombay speed record with a passage time of seventeen days, one hour, forty-two minutes.

On 23 November 1929 the *Viceroy of India* came to the aid of the Italian cargo ship *Maria Luisa* when it foundered in a storm off Egypt in the Mediterranean. All the crew were safely rescued by the liner and landed at Marseilles. A year later on 31 December 1930 the *Viceroy of India* was inbound from Bombay under the command of Captain William Townshend when a distress message was received from the Greek cargo vessel *Theodoros Bulgaris*, which was sinking in stormy weather in the Bay of Biscay. The *Viceroy of India* immediately diverted course and steamed 135 miles to the stricken vessel. The ship arrived just in time and Captain Townshend ordered oil to be pumped over the water in a bid to ease the tempestuous seas. A lifeboat was then lowered and sent away in charge of the third officer and half the crew were rescued. The remainder made it to the liner in their own lifeboat and the *Theodoros Bulgaris* sank without any loss of life. Captain Townshend and members of his crew were later presented with gallantry awards from the Greek government.

In April 1937 the *Viceroy of India* herself need rescuing when the ship ran aground northbound in the Suez Canal during a spell of bad weather. The ship was towed off by the tug *Hercule*, only to run aground once more, causing damage to the rudder. The canal traffic was held up for five hours, but eventually the *Viceroy of India* was able to get underway again.

Following the outbreak of the Second World War, the *Viceroy of India* continued to make passenger sailings to the Far East, the last of which sailed from Liverpool on 22 July 1940 via Cape Town.

During the voyage the *Viceroy of India* came to the assistance of the Shaw, Savill & Albion liner *Ceramic*, which had collided with the Bank Line cargo liner *Testbank* off Walvis Bay. All of *Ceramic*'s passengers were transferred to *Viceroy of India* as a precaution.

Shortly after her return to England in November the *Viceroy of India* was requisitioned for war service as a troopship. Following a partial modification on the Clyde the ship made one return voyage to Port Said via the Cape, after which a more comprehensive conversion was completed in March 1941. From then on the *Viceroy of India* made regular trooping voyages to the Far East and Suez, sometimes in convoy, but often sailing independently.

On 26 October 1942 the *Viceroy of India* sailed from the Clyde under the command of Captain Sidney French in convoy KMF.1, with 2,800 Allied troops bound for Algiers for the invasion of French North Africa as part of Operation Torch. The ship arrived safely on 7 November and sailed unescorted on the return voyage three days later, with just twenty-two passengers remaining on board. In the early hours of 11 November the *Viceroy of India* was about 40 miles north of Oran when the ship came under attack from *U-407* (Ernst-Ulrich Brüller). The submarine fired four torpedoes, two of which hit the target, causing an explosion in the engine room and the ship to lose power. Before the ship was abandoned at 7 a.m., Chief Officer Kenneth Cummins was sent to conduct a search of the ship by torchlight. He later said that the memory of the echoing sound in the lower decks of water rushing into the hull haunted him for the rest of his life.

Five lives were lost: the third engineer, a junior engineer and three Indian crew. The survivors were soon picked up by the destroyer HMS *Boadicea* and landed at Gibraltar from where they were repatriated by the *Llangibby Castle*. The *Viceroy of India* was one of the largest vessels sunk in the war and a great loss to P&O.

– *Cathay* (2) –

1925–1942, Algeria

Cathay (2) (15,104 tons) was built for P&O by Barclay, Curle & Co., Glasgow, and launched by Lady Inchcape, wife of the P&O chairman, on 31 October 1924. The length was 523.5ft (159.6m) and beam 70.2ft (21.4m). Twin screws were powered by quadruple-expansion steam engines, giving a service speed of 16 knots. There was accommodation for 203 first- and 103 second-class passengers, with a crew of 278.

The maiden voyage of the *Cathay* (2) sailed for Sydney on 27 March 1925, and for the next three years the ship became a regular on the Australia service, along with her sister ships, *Comorin* (1) and *Chitral* (1). From 1932 onwards the *Cathay* (2) also made occasional voyages to India and the Far East.

On 17 November 1933 *Cathay* (2) sailed for Australia with 40,000 bags of Christmas mail, but later in the voyage she lost her port propeller in the Indian Ocean, three days out from Colombo. Despite the mishap the ship was still able to make a steady 12 knots and arrived in Fremantle just a few days behind schedule on 21 December. However, the delays meant that the *Cathay* (2) did not reach the eastern Australian ports in time to deliver the mail for Christmas.

The *Cathay* (2) was the first of the three C-class vessels to be requisitioned by the Admiralty for service as an AMC on 25 August 1939. At the time the vessel was east of Suez so the conversion took place in Bombay, where the ship was commissioned as HMS *Cathay* (F 05). For the next year the *Cathay* (2) undertook patrol and escort duties in the Indian Ocean, after which the vessel transferred to the Freetown escort force.

Towards the end of 1941 the Admiralty decided that the *Cathay* (2) should be refitted as a troopship and the vessel was sent to the US Navy yard at Brooklyn for conversion, after which the ship was returned to P&O. The *Cathay* (2) commenced her new role carrying troops in May 1942 and spent the next five months making voyages to South Africa, the Middle East and India.

On 26 October 1942 the *Cathay* (2) sailed from the Clyde under the command of Captain Douglas Stuart in convoy KMF.1 as a participant in the Operation Torch landings in North Africa. The large convoy also included the P&O ships *Ettrick*, *Mooltan* (3), *Strathnaver* (1) and *Viceroy of India*. *Cathay* (2) disembarked the first of her troops at Algiers on 7 November, then proceeded east along the Algerian coast to Bougie where she arrived at anchor on the morning of 11 November. Later that afternoon, while the remainder of the troops

The *Cathay* (2) was one of many P&O vessels that took part in Operation Torch and was sunk less than twenty-four hours after the *Viceroy of India*. (Allan C. Green/State Library of Victoria)

were being discharged, the anchorage came under heavy attack from German aircraft. The *Cathay* (2) sustained several direct hits and was abandoned at 7 p.m. Three hours later a delayed-action bomb exploded in the galley, starting a fire which raged out of control throughout the night. At 7 a.m. the following morning there was a massive explosion of ammunition, which blew off the stern, and three hours later the *Cathay* (2) sank. There had been one fatality, Sub-Lieutenant Dudley Ward of the Royal Naval Volunteer Reserve. Most of the *Cathay* (2)'s crew were taken on board the British India ship *Karanja*, but after she too was bombed both crews were transferred to the *Strathnaver* (1).

The loss of the *Cathay* (2) came less than twenty-four hours after the *Viceroy of India* was sunk by a torpedo off Algiers.

– *Narkunda* –

1920–1942, Algeria

Narkunda (16,227 tons) was built for P&O by Harland & Wolff, Belfast, launched on 25 April 1918, but not completed until 1920. The length was 581.4ft (177.2m) and beam 69.4ft (21.2m). Twin screws were powered by quadruple-expansion four-cylinder engines, giving a service speed of 17 knots. There was accommodation for 426 first- and 247 second-class passengers.

In November 1913 and early 1914 P&O placed orders for two new mail steamers, *Naldera* and *Narkunda*, but due to the outbreak of the First World War work was suspended before much progress on construction could be made. After sitting idle on the stocks for three years, both vessels were taken over by the government, with a view to commissioning them for war service. The *Narkunda* was eventually launched in April 1918 and work commenced to complete the ship as an AMC. By the time of the armistice in November 1918 the conversion had only been partially completed and the *Narkunda* was handed back to P&O.

The finished *Naldera* and *Narkunda* were finally delivered to P&O in March 1920 and were the first new mail steamers to be completed after the war. The design of both vessels also introduced several firsts for the P&O fleet: first to exceed 15,000 tons, first to feature three funnels and first to possess cruiser sterns. The maiden voyage of the *Narkunda* sailed from London for Bombay on 24 April 1920,

and was followed in June by the first of many sailings on the Australia service.

The maiden arrival of a new P&O passenger liner in Australia always generated a great deal of public interest and the *Narkunda* was certainly no exception. The day after the vessel arrived in Sydney on 24 August the *Daily Commercial News and Shipping List* described the magnificent interiors of the 'palatial liner':

The dining saloons, extending over the width of the vessel, are served from elaborate kitchens fitted with the latest utensils, ensuring hygiene. Liberal provision is made for promenading. An artistic feature of the vessel is the oval well, where a deep frieze depicts nymphs and dryads sporting in woodland surroundings under a gorgeous Eastern sunset, from the brush of Professor Gerald Moira. This decorative effect is reflected into the music-room, which is divided from the divan by a light wooden bulkhead with plate-glass doors. The gymnasium is conveniently situated on the promenade deck, and includes all the latest appliances for exercise. Two electric passenger lifts are at the disposal of the first saloon passengers. At the after end of the promenade deck is the first saloon smoking-room, the furniture of which is in the style of the period of William III and Mary. There are deep, roomy lounges and big arm-chairs upholstered in green morocco leather, the walls being panelled between fluted pilasters having carved caps. All cabins throughout the ship have lavatory basins, wardrobes, and in many cases writing tables. The public rooms of the *Narkunda* are panelled in dull finished brown oak, with the exception of the first-class dining saloon, where the walls have been painted to imitate old ivory. In pleasant contrast with these vellum-like walls are the movable chairs in natural coloured oak, with oval backs, pierced centre panels, the seats in green morocco leather.

In 1927 the *Narkunda* was taken out of service for several months in order to undergo conversion from using coal to more economical oil fuel. The change resulted in the stokehold crew being reduced significantly from 136 to fifty-three men, along with a slight speed increase of ¼ knot. The *Naldera* did not undergo the same changes and following a number of mishaps in the 1930s the vessel was scrapped in 1938. Meanwhile the *Narkunda* continued to provide reliable services to Australia and the Far East.

The *Narkunda* sailed from London on her last peacetime voyage on 23 June 1939, bound for Brisbane. Just as the ship was approaching Colombo Harbour a fire broke out in No. 6 hold. A local fireboat came

The 16,227-ton *Narkunda* was ordered in 1914 but not completed until 1920. The ship was sunk in November 1942 during Operation Torch and is the largest P&O wreck accessible to scuba divers.

alongside and assisted the crew in fighting the flames but before the fire could be contained there was a blinding flash accompanied by a big explosion. Four crew members were killed by the blast and many more were seriously injured. None of the passengers were hurt but one man was blown through an open doorway while he was shaving. The fire was eventually extinguished and the *Narkunda* was able to continue her voyage to Australia a few days later, leaving fifteen crew behind in Colombo hospital. The official inquiry into the mystery explosion attributed it to gas from fermenting cargo, not a bomb, as many people had suspected.

Following the outbreak of the Second World War, the *Narkunda* continued to make regular passenger voyages. In May 1940 the ship came under fire from an unknown vessel off Gibraltar, following an aborted call to Marseilles. Fortunately the *Narkunda* was able to outrun her attacker and made it safely to London without further incident. In November 1940 the *Narkunda* carried a mixed complement of passengers and troops on a voyage to Penang via Cape Town, after which the ship was employed primarily as a troopship.

Following the Japanese invasion of Malaya the British Army was forced into retreat and in January 1942 the *Narkunda* embarked a large number of women and children during the evacuation of

The *Narkunda* and her sister ship *Naldera* were the first P&O liners to have three funnels.

The first-class cabins on the *Narkunda* had en suite bathrooms.

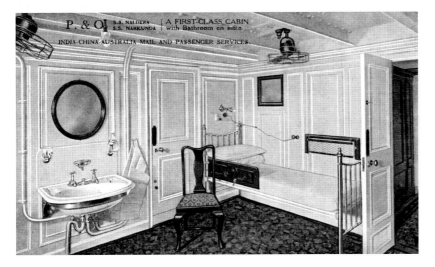

Singapore. Later in August the same year, the ship was required to repatriate British diplomats from Lourenço Marques, Mozambique, following an exchange with the Japanese. After arriving safely in Liverpool on 9 October, the *Narkunda* made for the Clyde to embark troops for the second Operation Torch invasion force.

On 1 November 1942 the *Narkunda* sailed for Algeria under the command of Captain Lewis Parfitt, in convoy KMF.2, which also included the P&O ships *Stratheden* (1) and *Strathmore* (1). The *Narkunda* arrived in Algiers on 12 November where the first of the troops disembarked. The ship then made for Bougie, where she arrived on the morning of 14 November. After spending the day transferring the remaining troops and stores ashore the ship sailed for home at 4 p.m.

Within an hour the *Narkunda* came under sustained bombardment from German Junkers Ju 88 aircraft. By 6.30 p.m. the ship had been abandoned and sank by the stern twelve minutes later.

The Italian submarine *Platino* (Roberto Rigoli) claimed to have damaged the *Narkunda* with one of four torpedoes fired at the merchant ship on 13 November at 3.26 a.m. Many sources also state that thirty-one crew lost their lives on the *Narkunda*, but only six crew members are listed in the Commonwealth War Graves Commission records: one European and five Indians. The survivors were picked up by HMS *Cadmus* and transferred to *Stratheden* (1) and the Orient Line *Ormonde* for repatriation to Britain. The *Narkunda* was the third P&O vessel to be lost during Operation Torch.

Diving the Wreck

The *Narkunda* is by far the largest P&O wreck to have been visited by scuba divers, a statistic that is immediately apparent when diving the wreck. Local divers had been aware for some time of the presence of a big wreck lying in a depth of 30m a short distance out from Boulimat on the Algerian coast, but the wreck was only formally identified as the *Narkunda* in 2011 following an extensive research expedition.

Despite the violent circumstances of the *Narkunda*'s demise, huge sections of the hull remain intact and tower above the flat, sandy seabed below. The water is the typical clear blue of the Mediterranean, allowing plenty of natural light to filter down through the wreckage. Much of the hull is adorned with marine growth and white sea fans, although the fish life is relatively sparse. There are many areas where it is possible to safely penetrate the wreck and explore the cavernous interiors but care needs to be taken not to stir up the thick layers of silt. The outline of the wreck has been distorted by the bomb damage and there are places where large hull plates lie flat across the wreck. Some of these still have some very substantial-looking portholes attached.

– *Ettrick* –

1938–1942, Atlantic

Ettrick (11,279 tons) was built for P&O by Barclay, Curle & Co., Glasgow, and launched on 25 August 1938. The length was 496.5ft (151.3m) and beam 63.2ft (19.3m). Twin screws were powered by two five-cylinder engines, giving a service speed of 20 knots. There was accommodation for 104 first- and ninety second-class passengers, 1,150 troops and 164 army families.

The *Ettrick* was an unusual vessel in that she was purpose-built as a troopship for charter to the British government. The ship was the third in a quartet, preceded by *Dilwara* (1936) and *Dunera* (1937) for the British India Line, and completed with *Devonshire* (1939) for the Bibby Line. When not required by the government, the ships were typically used for cruising and educational purposes. The maiden voyage of the *Ettrick* sailed from Southampton on 13 January 1939, bound for the West Indies, carrying men of the King's Shropshire Light Infantry, accompanied by their wives and children.

The *Ettrick* was kept busy with a variety of wartime duties. In May 1940 the ship was sent empty from Gibraltar to evacuate 250 refugees from Bordeaux to the Clyde. The following month *Ettrick* was sent to Saint Nazaire but, upon learning that the town had fallen to the Germans, was diverted to Bayonne. Upon arrival in Bayonne on 22 June 1940 the ship managed to evacuate 2,000 people from Saint-Jean-de-Luz for repatriation to Plymouth. Captain John Legg, master of the *Ettrick*, was later awarded with the Cross of Valour in recognition of the large number of Polish troops that were taken on board.

On 26 October 1942 *Ettrick* was one of five P&O vessels to sail from the Clyde as part of convoy KMF.1 for the Operation Torch landings in North Africa. The ship reached Arzeu on 8 November and, after safely landing all her troops, made for Gibraltar, from where she

The *Ettrick* was purpose-built in 1938 as a troopship for charter to the British government. (Bert Moody)

sailed on 14 November in convoy MKF.1Y for the return voyage to the Clyde. In the early hours of the following morning the convoy came under attack from *U-155* (Adolf Cornelius Piening), during which the *Ettrick* and the escort HMS *Avenger* were both fatally struck. A resulting munitions explosion caused HMS *Avenger* to sink within just two minutes and over 500 lives were lost, leaving just a small number of survivors. The *Ettrick* lost six crew and eighteen naval ratings but Captain Legg survived and was decorated with an OBE the following year. The survivors were picked up by the Norwegian destroyer *Glaisdale* and taken to Gibraltar, from where they were transferred to the *Mooltan* (3) for repatriation to the UK.

The *Ettrick* was the fourth P&O vessel to be lost in Operation Torch and the fifth ship to be sunk within the space of two weeks.

– *Strathallan* –

1938–1942, Mediterranean Sea

Strathallan (23,722 tons) was built for P&O by Vickers-Armstrongs, Barrow, and launched by the Countess of Cromer on 23 September 1937. The length was 639.5ft (194.9m) and beam 82.2ft (25.1m). Twin screws were powered by six single-reduction-geared steam turbines, giving a service speed of 21 knots. There was accommodation for 448 first- and 563 tourist-class passengers, with a crew of 519.

The *Strathallan* was the final vessel in a group of five new 22,500-ton passenger liners and followed *Strathnaver* (1) (1931),

The *Strathallan* was the last of the five Strath liners built in the 1930s and the only one lost during the Second World War. (Allan C. Green/ State Library of Victoria)

Strathaird (1) (1932), Strathmore (1) (1935) and Stratheden (1) (1937). All five vessels marked a departure from the traditional P&O livery, as they were painted with white hulls and buff funnels, earning them the nickname 'White Sisters'.

The maiden voyage of the Strathallan sailed from Tilbury for Brisbane on 18 March 1938, after which the ship spent the summer months cruising to the Mediterranean and Norway. The next trip to Australia sailed in September and incorporated a call at the Cocos Islands on the return voyage. In 1939 the Strathallan made three round-trip voyages to Australia, the first of which featured a cruise from Sydney to New Zealand and the second a cruise from Brisbane to Fiji. After the outbreak of the Second World War the Strathallan continued to make passenger sailings and it was not until February 1940 that she was requisitioned for service as a troopship.

Captain John Henry Biggs had been the regular master of the Strathallan since the vessel first came into service and he was in command when the ship was ordered to the Clyde in October 1942 to take part in Operation Torch. On 14 November the Strathallan joined her elder sister Strathaird (1), along with many other merchant vessels in convoy KMF.3, bound for Algiers. After successfully landing 4,636 troops, Strathallan returned safely to the Clyde and sailed again on 12 December in convoy KMF.5 with a complement of 5,122, which included 296 British and American nurses. The ship arrived at Gibraltar on 20 December, where the convoy split in two, with Strathallan continuing in KMF.5A for Algiers.

Above: Following the torpedo attack in December 1942 by *U-562* the *Strathallan* was taken in tow by a navy vessel. (Mick Lindsay)

Right: After an uncontrollable fire broke out on the *Strathallan* all further hopes of saving the vessel had to be abandoned. (Mick Lindsay)

In the early hours of 21 December the *Strathallan* was about 40 miles north of Oran when the convoy came under attack from *U-562* (Horst Hamm). A spread of four torpedoes were fired, one of which struck the *Strathallan* on the port side in the engine room, resulting in an explosion which killed two third-engineer officers and several Indian crew. All power was lost, the lights went out and the ship soon listed 15 degrees to port. Captain Biggs ordered the alarm to be sounded for 'boat stations' and the troops and nurses calmly made their way up on deck, guided by emergency lighting. Fortunately the sea remained smooth and it wasn't long before most of the lifeboats were away. An inspection of the watertight bulkheads revealed that only one had been breached, and with the pumps working effectively, the ship did not seem likely to sink very quickly. Consequently, Captain Biggs halted the evacuation and ordered all the remaining troops to the starboard side of the liner, which helped stabilise the list.

At 6 a.m. HMS *Laforery* managed to secure a line to the *Strathallan* and the destroyer commenced a slow tow towards Oran. Meanwhile, around 1,300 survivors in the boats were picked up by HMS *Verity*. Since there were still several thousand people remaining on board, HMS *Lightning*, HMS *Panther* and HMS *Pathfinder* all assisted with taking them off, and by 2 p.m. the disembarkation was complete. Just as it was beginning to look as though the *Strathallan* might make it to Oran, flames were seen shooting high out of the funnel and an inspection quickly revealed that oil fuel had come into contact with the hot boilers, igniting a fire. The fire pumps were started, the tug HMS *Restive* came alongside with her fire hoses and the ammunition was discharged overboard, but the blaze proved impossible to contain. All the remaining crew were transferred to HMS *Laforery* and the tow was taken up by HMS *Restive*, but at 4 a.m. on 22 December the *Strathallan* finally succumbed and sank 12 miles short of Oran.

Witness reports vary as to the total number of lives lost. In addition to six crew members it appears that around a dozen nurses and troops also perished, but since there were over 5,000 souls on board the tragedy could have been a lot worse. Captain John Biggs was later awarded the CBE and the Lloyd's War Medal for Bravery at Sea for his actions. The *Strathallan* was the second largest vessel to be sunk by a German submarine in the Second World War (the 42,348-ton Canadian Pacific *Empress of Britain* being the largest) and the fifth and final P&O vessel to be lost during Operation Torch.

– *Shillong* (1) –

1939–1943, North Atlantic

Shillong (1) (5,529 tons) was a general-cargo liner built for P&O by Alexander Stephen & Sons, Glasgow, and launched on 11 August 1938. The length was 442.2ft (134.7m) and beam 57.9ft (17.6m). A single screw was powered by a four-cylinder diesel engine, giving a service speed of 12 knots.

The *Shillong* (1) was delivered to P&O in February 1939 and followed an identical sister ship *Surat* (2), which had been completed by the same yard a few months earlier. Both vessels were deployed on the London–Calcutta service, with the *Shillong* (1) making her first sailing from London on 12 March 1939.

On 25 March 1943 the *Shillong* (1) sailed from New York for Liverpool in Atlantic convoy HX.231 under the command of Captain James Hollow, with a cargo consisting mainly of zinc concentrates and grain. The convoy's northerly route carried the *Shillong* (1) into cold and heavy weather, which was severe enough to cause extensive icing on the ship's upper works, resulting in damage to the mast, davits and boats. Captain Hollow was therefore forced to haul the *Shillong* (1) out of line while temporary repairs were carried out, but the ship was later able to resume her station in the convoy.

Late in the evening of 4 April, while south-east of Greenland, the convoy came under attack from enemy submarines, which resulted in the *Shillong* (1) being struck by a torpedo fired from *U-635* (Heinz Eckelmann). With the ship rapidly sinking by the head in stormy weather, the crew struggled to abandon ship, but eventually managed to get away in a raft and lifeboat No. 3. A few hours later the *Shillong* (1) was sent to the bottom by a second torpedo from *U-630* (Werner Winkler).

Worse was yet to come for the surviving officers and crew of the *Shillong* (1). Captain Hollow along with over twenty other men on the packed life raft struggled bravely in the mountainous seas, which frequently swamped them, causing the raft to overturn multiple times. Less than half the men managed to cling on and of those the captain, chief officer and two others all died during the bitterly cold night. When daylight broke, the raft was found by the *Shillong* (1)'s lifeboat, which transferred the remaining few men. Overnight the lifeboat had been able to communicate with one of the escort destroyers, which had promised to return to pick them up, but no help came.

The general-cargo liner *Shillong* (1) was delivered to P&O in February 1939 and torpedoed in the North Atlantic in April 1943. (World Ship Society Photo Library)

Thirty-eight men from the *Shillong* (1)'s crew of seventy-eight now remained huddled together in one solitary lifeboat, abandoned and struggling in the freezing North Atlantic weather. Their difficulties were further compounded by flotsam from the wreck which threatened to stove-in their boat. Third Engineer William MacRae valiantly fought to fend off the wreckage with a boathook, and although they eventually managed to pull clear of the danger, the exertions proved too much and MacRae passed away soon afterwards. The cold and damp took a heavy toll on all the men, but it was particularly harsh for the lascar seamen, who were the most severely affected by it. As the days passed with fading hopes of rescue and dwindling supplies of water and provisions, more and more men perished. By the fourth day the weather had begun to moderate a little but it was still a constant struggle to man the oars and bail the boat. Four days later, the lifeboat was finally sighted by a Catalina aircraft but the crew still had to brave one last night before finally being picked up by the diverted convoy ON.177 rescue vessel *Zamalek*. Only two cadets and five DEMS gunners survived the ordeal, but all suffered badly from the effects of frostbite and gangrene. It was so bad that three men required amputation of both legs and another of both feet, leaving just three with all limbs intact.

– *Peshawur* (3) –

1919–1943, Indian Ocean

Peshawur (3) (7,943 tons) was a standard G-class refrigerated cargo liner, built for the Shipping Controller by Barclay, Curle & Co., Glasgow, and launched as *War Diane* on 26 June 1919. The ship was purchased by P&O and renamed prior to completion. The length was 449.5ft (137m) and beam 58.2ft (17.7m). Twin screws were powered by triple-expansion three-cylinder engines, giving a service speed of 13 knots. There was limited accommodation for twelve passengers.

In December 1922 the *Peshawur* (3) was chartered to the Federal Steam Navigation Company and spent the next twelve years importing Australian meat to the UK.

On 19 December 1943 *Peshawur* (3) sailed from Colombo for Calcutta under the command of Captain J.C. Mellonie, in convoy JC.30, along with seventeen other merchant vessels but no escorts. The voyage had originated from Swansea and the ship was carrying a cargo of government stores that included tin plate, explosives and bleaching powder. On 23 December the *Peshawur* (3) was sunk off the east coast of India by an unseen, wakeless torpedo fired from the Japanese submarine *RO-111* (Nakamura Naozo). Captain Mellonie and all hands were able to make it into the lifeboats before the ship sank two hours later. They were soon rescued by the Australian minesweeper HMAS *Ipswich* and landed at Madras the next morning.

The *Peshawur* (3) was the last P&O vessel to be lost during the Second World War.

The refrigerated cargo liner *Peshawur* (3) was sunk by the Japanese submarine *RO-111* in December 1943 and was the last P&O loss of the Second World War. (Bert Moody)

– *Tresillian* –

1944–1954, Celtic Sea

The general-cargo liner *Tresillian* (7,373 tons) was built as *Registan* for the Strick Line by William Doxford & Sons, Sunderland, and launched on 9 August 1944. The length was 431ft (131.4m) and beam 56.5ft (17.2m). A single screw was powered by two three-cylinder diesel engines, giving a service speed of 11 knots.

In July 1945 *Registan* was sold to the Hain Steamship Company, which had become a wholly owned subsidiary of P&O in 1917, following the death of Sir Edward Hain. In January the following year the vessel was renamed *Tresillian* and the ship was often used by P&O as replacement tonnage on their cargo liner services. In 1951 the ownership of the *Tresillian* was transferred to P&O, but the operation and management remained under Hain Steamship Company.

The last voyage of the *Tresillian* sailed from Urangan, Queensland, on 28 August 1954 under the command of Captain W.J. Winter. After calling at Suva in September, the ship proceeded to Canada, sailing from Sorel on 17 November for the final leg of the voyage to the UK, carrying a cargo consisting of 7,350 tons of barley and 2,000 tons of wheat. The weather remained normal for the Atlantic crossing but it rapidly deteriorated on 29 November when the vessel was 44 miles off the south coast of Ireland. By the evening the winds had reached gale force 10, with squalls up to force 12, and the *Tresillian* took on a heavy list to port. Captain Winter turned

the ship about to face the head into the sea but the list increased to such an extent that water soon came rushing in. An SOS distress call was sent at 5.51 a.m. and the crew prepared to abandon ship. Both port boats were found to have been washed away in the storm and one of the starboard boats broke away while it was being lowered, so the men ended up taking to the water in their lifejackets. Thirteen men were rescued by the tanker *Liparus* and another four by the *Ardglen*. Although many other ships assisted in the search for survivors no more where found and a total of twenty-four lives from the crew of forty were lost, including Captain Winter who died soon after being rescued.

Although owned by P&O, the *Tresillian* was operated by the Hain Steamship Company. (Bert Moody)

– *Shillong* (2) –

1949–1957, Red Sea

The general-cargo liner *Shillong* (2) (8,934 tons) was built for P&O by Vickers-Armstrongs, Newcastle, and launched on 9 June 1948. The length was 497.7ft (151.7m) and beam 67.3ft (20.5m). A single screw was powered by three geared steam turbines, giving a service speed of 17 knots. There was accommodation for twelve passengers and the crew numbered eighty-seven. The ship was delivered to P&O in March 1949 and employed on services to the Far East.

On 7 October 1957 the *Shillong* (2) sailed from Southampton bound for the ports of Penang, Port Swettenham, Singapore, Manila, Hong Kong, Japan and China. The ship was fully loaded with 11,700 tons of general cargo that included beer, whisky, gin, motor parts and Christmas toys. Additional cargo consisting of heavy machinery, cranes and JCBs was secured on the open decks. Most precious of all were fifteen racehorses, two of which were the highly valued thoroughbreds Donati and My Guinness, both of which had won races in England. There were six passengers on board and the ship was under the command of Captain Eric Spurling, an experienced master with over thirty years' service at P&O.

The cargo liner *Shillong* (2) sank in the Red Sea following a collision with the *Purfina Congo* on 22 October 1957. It was the last shipwreck in the history of P&O. (Newall Dunn Collection)

En route the *Shillong* (2) called at Almeria where she took on a cargo of grapes. After making one further Mediterranean call at Genoa the ship proceeded to Port Said and commenced the southbound transit through the Suez Canal. By the afternoon of 22 October the *Shillong* (2) had cleared the canal and was making her way steadily down through the Gulf of Suez. It was a warm, clear and starlit night when the watch changed over at 8 p.m. The course was set for Ras Gharib light, and Captain Spurling had left instructions with the officer of the watch to call him when the ship reached the light, which was still about 40 miles ahead. When the flashing light of Ras Gharib came into view shortly after 10 p.m. the shipping lanes were still very busy and the *Shillong* (2) was surrounded by other vessels on all sides.

Two ships were approaching from the south and were observed off the port bow with their green starboard lights clearly showing. In accordance with the International Regulations for Preventing Collisions at Sea, this made the northbound ships the 'give way' vessels and the *Shillong* (2) the 'stand on' vessel. As such, it was the duty of both approaching vessels to keep clear while the *Shillong* (2) maintained her course and speed. Accordingly, the second officer on watch had no immediate cause for concern. Meanwhile, the passengers were still up on deck enjoying a late-night singsong under the stars, oblivious to the events that were unfolding.

One of the approaching ships eventually altered course and crossed to the *Shillong* (2)'s starboard bow, but the other vessel still did not show any sign of changing course. The distance was now reduced to just 3 miles and the second officer became increasingly anxious. With a collision now seeming imminent he ordered the helm hard over starboard. The approaching vessel should have taken the same action, but instead also altered course to port, making a collision inevitable.

The engines were ordered full-astern, but it was too late; the bow of the Belgian tanker *Purfina Congo* (11,134 tons) pierced deep into the port side of the *Shillong* (2) and ripped a gaping hole in the hull 30m wide. Water flooded into the engine room, causing the ship to take on an alarming 30-degree list. Much of the officer accommodation was destroyed by the impact and Chief Steward Jack French was killed instantly whilst still asleep. One of the cadets, 18-year-old Derek Palmer, was also killed, but two other cadets miraculously escaped from their wrecked cabin.

Captain Spurling gave the order to abandon ship but the starboard boats were rendered useless due to the list and one of the port boats had been smashed. While the crew struggled to release the remaining boat, which was jammed due to a bent davit, Third Officer Miller was sent to prepare the inflatable dinghy for the passengers. One elderly passenger with an artificial leg found it impossible to make his way up the sloping deck so he had to remove the prosthetic and jump into the water. The jammed boat was eventually released, but when Pakistani fireman Fakir Khosia leaped in he was crushed against the ship's side and died from his injuries soon after. As the *Shillong* (2) settled deeper into the water the list began to decrease a little, allowing one of the starboard boats to be lowered. All the remaining crew got off safely and the captain was the last to leave the ship, which sank stern first shortly after midnight, along with all the horses.

The occupants of the dinghy were transferred to one of the lifeboats and it wasn't long before the survivors were able to signal the attention of the Danish tanker *Skotland*. They were all well cared for by the crew, who supplied them with hot coffee, food and warm blankets before landing them at Suez. The passengers were unanimous in their praise for how the shipwreck was handled by Captain Spurling and his crew, European and Asian alike.

Two months after the loss of the *Shillong* (2), Captain Spurling took command of the *Socotra* (2) but retired from the sea in July the following year to take up a position within P&O as nautical inspector, a post he held until his retirement in 1969, after forty-six years with the company.

The *Shillong* (2) was the last vessel to be wrecked in the history of the Peninsular and Oriental Steam Navigation Company.

SHIPWRECKS POST P&O OWNERSHIP

The following vessels were lost after they had been sold by the Peninsular and Oriental Steam Navigation Company.

– Adria –

Adria (1873, 1,225 tons), single-screw general-cargo liner. Sold to Hajee Cassum Joosub of Bombay in 1881. Wrecked on 6 May 1886 off Pemba Island, Tanzania.

– Alhambra –

Alhambra (1855, 730 tons), single-screw passenger liner. Sold in 1862 and underwent three further ownership changes between 1882 and 1884, the last recorded owner being Aaron Wheeler Junior of Sydney. On 30 June 1888 the *Alhambra* was wrecked off Port Stephens, New South Wales, after striking a derelict vessel.

– Ancona –

Ancona (1879, 3,081 tons), single-screw passenger liner. Sold to Hajee Cassum Joosub of Bombay in 1899 and renamed *Taher*. Wrecked on 22 March 1901 near Port Louis, Mauritius, while on charter to P&O.

– Azof –

Azof (1855, 700 tons), single-screw passenger/cargo liner. Sold in 1871 to new owners in Hong Kong. Wrecked 1 November 1871 off Amoy.

– Bangalore –

Bangalore (1867, 2,063 tons), single-screw passenger liner. Sold to Hajee Cassum Joosub of Bombay in 1886 and sold again several more times, the last to Norwegian owners in 1891 who renamed the ship *Coringa*. Foundered off the Azores on 18 March 1905 while on passage to Halifax.

– Bengal (1) –

Bengal (1) (1853, 2,185 tons), single-screw iron passenger liner. Sold in 1870 and subsequently underwent multiple ownership changes, the last in 1884 to Gellatly, Hankey, Sewell and Co. of London. Wrecked on 2 March 1885 off Milton Reef, Bawcan Island, Java.

– Bombay (2) –

Bombay (2) (1852, 1,186 tons), single-screw iron passenger liner. Sold in 1878 to Hong Kong owners. Destroyed by fire off Woosung on 24 December 1880 and subsequently had to be scrapped.

– Bulan –

Bulan (1924, 1,048 tons), general-cargo ship. Sold in 1952 to Hong Kong owners and renamed *Sunon*. Sold again in 1958 and once more in 1960 to Kum Luei Ltd SA, Panama. Wrecked on 15 July 1961 off Britto Bank during a voyage from Phnom Penh to Hong Kong.

– Ceylon (2) –

Ceylon (2) (1894, 4,094 tons), single-screw passenger/cargo liner. Sold in 1913 and underwent numerous further owner and name changes, the last of which was to the French government in 1916 when the vessel was renamed *Depute Pierre Goujon*. Torpedoed by *U 103* on 12 December 1917 off Belle Île.

– Deccan –

Deccan (1868, 3,128 tons), single-screw iron passenger liner. Sold in 1889 to Hajee Cassum Joosub of Bombay. Sailed from Mauritius for Bombay on 9 February 1892 and disappeared without trace.

– Delta (3) –

Delta (3) (1859, 1,618 tons), iron paddle steamer. Sold to the Japanese government in 1874. Sold again in 1875 and renamed *Takasago Maru*, then again in 1898 to American owners who renamed the ship *Centennial*. Captured by Japanese forces in 1905 and disappeared after sailing from Muroran for San Francisco on 24 February 1906. Wreck reportedly found locked in ice north of Sakhalin in 1913.

– Emeu –

Emeu (1854, 1,538 tons), single-screw iron passenger liner. Sold at auction to William McArthur of London in 1873 and subsequently had numerous London owners, one of whom renamed the ship *Winchester*. Final sale to G. Crowshaw in 1879. Lost in the Makassar Strait on 14 July 1880.

– Euxine –

Euxine (1847, 1,165 tons), iron paddle steamer. Sold to Edward Bates of Liverpool in 1868 and reduced to a sailing vessel. Destroyed by fire in the South Atlantic on 5 August 1874. Although two lifeboats landed safely at St Helena, a third became separated and the occupants had resorted to cannibalism by the time of their rescue by a passing ship.

– Frodingham –

Frodingham (1914, 1,081 tons), general-cargo liner. Originally launched as *Gyula* for French owners, then purchased and renamed by P&O in 1915. Sold in 1923 to Neville Shipping Co. and renamed *Neville*. Foundered off the Runnelstone, Cornwall, on 1 April 1927.

– Geelong (1) –

Geelong (1) (1866, 1,584 tons), single-screw iron passenger/cargo liner. Sold in 1887 to Hajee Cassum Joosub of Bombay, then again in 1890 to Japanese owners and renamed *Ishizaki Maru*. Wrecked on 8 June 1891 while on a voyage from Otaru to Yokohama.

– Granada –

Granada (1857, 561 tons), single-screw iron passenger/cargo liner. Sold in 1866 to Prince of Hijo, Japan, and renamed *Ryoun Maru*. Sunk in 1870 after a collision with the steamer *Fusiyama* off Japan.

– Gwalior –

Gwalior (1873, 2,733 tons), single-screw iron passenger liner. Sold in 1894 to Japanese owners and renamed *Shinshu Maru*. Wrecked at Chemulpo on 2 March 1904 while serving as a transport during the Russo–Japanese War.

– Haddington –

Haddington (1846, 1,648 tons), iron paddle steamer, re-registered as a barque in 1854. Sold in 1870 to Thomas Haviside of London and underwent multiple further ownership changes, the last of which was Adolphus Kinnear of London in 1884. Lost following a fire at sea in the Bay of Bengal on 9 February 1888.

– Himalaya (1) –

Himalaya (1) (1854, 3,438 tons), single-screw iron passenger liner. Laid claim to be the largest ship in the world when launched. Sold to the government in July 1854 for use as a troopship after just six months in P&O service. After an eventful career the *Himalaya* (1) was placed in reserve in 1894 and reduced to HM *Hulk C60* at Devonport the following year. In 1920 the vessel was sold to Portland & Weymouth Coaling Company Ltd and towed to Portland. Wrecked in Portland Harbour on 4 July 1940 aftering being bombed by German aircraft. The wreck lies in 12m and is a popular habitat for lobsters.

– *Khedive* –

Khedive (1871, 3,742 tons), single-screw iron passenger liner. Sold to Duda, Abdullah & Co. of Bombay in 1896. Wrecked off Porbandar in the Arabian Sea on 11 January 1897, just five days after formal delivery from P&O.

– *Khiva* (1) –

Khiva (1) (1873, 2,609 tons), single-screw iron passenger liner. Sold in 1890 to Hajee Cassum Joosub of Bombay. Caught fire off Ras Marbet in the Red Sea on 17 April 1893 and although beached became a total loss.

– *Mata Hari* –

Mata Hari (1915, 1,020 tons), single-screw general-cargo liner. Entered service for British India but ownership transferred to P&O in 1924. Captured by Japanese forces on 15 February 1942, bombed and sunk, then refloated and commissioned as *Yumihara*. Transferred to Japanese civilian owners in December 1943 and renamed *Nichirin Maru*. Bombed by US aircraft in the East China Sea on 2 March 1943.

– *Mazagon* (3) –

Mazagon (3) (1894, 4,997 tons), single-screw collier. Sold to British India in 1907, then to Japanese owners in 1913 and renamed *Teikoku Maru*. After one further sale the ship was purchased by the French government in 1918 and renamed *Saint Nicholas*. Stranded near Bénodet while under tow on 18 December 1922, refloated and scrapped.

– *Mooltan* (1) –

Mooltan (1) (1861, 2,257 tons), single-screw iron passenger liner. Sold in 1880 to J. Ellis & Co. of Liverpool. After a third change of owner in 1884 the ship was renamed *Eleanor Margaret* then sold a final time to German owners in 1888. Disappeared without trace in the North Atlantic after sailing from Newcastle-upon-Tyne for Valparaíso on 28 June 1891.

– *Mutlah* –

Mutlah (1948, 6,652 tons), single-screw general-cargo liner, built for James Nourse. Transferred to P&O in June 1957 but reverted to James Nourse in September 1957. Sold to Zephyr Steamship Co. in 1963 and renamed *Delwind*. Wrecked on Bombay Reef 19 March 1965 and broken up in situ.

– *Nankin* (1) –

Nankin (1) (1888, 3,960 tons), single-screw passenger/cargo liner. Built as *Rufford Hall* for Sun Shipping Co. and purchased by P&O in 1898. Sold to Japanese owners in 1904 and renamed *Kotohira Maru No 2*. Wrecked in the Soya Strait on 12 September 1907.

– *Nankin* (2) –

Nankin (2) (1912, 6,853 tons), twin-screw passenger/cargo liner. Sold to Eastern and Australian Steam Navigation Co. in 1931. Captured by Germany in 1942 and renamed *Leuthen*. Destroyed by fire on 20 November 1942.

– *Narrung* –

Narrung (1896, 5,078 tons), single-screw passenger liner. Purchased from Blue Anchor Line in 1910. Sold to Mexico Steamship Co. in 1913 and renamed *Mexico City*. Torpedoed off Holyhead by *U 101* on 5 February 1918.

– Nellore –

Nellore (1913, 6,853 tons), twin-screw passenger/cargo liner. Sold to Eastern and Australian Steam Navigation Co. in 1929. Torpedoed by Japanese submarine *I8* in the Indian Ocean on 29 June 1944.

– Northam –

Northam (1858, 1,330 tons), single-screw iron passenger liner. Sold to C.A. Day & Co. in December 1868 who sold the ship on to the Union Steamship Co. in January 1869. Sold to Sir James Malcolm of Liverpool in 1876, reduced to a sailing ship and renamed *Stars and Stripes*. Caught fire in the South Atlantic on 21 December 1878 on a voyage from London to Sydney.

– Ottawa (1) –

Ottawa (1) (1854, 1,275 tons), single-screw iron passenger liner. Purchased from the Canadian Steam Navigation Co. in 1857. Sold in 1872 to R.W. Hutchinson of Hong Kong then again in 1873 to Peter Landberg & Sons of Batavia, who renamed the ship *Generaal van Swieten*. Scuttled by gunfire off Atjeh on 29 April 1881.

– Pekin (2) –

Pekin (2) (1871, 3,777 tons), single-screw iron passenger liner. Sold in 1897 to Hajee Cassum Joosub of Bombay and renamed *Jubedu*. Beached in the River Hooghly, India, on 16 September 1900 and broke in two.

– Pera (2) –

Pera (2) (1855, 2,014 tons), single-screw iron passenger liner. Sold to William Ross of London in 1880. Struck an iceberg 50 miles south-west of Cape Race on 11 June 1882.

– Peshawur (1) –

Peshawur (1) (1871, 3,782 tons), single-screw iron passenger liner. Sold to Hajee Cassum Joosub of Bombay in 1900 and renamed *Ashruf*. Wrecked in Tamatave Harbour entrance, Madagascar, on 8 May 1905.

– Rajah (1) –

Rajah (1) (1853, 537 tons), single-screw iron collier. Sold to R.D. Sassoon of Hong Kong in 1861, then to Shanghai owners in 1864 and finally to G. Elliot of London in 1865. Sank following a collision with *Hugh Streatfield* off Yarmouth on 6 June 1875.

– Ravenna –

Ravenna (1880, 3,340 tons), single-screw passenger liner. Sold to George Paget Walford of London in April 1898. Found abandoned off Newfoundland one month later with a cargo of munitions, seized by the United States and renamed *Scipio*. Sold in 1899 and again in 1900 to Italian owners. Caught fire in the Mediterranean on 3 March 1902.

– Ripon –

Ripon (1846, 1,508 tons), iron paddle steamer. Sold to Caird and Co. in 1870 who sold the ship to London owners the same year. Sold again in 1871 to George Turnbull and J.R. Greig of Glasgow. By 1880 the *Ripon* had been reduced to a hulk at Trinidad and was ultimately scuttled off Port of Spain.

– Rohilla –

Rohilla (1880, 3,511 tons), single-screw iron passenger liner. Sold in 1900 to Japanese owners and renamed *Rohilla Maru*. Purchased by the Japanese government in 1904, who sold the ship to Toyo Kisen KK in 1905. Wrecked at Ujina in the Inland Sea of Japan on 7 July 1905.

– *Shanghai* (1) –

Shanghai (1) (1851, 546 tons), single-screw iron passenger/cargo liner. Sold to John Dickinson of London in 1862 then underwent numerous ownership and name changes. Sold for the final time in 1872 to the Pacific Mail Steamship Co. and renamed *Relief*. Wrecked near Nagasaki in January 1874.

– *Simla* (1) –

Simla (1) (1854, 2,441 tons), single-screw iron passenger liner. Sold to J. Howden & Co., Glasgow, in 1875, then to E.L. Alexander & Co. in 1877. Reduced to sail in 1878 and sold to Devitt & Moore of London in 1882. Collided with the *City of Lucknow* off the Isle of Wight on 25 January 1884 while outward-bound from London to Sydney, Australia. The wreck lies in a depth of 40m and interesting items from the general cargo are often found by divers.

– *Sumatra* (1) –

Sumatra (1) (1867, 2,202 tons), single-screw iron passenger liner. Sold to Hajee Cassum Joosub of Bombay in 1886. Sold again in 1888 and finally to James R. Brady of Belfast in 1889. Destroyed by fire in the Mediterranean on 4 March 1889.

– *Sumatra* (2) –

Sumatra (2) (1895, 4,607 tons), single-screw passenger/cargo liner. Sold to Arab Steamers in 1914 then a year later to Portuguese owners and renamed *Mossamedes*. In 1918 ownership was transferred to Cia. Nacional de Navegação, Portugal. Wrecked at Cape Fria on the coast of south-west Africa on 24 April 1923.

– *Sunda* (2) –

Sunda (2) (1895, 4,674 tons), single-screw passenger/cargo liner. Sold in 1914 to Minami Manshu Kisen KK, Japan, and renamed *Hokoku Maru*. Sailed from Singapore on 22 December 1915 bound for the UK but never heard of again.

– *Syria* (1) –

Syria (1) (1863, 1,932 tons), iron paddle steamer. Sold to Caird & Co. in 1870 who sold the ship to the Union Steamship Co. a few months later. Sold again to J. Laing of Sunderland in 1878. Abandoned in the Atlantic on 4 April 1880 after being badly damaged in a storm.

– *Teheran* –

Teheran (1874, 2,589 tons), single-screw iron passenger liner, converted to cargo in 1889. Sold to Chuyetsu Kisen Kabushiki Kaisha of Japan in 1894 and renamed *Toyei Maru*. Wrecked at the entrance to Ujina Harbour, Japan, on 3 November 1905.

– *Tientsin* –

Tientsin (1888, 3,950 tons), single-screw passenger/cargo liner. Completed as *Branksome Hall* for Sun Shipping Co. and purchased by P&O in 1898. Sold to Shah Steam Navigation of India in 1906 and renamed *Shah Nasir*. In 1909 transferred to Bombay and Hujaz Steam Navigation Co. of India and renamed *Fakhri*. Wrecked at Perim in the Red Sea on 20 December 1911.

– *Trevean* –

Trevean (1945, 7,308 tons), single-screw cargo liner. Completed as *Empire Tilbury* for the Ministry of War Transport, sold to Hain Steamship Co. in 1946 and renamed *Trevean*. Ownership briefly transferred to P&O in 1957 before reverting once more to Hain. Sold to Willow Shipping Company in 1963 and renamed *Kawana* the following year. Beached near Chittagong on 4 June 1966 following a fire.

APPENDIX 2

WRECK DIVES

Divers contemplating diving any of the P&O wrecks are strongly encouraged to contact local dive operators and clubs for further advice, and to consult any specialised books and publications that cover the area and wrecks, a selection of which can be found listed in the bibliography.

For the latest information on the wrecks, maps, links to websites and details of any new discoveries please refer to the companion website, www.linerwrecks.com.

Name	Location	Depth (m)	Notes
Alma	Hanish Islands, Red Sea	10 (est.)	
Australia (2)	Port Phillip, Australia	8	Very tidal
Ava	Trincomalee, Sri Lanka	12	Known locally as the 'Irrakandy Shipwreck'
Ballarat (1)	Lizard, Cornwall, England	73	
Candia (2)	Sussex, England	45	
Carnatic	Sha'ab Abu Nuhâs, Red Sea, Egypt	27	
Don Juan	Tarifa, Spain	32	Known locally as 'San Andrés'
Egypt	Ushant, France	130	Specialist technical dive
Eston	Tyneside, England	24	
Great Liverpool	Gures Beach, Finisterre, Spain	7	Archaeologically sensitive
Indus (2)	Muliative, Sri Lanka	10	Archaeologically sensitive
Maloja (1)	Dover, Kent, England	21	
Medina	Devon, England	60	
Moldavia (1)	English Channel	50	

Name	Location	Depth (m)	Notes
Narkunda	Algeria, Mediterranean	30	
Nepaul (2)	Plymouth, England	13	Very little remains, covered in kelp most of year
Oceana	Sussex, England	25	
Peshawur (2)	Irish Sea	58	
Rangoon	Point de Galle, Sri Lanka	32	
Salsette (2)	Lyme Bay, Dorset, England	45	
Sobraon	Tung Ying Island, Taiwan	30	Restricted access
Socotra (1)	Le Touquet, France	1	Can be visited by foot during extreme low tides
Somali (2)	Farne Islands, England	28	
Tasmania	Des Moines, Corsica	10	Diving currently prohibited
Tiber	Oporto, Portugal	33	Also known as '*Navio do Norte*' or 'North Wreck'
Travancore	Castro Bay, Otranto, Italy	15	

APPENDIX 3

FLEET LIST

This fleet list covers all ocean-going vessels that at one time belonged in the Peninsular and Oriental Steam Navigation Company fleet, commencing in 1837 and ending with *Canberra* in 1961.

Ship	Built	Tonnage	Fate	Note
Achilles	1839	820	Scrapped	
Aden (1)	1856	812	Hulk	Launched as *Delta* (2)
Aden (2)	1892	3,925	Wrecked	
Adria	1873	1,225	Wrecked	Sold 1881
Alhambra	1855	642	Wrecked	Sold 1862
Alipore	1920	5,273	Torpedoed (*U-516*)	
Alma	1855	2,165	Wrecked	Launched as *Pera* (1)
Ancona	1879	3,081	Wrecked	Sold 1899
Arabia	1898	7,903	Torpedoed (*UB 43*)	
Arcadia (1)	1888	6,603	Scrapped	
Arcadia (2)	1954	29,734	Scrapped	
Ariel	1846	709	Wrecked	
Assam	1873	3,033	Scrapped	
Assaye	1899	7,396	Scrapped	
Australia (1)	1870	3,648	Scrapped	Sold 1889
Australia (2)	1892	6,901	Wrecked	
Ava	1855	1,613	Wrecked	
Avoca	1866	1,482	Scrapped	Sold 1882
Azof	1855	700	Wrecked	Sold 1871
Ballaarat	1882	4,764	Scrapped	

Ship	Built	Tonnage	Fate	Note
Ballarat (1)	1911	11,120	Torpedoed (*UB 32*)	
Ballarat (2)	1921	13,033	Scrapped	
Ballarat (3)	1954	8,792	Scrapped	Renamed *Pando Cape* in 1968. Sold 1972
Balranald (1)	1922	13,039	Scrapped	
Banca	1900	5,995	Scrapped	Sold 1923
Bangalore	1867	2,063	Wrecked	Sold 1886
Baradine (1)	1921	13,144	Scrapped	
Baroda	1864	1,874	Scrapped	
Barrabool	1922	13,148	Scrapped	
Behar	1855	1,603	Scrapped	Sold 1874
Beltana	1912	11,120	Scrapped	Sold 1930
Benalla	1913	11,118	Scrapped	
Benares	1858	1,491	Wrecked	
Bendigo (1)	1922	13,039	Scrapped	
Bendigo (2)	1954	8,782	Scrapped	Renamed *Pando Sound* in 1968
Bengal (1)	1853	2,185	Wrecked	Sold 1870
Bengal (2)	1885	4,499	Scrapped	Sold 1906
Bentinck	1843	1,975	Unknown	Sold 1860
Berrima	1913	11,137	Scrapped	
Bokhara	1873	2,932	Wrecked	
Bombay (1)	1849	1,194	Unknown	Sold 1851
Bombay (2)	1852	1,186	Fire/Hulked	Sold 1878

Ship	Built	Tonnage	Fate	Note
Bombay (3)	1889	3,168	Scrapped	Sold 1903
Borda	1914	11,136	Scrapped	
Borneo	1895	4,573	Scrapped	Sold 1914
Braganza	1836	688	Scrapped	
Brindisi	1880	3,553	Scrapped	Sold 1899
Britannia	1887	6,525	Scrapped	
Bulan	1924	1,048	Wrecked	Sold 1952
Cadiz	1853	816	Scrapped	Sold 1870
Caledonia	1894	7,558	Scrapped	
Canberra	1961	45,733	Scrapped	
Candia (1)	1854	1,961	Scrapped	
Candia (2)	1896	6,482	Torpedoed (*UC 65*)	
Cannanore	1949	7,065	Scrapped	
Canton (1)	1848	348	Wrecked	
Canton (2)	1889	3,171	Scrapped	Sold 1903
Canton (3)	1938	15,784	Scrapped	
Carnatic	1863	2,014	Wrecked	
Carthage (1)	1881	5,013	Scrapped	
Carthage (2)	1931	14,304	Scrapped	
Cathay (1)	1872	2,983	Scrapped	Sold 1895
Cathay (2)	1925	15,104	Bombed	
Cathay (3)	1957	13,809	Scrapped	Sold 1976
Ceylon (1)	1858	2,110	Scrapped	Sold 1881
Ceylon (2)	1894	4,094	Torpedoed (*U 103*)	Sold 1913
China (1)	1856	2,009	Scrapped	Sold 1882
China (2)	1896	7,899	Scrapped	
Chitral (1)	1925	15,248	Scrapped	
Chitral (2)	1956	13,821	Scrapped	
Chusan (1)	1852	700	Hulk	Sold 1861
Chusan (2)	1884	4,636	Scrapped	Sold 1906
Chusan (3)	1950	24,215	Scrapped	
City of Londonderry	1827	319	Scrapped	

Ship	Built	Tonnage	Fate	Note
Clyde	1881	4,136	Scrapped	Sold 1901
Colombo	1853	1,865	Wrecked	
Columbian	1855	2,180	Scrapped	Sold 1877
Commonwealth	1902	6,616	Scrapped	
Comorin (1)	1925	15,116	Fire	
Comorin (2)				See *Singapore* (2)
Corea	1864	610	Wrecked	
Corfu	1931	14,293	Scrapped	
Coromandel (1)	1885	4,499	Scrapped	Sold 1906
Coromandel (2)	1949	7,065	Scrapped	Sold 1969
Deccan	1868	3,128	Wrecked	Sold 1889
Delhi (1)				See *Nemesis*
Delhi (2)	1864	2,178	Scrapped	Sold 1881
Delhi (3)	1905	8,090	Wrecked	
Delta (2)				See *Aden* (1). *Delta* (1) was a River Steamer
Delta (3)	1859	1,618	Wrecked	Sold 1874
Delta (4)	1905	8,089	Scrapped	
Devanha (1)	1906	8,092	Scrapped	
Devanha (2)	1947	7,367	Scrapped	Sold 1961
Don Juan	1837	932	Wrecked	First P&O shipwreck
Dongola (1)	1905	8,038	Scrapped	
Dongola (2)	1946	7,371	Scrapped	Sold 1961
Douro	1853	810	Wrecked	
Egypt	1897	7,912	Wrecked	
Ellora	1855	1,574	Hulked	Sold 1876
Emeu	1854	1,538	Wrecked	Sold 1873
Erin	1846	798	Wrecked	
Essex (1)	1936	11,063	Scrapped	Renamed *Paringa* in 1946
Eston	1919	1,487	Mined (*U-22*)	
Ettrick	1938	11,279	Torpedoed (*U-155*)	
Euxine	1847	1,165	Wrecked	Sold 1868
Faid Rabany	1852	274	Unknown	Sold 1853

Ship	Built	Tonnage	Fate	Note
Formosa (1)	1852	637	Unknown	Sold 1870
Formosa (2)	1892	4,045	Scrapped	
Frederick VI	1785	755	Wrecked	
Frodingham	1914	1,081	Wrecked	Sold 1923
Ganges (1)	1849	1,285	Unknown	Sold before completion
Ganges (2)	1850	1,189	Hulked	Sold 1871
Ganges (3)	1882	4,196	Wrecked/ Scrapped	
Garonne	1959	24,513	Scrapped	ex-Orient Line
Geelong (1)	1866	1,584	Wrecked	Sold 1887
Geelong (2)	1904	7,951	Wrecked	
Golconda	1863	1,909	Scrapped	
Granada	1857	561	Wrecked	Sold 1866
Great Liverpool	1838	1,382	Wrecked	
Gwalior	1873	2,733	Wrecked	Sold 1894
Haddington	1846	1,648	Wrecked	Sold 1870
Harlington (1)	1895	1,032	Wrecked	
Harlington (2)	1913	1,089	Mined (UC 11)	
Himalaya (1)	1854	3,438	Bombed	Sold 1854
Himalaya (2)	1892	6,898	Scrapped	Sold 1922
Himalaya (3)	1949	27,955	Scrapped	
Hindostan (1)	1842	2,019	Wrecked	
Hindostan (2)	1869	3,113	Wrecked	
Hong Kong	1889	3,174	Wrecked	
Hydaspes	1872	2,984	Scrapped	
Iberia (1)	1836	516	Scrapped	
Iberia (2)	1954	29,614	Scrapped	
India (1)	1839	871	Scrapped	Sold 1849
India (2)	1896	7,911	Torpedoed (U 22)	
Indus (1)	1847	1,386	Hulked/ Scuttled	Sold 1869
Indus (2)	1871	3,462	Wrecked	
Indus (3)	1954	7,049	Scrapped	Sold 1957

Ship	Built	Tonnage	Fate	Note
Isis	1898	1,728	Scrapped	HMS Isonzo 1915–1920. Sold 1920
Japan	1893	4,319	Scrapped	Sold 1910
Java	1892	4,093	Scrapped	Sold 1910
Jeddo	1859	1,631	Wrecked	
Jeypore	1920	5,318	Torpedoed (U-89)	
Jupiter	1835	610	Scrapped	
Kaisar-I-Hind (1)	1878	4,023	Scrapped	
Kaisar-I-Hind (2)	1914	11,430	Scrapped	
Kallada	1946	6,607	Scrapped	Sold 1957
Kalyan	1915	8,987	Scrapped	
Karmala (1)	1914	8,983	Scrapped	
Karmala (2)	1945	7,673	Scrapped	
Kashgar (1)	1874	2,621	Scrapped	Sold 1889
Kashgar (2)	1914	8,840	Scrapped	
Kashmir	1915	8,841	Scrapped	
Khedive	1871	3,742	Wrecked	Sold 1896
Khiva (1)	1874	2,609	Wrecked (Fire)	Sold 1890
Khiva (2)	1914	8,947	Scrapped	
Khyber (1)	1914	8,946	Scrapped	
Khyber (2)	1945	7,675	Scrapped	Sold 1964
Kidderpore	1920	5,334	Scrapped	
Lady Mary Wood	1842	553	Scrapped	Sold 1858
Lahore	1920	5,252	Torpedoed (U-124)	
Liverpool	1830	330	Scrapped	
Lombardy	1873	2,723	Scrapped	Sold 1893
Macedonia	1904	10,512	Scrapped	
Madras	1852	1,185	Hulked	Sold 1874
Madrid	1845	479	Wrecked	
Malabar	1858	917	Wrecked	

Ship	Built	Tonnage	Fate	Note
Malacca (1)	1866	1,584	Scrapped	Sold 1882
Malacca (2)	1892	4,045	Scrapped	
Maloja (1)	1911	12,431	Mined (UC 6)	
Maloja (2)	1923	20,837	Scrapped	
Malta (1)	1848	1,217	Scrapped	
Malta (2)	1895	6,064	Scrapped	
Malwa (1)	1873	2,933	Scrapped	Sold 1894
Malwa (2)	1908	10,883	Scrapped	
Manila	1892	4,210	Scrapped	Sold 1910
Manilla	1853	646	Unknown	Sold 1861
Mantua (1)	1909	10,885	Scrapped	
Marmora	1903	10,509	Torpedoed (UB 64)	
Massilia (1)	1860	1,640	Unknown	Sold 1877
Massilia (2)	1884	4,908	Scrapped	
Mata Hari	1915	1,020	Bombed	Captured 1942
Mazagon (3)	1894	4,997	Wrecked	Mazagon (1) was a tug, Mazagon (2) was a launch. Sold 1907
Medina	1911	12,350	Torpedoed (UB 31)	
Mirzapore (1)	1871	3,763	Scrapped	Sold 1897
Mirzapore (2)	1921	6,715	Scrapped	
Moldavia (1)	1903	9,500	Torpedoed (UB 57)	
Moldavia (2)	1922	16,449	Scrapped	
Mongolia (1)	1865	2,799	Scrapped	
Mongolia (2)	1903	9,505	Mined (Wolf)	
Mongolia (3)	1923	16,504	Scrapped	Renamed Rimutaka in 1938. Sold 1950
Montrose	1837	603	Unknown	Sold 1852
Mooltan (1)	1861	2,257	Missing	Sold 1880
Mooltan (2)	1905	9,621	Torpedoed (UC 27)	
Mooltan (3)	1923	20,847	Scrapped	
Morea	1908	10,890	Scrapped	

Ship	Built	Tonnage	Fate	Note
Mutlah	1947	6,652	Wrecked	Transferred to James Nourse 1957 and sold 1963
Nagoya	1913	6,854	Scrapped	
Nagpore	1920	5,283	Torpedoed (U-509)	
Naldera	1918	15,825	Scrapped	
Namur	1906	6,694	Torpedoed (U 35)	
Nankin (1)	1888	3,960	Wrecked	Sold 1904
Nankin (2)	1912	6,853	Fire	Sold 1931
Narkunda	1920	16,227	Bombed	
Narrung	1896	5,078	Torpedoed (U 101)	Sold 1913
Nellore	1913	6,853	Torpedoed (I8)	Sold 1929
Nemesis	1857	2,018	Scrapped	Launched as Delta (1). Sold 1867
Nepaul (1)	1858	796	Unknown	Sold 1867
Nepaul (2)	1876	3,536	Wrecked	
Nile	1906	6,694	Wrecked	
Niphon	1865	695	Wrecked	
Nizam	1873	2,725	Scrapped	
Nore	1907	6,696	Scrapped	
Norna	1853	970	Scrapped	Sold 1871
Northam	1858	1,330	Fire	Sold 1868
Novara	1912	6,850	Scrapped	
Nubia (1)	1854	2,096	Scrapped	Sold 1877
Nubia (2)	1895	5,914	Wrecked	
Nyanza (1)	1864	2,982	Scrapped	Sold 1873
Nyanza (2)	1906	6,695	Scrapped	
Oceana	1888	6,610	Wrecked	
Orcades	1948	28,396	Scrapped	ex-Orient Line
Oriana	1960	41,915	Scrapped	ex-Orient Line. Sold 1986
Oriental (1)	1840	1,673	Scrapped	

Ship	Built	Tonnage	Fate	Note
Oriental (2)	1889	4,971	Scrapped	Sold 1915
Orion	1935	23,696	Scrapped	ex-Orient Line
Orissa (1)	1856	1,647	Scrapped	Sold 1878
Oronsay	1951	27,632	Scrapped	ex-Orient Line
Orontes	1929	20,186	Scrapped	ex-Orient Line
Orsova	1954	28,790	Scrapped	ex-Orient Line
Osiris	1898	1,728	Scrapped	Renamed Osiris II in 1916
Osiris II				See Osiris
Ottawa (1)	1854	1,275	Scuttled	Sold 1872
Pacha	1842	548	Wrecked	
Padua	1912	5,907	Scrapped	
Palana				See Sussex (1)
Palawan	1895	4,686	Scrapped	Sold 1914
Palermo	1903	7,597	Scrapped	
Palma	1903	7,632	Scrapped	
Pando Cape				See Ballarat (3)
Pando Cove				See Singapore (2)
Pando Head				See Surat (3)
Pando Sound				See Bendigo (2)
Pando Strait				See Sunda (3)
Paringa				See Essex (1)
Parramatta	1882	4,771	Scrapped	
Patonga	1953	10,071	Scrapped	Renamed Strathlauder in 1975
Pekin (1)	1847	1,182	Scrapped	Launched as Sultan (1)
Pekin (2)	1871	3,777	Beached	Sold 1897
Pekin (3)	1888	3,957	Scrapped	Sold 1906
Peninsula	1836	113	Unknown	Sold 1837
Peninsular	1888	5,294	Scrapped	
Pera (1)				See Alma
Pera (2)	1855	2,014	Wrecked	Sold 1880
Pera (3)	1903	7,635	Torpedoed (UB 48)	
Perim (1)	1916	7,648	Scrapped	

Ship	Built	Tonnage	Fate	Note
Perim (2)	1945	9,550	Scrapped	
Persia	1900	7,951	Torpedoed (U 38)	
Peshawur (1)	1871	3,782	Wrecked	Sold 1900
Peshawur (2)	1905	7,634	Torpedoed (U 96)	
Peshawur (3)	1919	7,934	Torpedoed (RO-111)	
Pinjarra	1944	9,892	Scrapped	Sold 1962
Plassy	1900	7,405	Scrapped	
Poona	1905	7,626	Scrapped	
Poonah	1863	2,596	Scrapped	
Pottinger	1846	1,350	Scrapped	
Precursor	1841	1,751	Scrapped	
Rajah (1)	1853	537	Wrecked	Sold 1861
Rajputana	1925	16,568	Torpedoed (U-108)	
Ranchi	1925	16,650	Scrapped	
Rangoon	1863	1,776	Wrecked	
Ranpura	1925	16,601	Scrapped	Sold 1944
Ravenna	1880	3,340	Wrecked	Sold 1898
Rawalpindi	1925	16,619	Sunk by battlecruisers	
Razmak	1925	10,602	Scrapped	Transferred to Union SS Co. of New Zealand in 1930
Redcar	1920	1,475	Scrapped	Sold 1946
Rimutaka				See Mongolia (3)
Ripon	1846	1,508	Scuttled	Sold 1870
Rohilla	1880	3,511	Wrecked	Sold 1900
Rome	1881	5,010	Scrapped	Renamed Vectis (3) in 1904
Rosetta	1880	3,502	Scrapped	Sold 1900
Royal Tar	1832	681	Unknown	
Salmara	1956	8,202	Scrapped	Renamed Strathloyal in 1975
Salsette (1)	1858	1,491	Scrapped	Sold 1871

Ship	Built	Tonnage	Fate	Note
Salsette (2)	1908	5,842	Torpedoed (*UB 40*)	
Salsette (3)	1956	8,202	Scrapped	Renamed *Strathlomond* in 1975. Sold 1977
Sardinia	1902	6,574	Scrapped	
Shanghai (1)	1851	546	Wrecked	Sold 1862
Shanghai (2)	1889	3,171	Scrapped	Sold 1904
Shannon	1881	4,189	Scrapped	
Shillong (1)	1939	5,529	Torpedoed (*U-630*)	
Shillong (2)	1949	8,934	Wrecked	Last P&O shipwreck
Siam	1873	3,026	Scrapped	Sold 1895
Sicilia	1901	6,696	Scrapped	
Simla (1)	1854	2,441	Wrecked	Sold 1875
Simla (2)	1894	5,884	Torpedoed (*U 39*)	
Singapore (1)	1850	1,189	Wrecked	
Singapore (2)	1951	9,236	Scrapped	Renamed *Comorin* (2) in 1964, *Pando Cove* in 1968
Sir Jamsetjee Jeejebhoy	1848	136	Scrapped	Sold 1859
Sobraon	1900	7,382	Wrecked	
Socotra (1)	1897	6,044	Wrecked	
Socotra (2)	1943	7,840	Scrapped	
Somali (1)	1901	6,708	Scrapped	
Somali (2)	1930	6,809	Bombed	
Somali (3)	1948	9,080	Scrapped	Sold 1969
Soudan (1)	1901	6,680	Scrapped	
Soudan (2)	1931	6,677	Mined	
Soudan (3)	1948	9,080	Scrapped	
Strathaird (1)	1932	22,544	Scrapped	
Strathallan	1938	23,722	Torpedoed (*U-562*)	
Stratheden (1)	1937	23,722	Scrapped	Sold 1964
Strathlauder				See *Patonga*

Ship	Built	Tonnage	Fate	Note
Strathlomond				See *Salsette* (3)
Strathloyal				See *Salmara*
Strathmore (1)	1935	23,428	Scrapped	Sold 1963
Strathnaver (1)	1931	22,547	Scrapped	
Sultan (1)				See *Pekin* (1)
Sultan (2)	1847	1,091	Hulked	Sold 1870
Sumatra (1)	1867	2,202	Fire	Sold 1886
Sumatra (2)	1895	4,607	Wrecked	Sold 1914
Sunda (1)	1866	1,682	Hulked	Sold 1882
Sunda (2)	1895	4,674	Missing	Sold 1914
Sunda (3)	1952	9,235	Scrapped	Renamed *Pando Strait* in 1968
Surat (1)	1866	2,578	Scrapped	Sold 1894
Surat (2)	1938	5,529	Torpedoed (*U-103*)	
Surat (3)	1948	8,925	Scrapped	Renamed *Pando Head* in 1968
Sussex (1)	1937	11,063	Scrapped	Renamed *Palana* in 1946
Sutlej	1882	4,205	Scrapped	
Syria (1)	1863	1,932	Wrecked	Sold 1870
Syria (2)	1901	6,660	Scrapped	
Tagus	1837	743	Scrapped	
Tanjore	1865	2,245	Scrapped	Sold 1888
Tartar	1853	293	Scrapped	
Tasmania	1884	4,488	Wrecked	
Teheran	1874	2,589	Wrecked	Sold 1894
Thames	1882	4,113	Scrapped	
Thibet	1874	2,593	Scrapped	Sold 1895
Tiber	1846	764	Wrecked	
Tientsin	1888	3,950	Wrecked	Sold 1906
Travancore	1868	1,900	Wrecked	
Tresillian	1944	7,373	Wrecked	
Trevean	1945	7,308	Wrecked	Transferred to Hain in 1958, sold 1963
Trevelyan	1943	7,289	Scrapped	Sold 1958

Ship	Built	Tonnage	Fate	Note
Trevethoe	1944	7,635	Scrapped	Sold 1958
Trevose	1944	7,365	Scrapped	Sold 1958
Trewellard	1942	7,264	Scrapped	Sold 1958
Treworlas	1942	7,262	Scrapped	Sold 1958
Union	1854	336	Hulked	Sold 1863
Valetta (1)	1853	833	Unknown	Sold 1865
Valetta (2)	1884	4,911	Scrapped	Sold 1903
Vectis (1)	1849	794	Unknown	Sold before completion
Vectis (2)	1853	751	Unknown	Sold 1865
Vectis (3)	1881		Scrapped	See *Rome*

Ship	Built	Tonnage	Fate	Note
Venetia	1873	2,726	Scrapped	
Verona	1879	3,069	Scrapped	
Viceroy of India	1929	19,648	Torpedoed (*U-407*)	
Victoria	1887	6,522	Scrapped	
Wakool	1898	5,004	Scrapped	Sold 1913
Wilcannia	1899	4,953	Scrapped	Sold 1914
William Fawcett	1828	206	Scrapped	First recognised P&O ship
Zambesi	1873	2,431	Scrapped	Sold 1888

BIBLIOGRAPHY

Books

Armitage, Albert B. *Cadet to Commodore*, Cassell, 1925

Bugg, Stan & Wealthy, Bob. *Shipwrecks around Port Phillip Heads*, J.L. Publications, 1995

Cable, Boyd. *A Hundred Year History of the P&O*, Ivor Nicholson & Watson, 1937

Cornewall-Jones, R.J. *The British Merchant Service*, Sampson Low, Marston & Co., 1898

Davis, Robert H. *Deep Diving & Submarine Operations*, Saint Catherine Press, 1962

Finidori, Charles. *Le Tasmania*, Alain Piazzola, 1994

Foot, John. *Marine Pilot*, Ian Henry Publications, 1995

Haws, Duncan. *Merchant Fleets in Profile (1)*, Patrick Stephens, 1978

Henderson, Robert et al. *A Photographic History of P&O Cruises*, The History Press, 2015

Hinchcliffe, John & Vicki. *Dive Dorset*, Underwater World Publications, 1999

Hinds, Fergus. *Riches From Wrecks: The Recovery of Sunken Cargoes*, Brown, Son & Ferguson, 1995

Hocking C. *Dictionary of Disasters at Sea during the Age of Steam*, Naval & Military Press Ltd, 1994

Hook, F.A. *Merchant Adventurers*, A&C Black, 1920

Howarth, David & Stephen. *The Story of P&O*, Weidenfeld & Nicolson, 1986

Jayawardena, Dharshana. *Ghosts of the Deep: Diving the Shipwrecks of Sri Lanka*, Vijitha Yapa Publications, 2016

Joncheray, Anne & Jean-Pierre. *50 Épaves en Corse*, Gap Editions, 2002

Kerr, George F. *Business in Great Waters: The War History of the P&O 1939–1945*, Faber & Faber, 1951

Larn, Richard & Bridget. *Shipwreck Index of British Isles Vol. 1*, Lloyd's Register, 1995

Larn, Richard & Bridget. *Shipwreck Index of Ireland*, Lloyd's Register, 2002

Malcolm, Ian M. *Shipping Company Losses of the Second World War*, The History Press, 2013

Maw, Neil. *World War One Channel Wrecks*, Underwater World Publications, 1999

McCart, Neil. *20th Century Passenger Ships of the P&O*, Patrick Stephens Ltd, 1985

McDonald, Kendall. *Dive Kent*, Underwater World Publications, 1994

McDonald, Kendall. *Dive South Devon*, Underwater World Publications, 1982

McDonald, Kendall. *Dive Sussex*, Underwater World Publications, 1999

McDonald, Kendall. *Great British Wrecks (1&2)*, Underwater World Publications, 1986

Middleton, Ned. *Shipwrecks from the Egyptian Red Sea*, Immel Publishing, 2006

Mitchell, Peter. *The Wrecker's Guide to South West Devon*, Sound Diving, 1986

Nicolson, John. *Arthur Anderson: A Founder of the P&O Company*, Lerwick, 1932

Padfield, Peter. *An Agony of Collisions*, Hodder & Stoughton, 1966

Padfield, Peter. *Beneath the House Flag of the P&O*, Hutchinson, 1981

Rabson, Stephen & O'Donoghue, Kevin. *P&O: A Fleet History*, World Ship Society, 1988

Roussel, Mike & Warwick, Sam. *The Union-Castle Line: Sailing Like Clockwork*, The History Press, 2015

Scott, David. *Seventy Fathoms Deep*, Faber & Faber, 1931

Scott, David. *The Egypt's Gold*, Faber & Faber, 1933

Scott, Peter. *The Eye of The Wind*, Houghton Mifflin, 1961

Shaw, David & Winfield, Barry. *Dive North East*, Underwater World Publications, 1988

Silvester, Bill. *Down Under Magic*, 2012

Twain, Mark. *Following the Equator: A Journey Around the World*, Hartford, 1897

Warwick, Sam & Roussel, Mike. *Shipwrecks of the Cunard Line*, The History Press, 2012

Woodman, Richard. *The Real Cruel Sea: The Merchant Navy in the Battle of the Atlantic 1939–1943*, Pen & Sword, 2011

Young, Ron. *Shipwrecks of the North East Coast Volume Two*, Tempus, 2001

Periodicals

Diver
Illustrated London News
SCUBA
The Times
Wreck Diving Magazine

Web Sites

trove.nla.gov.au
www.britishnewspaperarchive.co.uk
www.convoyweb.org.uk
www.poheritage.com
www.uboat.net
www.wrecksite.eu

INDEX

Page references in italics indicate illustrations.